CHANGING EXPECTATIONS

A Key to Effective Psychotherapy

36,42

CHANGING EXPECTATIONS

A Key to Effective Psychotherapy

IRVING KIRSCH

University of Connecticut

Brooks/Cole Publishing Company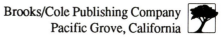
Pacific Grove, California

Consulting Editor: *C. Eugene Walker, University of Oklahoma*

Brooks/Cole Publishing Company A Division of Wadsworth, Inc.
© 1990 by Wadsworth, Inc., Belmont, California 94002. All rights reserved. No part of this book may be reproduced, stored in a retrieval system, or transcribed, in any form or by any means—electronic, mechanical, photocopying, recording or otherwise—without the prior written permission of the publisher, Brooks/Cole Publishing Company, Pacific Grove, California 93950, a division of Wadsworth, Inc.

Printed in the United States of America
10   9   8   7   6   5   4   3   2   1

Library of Congress Cataloging in Publication Data
Kirsch, Irving.
   Changing expectations : a key to effective psychotherapy / Irving Kirsch.
     p.   cm.
  Bibliography: p.
  Includes index.
  ISBN 0-534-12648-0
  1. Psychotherapy.   I. Title.
RC480.K543   1990
616.89'14—dc20   89-35604
                                                      CIP

#20017036

Sponsoring Editor: *Claire Verduin*
Editorial Assistant: *Gay C. Bond*
Production Editor: *Timothy A. Phillips*
Manuscript Editor: *Hal Straus*
Permissions Editor: *Carline Haga*
Interior and Cover Design: *Lisa Thompson*
Jacket Photo: *George Savic*
Art Coordinator: *Lisa Torri*
Interior Illustration: *Maggie Stevens-Huft*
Typesetting: *Phyllis Larimore Publication Services*
Cover Printing: *Phoenix Color Corporation, Long Island City, New York*
Printing and Binding: *Arcata Graphics/Fairfield, Fairfield, Pennsylvania*

FOREWORD

In this book Irving Kirsch introduces a new construct, response expectancies, and integrates this notion into social learning theory. In doing so he follows a tradition of theory-building by addition of new constructs only when they have empirically been demonstrated to be useful by providing explanations and prediction for events not adequately handled by the original set of construct. For the most part the development of theories of personality and psychopathology have followed one of two strategies. The first strategy might be called the "intuitive approach," where one or two major insights into human nature are hypothesized as central to the development of personality. These theories elaborate on these insights and describe how they influence a wide variety of behaviors. When two or more principles are so enunciated, the interaction of these principles may produce additional predictions about behavior. The psychoanalytic theories and neoanalytic theories, along with that of Carl Rogers, are examples of this approach.

Such theories are illustrated mainly by means of case histories and anecdotal evidence; the careful definition of terms in ways that can lead to agreed-upon measurements come later, if at all. The popularity of these theories may last for a long time, but they ultimately lose vigor and influence because they never produce a body of convincing data that can be replicated under controlled scientific conditions; each clinician revises the theory to suit his or her personality and experience. When practitioners can read their own meanings into a set of terms or concepts, they are more likely to embrace them than if they are forced to accept the more precisely delimited definitions of the theorist. This is true since the precise definitions are more likely to be different from the way in which they have been previously thinking about the same concept.

Such broad insights are not to be disparaged. They may often have considerable heuristic value and lead to the acquisition of valuable scientific knowledge, but only if the terms in which they are described are anchored in reliable, generally accepted measurements. Otherwise, they are ultimately discarded because the conditions under which they are predictive cannot be carefully specified and post-hoc explanations replace predictions.

The second approach to theory-building is to start with a few carefully defined concepts and to carefully describe the direction of relationships among the constructs. Although, ultimately, the operations for measurement may turn out to be inadequate, it is necessary from the beginning to attempt to specify the methods of measurement as clearly as one specifies the definitions. Indeed, in psychology, in the early stages of such theory-building much more attention is usually paid to the problems of measurement than to elaboration of theory. Of course, there are problems with this approach also. Because measurement is so difficult and the conditions under which particular operations will work are so limited, there is a tendency to avoid complex natural settings and to avoid adding new concepts and subconcepts because of the new and difficult problems of measurement. There is also a tendency to avoid studying behaviors that are more complex and produce difficult problems of measurement. Experimental studies tend to try to control for conditions and variables that are normally present in typical human interactions, so that even though the theories may be tested, they can provide prediction only under extremely limited conditions.

It seems clear that theories that will ultimately provide understanding and prediction of complex human behavior need to be constantly growing and changing. The adherents of the theory must accept both the complexity of human behavior and the necessity for precise measurement of person variables and the psychological situations in which behavior is expected to occur. It is just such growth that Kirsch has achieved with his addition of the concept of response expectancies to social learning theory.

The social learning theory developed by me, my colleagues, and students (Rotter, 1954, 1982; Rotter, Chance, & Phares, 1972) has followed the latter tradition. It is an attempt to combine or integrate the two great traditions of cognitive psychology and behavioral psychology. Initially, we set out four sets of basic variables: behavior potentials, expectancies, reinforcement values, and the psychological situation. Over the 35 years since the initial publication of the theory, we have attempted to refine and add concepts, always with careful definitions, concern for overlap, and with operations for measurement specified.

It can be demonstrated that the more narrow and delimited a construct, the greater is the probability of significant prediction. So, for example, achievement need as a broad construct will not predict behavior in a competitive sport as well as the more specific construct of need for achievement in physical skills. Dependency on peers will predict interaction with roommates more accurately than would a broader construct of dependency. Similarly, more specific constructs, dealing with classes of responses, expectancies, reinforcements, or psychological situations can produce more precise prediction, and a useful theory must continually grow by the addition of such concepts.

This book is concerned with expectancies. Initially, in social learning theory, we identified three classes of expectancies: expectancies for behavior-reinforcement sequences, expectancies for reinforcement-reinforcement sequences, and expectancies that have been generalized over a set of similar reinforcements, which we call freedom of movement. To this, we have added expectancies regarding the nature of stimuli, social or otherwise, which we call "simple cognition," and expectancies that are generalized over similar situations, in that these situations provide a similar problem requiring solution, which we called "generalized expectancies for problem solving."

All of these expectancies are subjectively held and it may be parenthetically added that Bandura's construct of self-efficacy has always been included in expectancies for behavior-reinforcement sequences, since they are not expectancies for whether or not someone else can perform the behavior in question, but for what would happen if the subject attempted to perform the behavior in question. Kirsch (1982, 1985) has shown that when typical operations for the measurement of self-efficacy and behavior-reinforcement expectancies are used that similar predictions are obtained.

Now Kirsch has added to our refinement of the concept of expectancies the construct of response expectancies. These are expectancies for nonvolitional responses, following particular kinds of stimulation. They could be observable or nonobservable responses, such as changes in the state of the organism (emotions, vascular reactions) or motoric responses. The person *believes* that he or she has no voluntary control of these responses if he or she allows or cannot avoid the stimulation. Such responses, Kirsch believes, are of considerable importance in understanding the effects of such interventions as placebos, hypnotic inductions, desensitization treatments, as well as the effects of psychotherapy more broadly considered.

This book carefully reviews and analyzes the literature of these fields and the methodology of research. Kirsch makes a strong case for the significance of response expectancies in examining a wide diversity of studies. His analysis of weaknesses and strengths of the research methodologies typically used in studies employing placebos is particularly illuminating.

Response expectancies for nonvolitional responses are a special case of expectancies for behavior-reinforcement sequences. The psychological situation sets off the expectancies for a response that also has negative or positive reinforcement consequences. The expectancies for such responses may lead to *voluntary* behavior to either avoid or not avoid involuntary response. It is apparent that this has important implications for individual differences in reaction to placebos, hypnosis, and other treatment procedures.

The reviews of the literature on hypnosis, placebos, credibility of treatment procedures, desensitization, the treatment of depression, and psychotherapy outcome are impressive. Kirsch attempts a carefully reasoned meta-analysis of these data and describes the part played by response expectancies, citing his own and others' research.

Kirsch has strongly supported his theories, both logically and with his own and his students' programmatic research. One cannot fail to be impressed and stimulated by this important addition to our understanding of the effects of psychotherapy procedures and the new light it sheds on much data already accumulated.

Julian B. Rotter
University of Connecticut

PREFACE

Philosophers of science sometimes distinguish between the "context of discovery" and the "context of justification." The process of discovery is much looser than the subsequent process of justification. Discoveries may begin with serendipitous observations, casual introspection, or even idle speculation and intuitive hunches. The rules of scientific evidence, however, are far more stringent. They require systematic and controlled observation to substantiate our hypotheses.

Accordingly, this book is devoted largely to presenting the controlled empirical evidence of the effects of response expectancies and to considering their implications for theory, research, and clinical practice. A preface, however, seems an appropriate place to share with you some of the process by which I became aware of the self-confirming power of response expectancy.

Mind over Taco

I always liked Mexican food, but I didn't like hot spicy food; in fact, I found the experience painful. Even a radish made me feel uncomfortable. I coped with this dilemma by frequenting Tex-Mex restaurants only in the gringo neighborhoods of Los Angeles, ordering just the safe foods—burritos, tostadas, cheese enchiladas, and frijoles. The hot sauce sat safely at the end of the table, untouched.

"Have you ever been to El Tippiac?," Mike Wapner asked, following one of our rambling afternoon excursions down the twisting lanes of theoretical psychology.

I shook my head.

"You've got to try it," he said exuberantly. "They make the best tacos in the world."

This was too promising to pass up. We collected Nancy, Michael's wife and colleague, and the three of us went to El Tippiac, where we ordered guacamole tacos. Mike and Nancy began eating theirs with gusto, and I bit into mine with eager anticipation.

When you take your first bite of a hot dish, there is a short period of time during which you can taste the flavor of the food, before it is eclipsed by the fiery sensation of the spice. During that brief delay, the delicious flavor of the guacamole taco came through. But then came the pain—excruciating pain! A familiar searing sensation spread through my mouth, and my eyes began to water.

Normally at that point, I would swallow the offending substance as quickly as possible and grope for a glass of water. But that afternoon, I did not. A sudden insight had occurred to me. Recalling the marvelous flavor that the pain had obscured, and seeing the expressions of pleasure on the faces of my friends, I thought: "Why am I experiencing pain while they are experiencing pleasure? The tacos are the same, and there is nothing *physically* different between them and me. We have the same kinds of taste buds, the same type of pain receptors. It's not fair! I too should be able to enjoy a guacamole taco."

Thinking back to that experience, I realize that my conclusions were not entirely sound. Perhaps there *is* a physiological difference between people who enjoy spicy foods and those who find them painful. Yet at the time, I had no doubts. I was certain that the difference was not physiological, and I decided to experience exactly what they were experiencing.

So I did not swallow as quickly, nor did I reach for a glass of water. Instead, I chewed slowly. I rolled the food around in my mouth. I savored it.

And then a strange thing happened. The taco still tasted spicy, but the spiciness was no longer painful. It began to feel pleasant, and finally, wonderful.

From that day on, my experience of spicy food has been different; it is no longer painful. When it is good and spicy, it is spicy and good.

A Ticklish Question

Some years later, I moved to the East Coast and began teaching at the University of Connecticut. One day, I received a phone call from Marilyn, an old high school friend. She was living in Cambridge now, and had heard that I had moved to Connecticut.

Marilyn came down for a visit, and while reminiscing and bringing each other up to date on how our lives had progressed, I told her of my experience with the guacamole taco.

"That reminds me of something that happened to me when I was a kid," she said. "I used to be very ticklish, and my father would often tickle me, while I laughed uncontrollably and tried to get away. He thought it was fun, and he just refused to believe that I hated it.

"One day when I was sixteen, I decided that I had had enough. I was not going to be ticklish any more. It was just a decision that I made, but I knew it was true. I was no longer ticklish.

"The next time he tried to tickle me, I didn't flinch or move away or laugh. I just stood there and looked at him, and after a little while, I calmly asked, 'Are you through yet?' Since then, I haven't been ticklish."

"May I try?" I asked, and I reached my fingers out toward her.

She lifted her arms, shrugged, and said, "Sure!"

She was right. She wasn't ticklish at all.

I thought for a few minutes about the story she had told me, and also about my experience with Mike and Nancy and the guacamole taco. I had always been ticklish and experienced it as beyond my control. It occurred to me that Marilyn's experience with tickling was similar to mine at the taco stand. Marilyn's story suggested that there was no physiological difference between people who are ticklish and those who are not, just as there is no physiological difference between those who enjoy spicy and those who find it painful. She had changed her experience of being tickled just as I had changed my experience of piquant food. And on the basis of those thoughts, I decided that I was no longer ticklish.

"I'm not ticklish any more," I said.

"Sure," said Virginia, a friend who had witnessed the exchange. I lifted my arms and Virginia tried to tickle me. I didn't flinch, and I didn't move away; I just stood there. And then I experienced something that I had never experienced before.

If you are uncontrollably ticklish, it is impossible for me to convey the nature of my experience to you. Having someone try to tickle you when you are not ticklish is a mildly unpleasant experience. Given a choice, you would prefer them to stop, but the sensation is certainly not unbearable. It is about as disagreeable and as tolerable as allowing an ant to walk around on the back of your hand.

I have not been ticklish since.

The Tickling Cure

Soon after I ceased being ticklish, a friend came for dinner with her 13-year-old daughter, who happened to be uncontrollably ticklish. I told them the stories that you have just read and asked the young girl to think about them. I told her that she could stop being ticklish if she chose to do so, but that she would only succeed if she believed quite firmly that she was no longer ticklish.

I gave her a minute to think about what I had said, and then I asked, "Are you still ticklish?"

She said that she was not.

I then asked her if she was certain, and she assured me that she was. Her mother and I then set about trying to tickle her, but to no avail. Finally, I asked her to be ticklish again. Once again, we tried to tickle her, but to her apparent surprise she found herself unable to be ticklish. We kept in touch for some years, and throughout that time, she remained tickle-free.

Because I had become curious about the reliability of this conversion process, I have since attempted hundreds of tickling cures. Most frequently, I have done so by telling people the story of my own conversion, just as I did with my friend's daughter. In other cases, I have used imagery instead. I ask people to close their eyes, to imagine that someone is approaching them and trying, without success, to tickle them. On occasion, I have coupled this with a hypnotic induction. If one method does not work, I sometimes try another.

I have not kept track of the exact number of times that this has been successful, but my perception is that the successes far outnumber the failures.

More importantly, people are very accurate at predicting their responses to these procedures. I always ask people whether they are still ticklish before testing to see if they are. If the answer is "Yes," I ask if they are sure. When people tell me that they are certain that they are no longer ticklish, they invariably are right.

As You Believe, So Shall You Be

When I first came to enjoy spicy food, I was reviewing the experimental literature on systematic desensitization, then the most widely touted behavioral treatment for anxiety disorders. When I stopped being ticklish, I was conducting research on the mechanisms by which desensitization achieved its effects. It seemed to me then that some common threads were running through my personal experiences and my academic research. I still believe this to be true.

The threads that link these seemingly diverse phenomena are expectancies and beliefs. More specifically, they are expectancies and beliefs about oneself. My experience of spicy food and of being tickled changed when I became firmly convinced that I was able to experience them differently. Desensitization therapies are effective when they succeed in convincing people that they are no longer afraid.

It has been proposed that the purpose of the brain is to anticipate events (Craik, 1943). This hypothesis may be an overstatement, but it seems clear that our ability to predict the consequences of our behavior developed because of its value for survival. Our ancestors learned to make tools and weapons, anticipating their uses, and they learned to cultivate the land in anticipation of a harvest. In short, their capacity to predict the results of their actions made it possible for them to exert greater control over their environment.

Similarly, much of what we do today is governed by expectancy. Although some of us are fortunate enough to enjoy our work, almost all of us are at least partly motivated by the income that it produces. But that income is generally obtained after the work is done. It is therefore an expectancy that keeps us working. More importantly, it is difficult to think of an occupation in which the work itself is not guided by expectations. We design bridges in anticipation of the loads they will carry, pour water on fires expecting to put them out, recommend investments that we think will yield sizeable returns, write advertisements in order to generate future sales, manufacture goods for people to buy and use in the future, and treat those who are suffering in the hope that they will improve.

This book is about people's expectations and beliefs. In particular, it focuses on people's beliefs about their own reactions to events, especially their emotional reactions. These beliefs, which I have termed *response expectancies,* are important because they are self-confirming. For example, people who are depressed often are locked into a vicious cycle in which they expect to be depressed forever and believe that there is nothing they can do to overcome their terrible fate. This very depressing thought is part of what keeps them depressed. It also keeps them from trying to do something to overcome depression. Further, when they do attempt to overcome their dysphoric mood, their negative expectations make it likely that their effort will not succeed. Their failure to overcome their depression then confirms the negative beliefs that help to maintain their problem.

This vicious cycle involving the anticipation of a negative consequence that, in turn, generates that consequence is not unique to depression. The belief that one will not be able to fall asleep can keep one awake; the belief that one is impotent can inhibit sexual arousal; and the belief that a panic attack is imminent can produce intense fear. These experiences strengthen and stabilize the expectancies by which they were generated, thereby convincing people that they are insomniac, sexually dysfunctional, or phobic. Treating depression, insomnia, erectile dysfunction, and anxiety disorders requires breaking this cycle, so that dysfunctional self-confirming beliefs are replaced by more benign expectations.

It is my opinion that the psychological theories that will be most useful in the long run are those that are short on speculation and long on experimental data. For that reason, this book devotes more attention to reviewing the pertinent data than to providing detailed instructions on how to treat clients. The purpose of the book is to summarize what is known about the effects of response expectancies, particularly as they relate to clinical concerns. These data indicate that response expectancy is an important factor in the etiology, maintenance, and treatment of many psychological disorders. By understanding expectancy effects, a therapist may be able to select or design therapeutic interventions more wisely, tailor them to match the belief systems of particular clients, and implement them more effectively.

Acknowledgments

Appreciation is due to Michael Wapner and Nancy Cobb, who introduced me to the great guacamole taco; to Marilyn Levin, who cured me of being ticklish; to Jules Rotter, who provided a theoretical framework, a language, and a foreword; to Jim Council, who critiqued but never doubted; to Christine Winter, who held my hand and suggested many important improvements; to David Winter Kirsch, who pushed the "enter" key on my computer; to Gene Walker, Perry London, and David Haaga, whose critiques of an earlier draft substantially improved the final product; to Steven Jay Lynn, George Allen, and John Teasdale, who read and commented on particular chapters; to the copy editor, Hal Straus, whose work reminded me of the sage maxim, "When in doubt, strike it out!"—perhaps I should have followed his advice more often than I did; to the production editor, Tim Phillips, who greased the wheels; to the graduate students with whom I have collaborated; to the therapists whom I have supervised and whose cases expanded my clinical database exponentially; and to the subjects and clients whose behavior confirmed some of my ideas and caused me to modify others. Thank you one and all!

Irving Kirsch

Contents

CHANGING EXPECTATIONS

A Key to Effective Psychotherapy

RESPONSE EXPECTANCY THEORY

EXPECTANCY, EXPERIENCE, AND BEHAVIOR

Theories of expectancy are not new to psychology. Expectancy was the basis of Tolman's (1932) cognitive learning theory, and it later became the central construct of social learning theory (Rotter, 1954). Response expectancy theory is part of this theoretical tradition. Rather than being a self-contained theory, it is an extension of social learning theory. This chapter describes the development of expectancy as a theoretical construct and introduces the basic concepts of response expectancy theory.

The Roots of Expectancy Theory

The link between expectancy and behavior has been a subject of considerable controversy. One of the reasons for this controversy was the prominence of behaviorism in American psychology from the 1920s through the 1960s. It was the opinion of most behavioral theorists that behavior could be explained adequately in terms of its actual consequences, without consideration of its anticipated consequences. It was proposed that terms like *expectancy* and other cognitive constructs were redundant and added nothing to the prediction and control of behavior. Learning, it was argued, was due to the mechanistic processes of operant and classical conditioning. These basic processes might be used to explain thought, conceptualized as a kind of covert and complex behavior, but they were not themselves thoughtful processes.

Dissenters emerged even during the height of the behaviorist *zeitgeist*. Although the most important of these dissenters, Edward Chace Tolman, called himself a behaviorist, his theory stretched the meaning of the term. Tolman (1932) saw the task of psychology as explaining behavior rather than mind, but he also believed that behavior could only be explained in terms of inferred mental processes, especially expectations.

If one wishes to demonstrate that behavior is linked to thought, it would seem easiest to do so with human beings rather than with other animals. Yet, during the heyday of behaviorism, Tolman worked with rats, trying to demonstrate that they thought, they formed cognitive maps of their environment, they were capable of showing insight, and their behavior was largely governed by their expectations.

Tolman and his intellectual descendents stood conditioning theory on its head. Instead of explaining thought as an outcome of conditioning, they explained conditioning in terms of thought. From a cognitive perspective, operant conditioning leads to knowledge about the consequences of behavior, and classical conditioning leads to knowledge about the sequence of events in the environment (Bolles, 1972). A rat in a Skinner box learns that pressing a bar produces food, and a classically conditioned dog learns that the sound of a bell is a signal for food. Bolles (1972) has termed these two kinds of information *response-stimulus (R-S)* expectancies and *stimulus-stimulus (S-S)* expectancies.

Social Learning Theory

When Tolman's expectancy theory was applied to socially and clinically significant human behavior, the result was social learning theory. Originally formulated by Julian B. Rotter in 1954, social learning theory has given rise to various modifications and extensions (Bandura, 1977; Kirsch, 1985a; Mischel, 1973). According to social learning theory, most significant human behavior is due to learning, and learning is a cognitive process involving the acquisition of information. Information can be acquired through direct experience, as in classical and operant conditioning situations, and it can also be acquired indirectly, through modeling and other forms of vicarious experience. Although most of our knowledge may be acquired vicariously, some evidence suggests that attitudes and expectations based on direct experience are held with greater certainty and therefore have greater impact on behavior (Fazio & Zanna, 1981; Wickless & Kirsch, in press).

The central constructs of social learning theory are *expectancy* and *reinforcement value* (Rotter, 1954). Expectancy is a person's estimate of the likelihood that an event will occur. Reinforcement value is the subjective value of the anticipated event. The occurrence of any particular behavior is hypothesized to be a joint function of these two variables. In other words, we perform actions that we think will lead to desired outcomes.

In social learning theory, the relationship between expectancy and reinforcement value as predictors of behavior is assumed to be multiplicative, rather than additive. This assumption has been validated empirically (Ajzen & Fishbein, 1980), and it is also in accord with common sense. Potential outcomes that are seen as having a zero probability of occurring should have no impact on behavior no matter what their values. Similarly, consequences that are of no importance to us—that is, their reinforcement value is zero—are unlikely to affect behavior no matter how certain their occurrence. When buying a car, for example, we do not consider the possibility of the company giving us a million-dollar rebate, nor the likelihood that buying the car will make the salesperson very happy. The first outcome is too unlikely to warrant consideration; the second, though virtually

4

certain, does not matter to us very much. In other words, these possible outcomes are not salient when deciding whether to buy a particular car.

Any given behavior is likely to have more than one consequence, and accurate prediction of behavior therefore requires consideration of all salient expected outcomes and their reinforcement values (Rotter, 1982). In many cases, a given action will be expected to produce some positive and some negative outcomes. For example, one may expect that seeing a therapist will entail some emotional discomfort, but also that it might enhance the quality of one's life. Whether one goes or not depends on the amount of discomfort and the degree of benefit that is anticipated, as well as the values of other anticipated consequences (for example, the cost of therapy).

To complicate matters further, in most situations we are confronted with a choice between alternate behaviors. For example, a student may face a choice between studying, going to the library, socializing with friends, playing softball, and so on. In order to accurately predict behavior, one would need to know the available alternatives and the expectancies and reinforcement values associated with each of them.

The basic formula of social learning theory, $BP = f(E \times RV)$, is situation-specific. It indicates that the probability (BP) of a particular behavior occurring *in a particular situation* is a multiplicative function of the expectancy *(E)* that it will lead to various outcomes and of the reinforcement value *(RV)* of those outcomes. However, expectancies formed in particular situations generalize to other situations. In other words, we develop *generalized expectancies* about broad classes of situations and behaviors. For example, we learn from experience that certain people are trustworthy in certain situations. When in a familiar situation with a familiar person, our specific expectancies will determine our level of trust. However, based on our accumulated experience with a wide range of people in different situations, we also develop generalized expectancies about how trustworthy people are. These generalized expectancies are particularly important in shaping our behavior in novel situations. They are the social learning theory equivalent of personality traits.

Of course, no situation is completely novel, nor are any two situations absolutely identical. For that reason, the decision to engage in a particular act is always a function of both generalized and specific expectancies. The more familiar the situation, the greater the role of specific expectancies. Conversely, in more novel situations, generalized expectancies are more important in predicting behavior.

The most widely studied generalized expectancy is "locus of control" (Rotter, 1966), a belief about the causes of outcomes. We see some events as being under our own control and others as chance occurrences. Many outcomes are viewed as controlled partially by ability and partially by luck. Winning at poker, for example, depends both on our skill at the game and the luck of the draw. As a generalized expectancy (or personality trait), locus of control refers to the degree to which people believe that important outcomes are determined by their own efforts and abilities (an *internal* locus of control) versus the extent to which they see them as due to chance or under the control of powerful others (an *external* locus of control). Neither extreme internality nor extreme externality is adaptive, as both entail serious distortions of reality. However, within normal bounds, an internal locus of control is associated with better adjustment, a greater sense of generalized self-efficacy, and a tendency to be more active in trying to achieve one's goals.

Social learning theory is open-ended, rather than closed, with room for expansion and elaboration. Walter Mischel (1973), for example, has drawn a distinction between *behavior-outcome* expectancies and *stimulus-outcome* expectancies. Behavior-outcome expectancies are beliefs that engaging in a particular behavior will lead to particular outcomes; they are the kind of expectancies that were hypothesized to interact with reinforcement value in the prediction of behavior (Rotter, 1954). Stimulus-outcome expectancies are beliefs that some events are predictors of others; for example, that a cloudy sky is a harbinger of rain.

Some stimulus-outcome expectancies affect behavior because they are determinants of behavior-outcome expectancies. Anticipating rain, for example, we might decide against going to the beach on a cloudy day. Other stimulus-outcome expectancies affect behavior via their influence on the values that we attach to certain outcomes. The value of an outcome is largely a function of the expectancy that it will lead to other consequences of value (Rotter, 1954). The value of a dollar to us, for example, depends on what we think it can buy, and a college degree is important because we expect it will enable us to get a better job.

In a similar vein, Bandura (1977) has added a distinction between expectancies that are based on judgements of one's capabilities, termed *self-efficacy* expectancies, and expectancies about environmental contingencies, which he terms *outcome expectancies*. Thus, one can believe that high grades in college will enhance one's chances of being accepted into graduate school (an outcome expectancy), but also believe that one is incapable of achieving those high grades (a self-efficacy expectancy). Though social learning theory had always considered both types of expectancy (see Kirsch, 1985b, 1986a), they had not been distinguished with different names before Bandura's contribution. The idea of response expectancies (Kirsch, 1985a), which is the central theme of this book, also can be regarded as an extension of social learning theory.

Expectancies and Emotions

One of the deficiencies of social learning theory, as it was originally formulated, is the scant attention that it paid to feelings. However, more recent cognitive theorists have developed hypotheses about emotional reactions that can be integrated quite easily into social learning theory. For example, Aaron Beck (1976) has proposed that different emotions are caused by different kinds of thoughts or cognitions. Anticipatory excitement or joy is the result of the expectancy of positively valued outcomes, anxiety is due to the expectation or threat of harm, and sadness results from the perception that important reinforcers have been lost irretrievably. In other words, besides affecting overt behavior, expectancies have emotional consequences. Beck's hypotheses not only have common sense appeal but have also been supported experimentally (Sewitch & Kirsch, 1984; Wickless & Kirsch, 1988).

Another cognitive theory of emotion that is consistent with social learning theory is the theory of "learned helplessness" (Seligman, 1975). Learned helplessness was first demonstrated in experiments in which dogs were subjected repeatedly to inescapable electric shocks. After numerous experiences of this sort, the dogs became passive and submissive. They lost their appetites and no longer tried to escape the shocks. Even when escape was possible once again, they sat passively and tolerated the continued shocks.

Seligman noted that the behavior displayed by these dogs was similar to symptoms of depression in humans, and he hypothesized that a common mechanism was involved. According to this hypothesis, people become depressed when inescapable aversive consequences teaches them that they cannot control their environment. In other words, depressed people have an extremely external locus of control, and their passivity is due to the expectation that bad things will happen no matter what they do.

In 1978, Seligman and his colleagues substantially revised their theory of learned helplessness (Abramson, Seligman, & Teasdale, 1978). As in the original theory, depression was seen as a consequence of an expectancy of uncontrollable negative outcomes. What was new were the conditions under which this expectancy was hypothesized to be acquired. In the reformulated model, the occurrence of inescapable negative events alone is not sufficient to produce feelings of depression but must be accompanied by certain attributions about the causes of those events. Specifically, people acquire generalized expectancies of helplessness when they attribute inescapable negative events to stable characteristics about themselves that could affect many other areas of their lives. In contrast, when aversive consequences are attributed to temporary external circumstances, neither learned helplessness nor depression should result.

To illustrate this revised theory of learned helplessness, students may find themselves receiving the same low grades in a class regardless of how much they study. If they interpret this as due to a lack of academic skill (or worse yet, as a reflection of their inability to do anything right in general), they are likely to develop the expectation that they cannot prevent anticipated negative events from happening; as a result, they may become depressed. However, if they interpret the same experience as due to unfair exams that were constructed or graded capriciously by the teacher, they are more likely to see this as an isolated incident with few implications for the future. With this latter interpretation, they will not acquire a generalized expectancy of helplessness, and they will not become depressed. According to the reformulated model of learned helplessness, depression is associated with a particular attributional bias. People who tend to attribute negative consequences to stable, global, internal factors (such as a pervasive lack of native ability) are most likely to become depressed.

The Theory of Reasoned Action

One of the traditional concerns of social psychology has been the measurement, formation, and change of people's attitudes. The assumption underlying this research was that behavior can be predicted from people's attitudes. However, when the research testing this assumption was reviewed, it was found that a demonstrable relationship between attitude and behavior was virtually nonexistent (Wicker, 1969). This discovery, quite naturally, led to a crisis in the field of attitude research and theory. Why bother measuring people's attitudes or discovering how they were formed if their relationship to behavior was negligible?

In response to this crisis, Martin Fishbein and Icek Ajzen developed their theory of reasoned action (Ajzen & Fishbein, 1980; Fishbein & Ajzen, 1975), which maintains that attitudes toward behaviors are better predictors of actions than are attitudes toward objects. For example, if you want to predict whether someone will hire Blacks, the question to ask is not whether that person likes or dislikes Blacks, but rather what his or her attitude is toward *hiring* Blacks. In reasoned action theory, attitudes toward behaviors are hypothesized to be a multiplicative function of expected outcomes and their values to the individual—the same variables from which behavior is predicted in social learning theory.

In developing reasoned action theory, Ajzen and Fishbein have made important methodological and conceptual contributions to expectancy theory. They have developed methods for eliciting the outcome expectancies that people are likely to consider in choosing to engage in particular actions, and they have also presented useful methods for scaling people's expectancies and values. On the conceptual level, they have added considerations of people's normative beliefs—that is, their beliefs about whether others think they should behave in a particular manner—to the prediction of behavior. They have also suggested that attitudes and norms predict behavior because of their impact on people's intentions, which are seen as the immediate determinants of actions. In other words, the best way to predict whether a person will do something is to ask whether he or she intends to do it.

Response Expectancy Theory

By calling their theory a "reasoned action" and emphasizing the importance of intentions, Fishbein and Ajzen have drawn explicit attention to a limitation of their theory and of earlier formulations of social learning theory. Expected outcomes and their values are good predictors of *volitional* actions, the things that people intend to do. Yet many responses are not fully under voluntary control, and the occurrence of these responses is not explained in reasoned action theory.

For example, when we read a book (a voluntary behavior) we may find ourselves turning the pages automatically, without any volitional effort. Similarly, when driving a car, eating dinner, writing, typing, or playing an instrument, we do not attend to each of the movements of which these acts are composed. We voluntarily intend to do each of these molar acts; our intentions then set off a chain of well-learned component responses that are experienced as occurring nonvolitionally. Although molar acts can be predicted accurately by evaluating expected outcomes and their associated values, the specific movements of which they are composed cannot be explained in the same way.

Sometimes, even molar acts become so well learned that they are performed automatically. Most of us have had the experience of driving home and realizing upon arrival that we have been totally unaware of following the route. We sometimes experience even greater surprise when we intended to drive someplace other than where we usually go and find ourselves at our usual, though unintended, destination. In such cases, it is clear that our behavior was involuntary—that is, unintended. When we mistakenly drive to the wrong destination, it is not because we are expecting a valued consequence at that location.

The components of well-learned actions are not the only responses that are experienced as occurring automatically. Subjective experiences and their physiological concomitants are another important category of nonvolitional response. We do not have direct control over how much pain we feel when physically injured, nor over our feelings of sadness, anger, anxiety, joy, tension, relaxation, alertness, pleasure, sexual arousal, or intoxication. This is not to say that we have no control whatsoever over these responses. In fact, we can do many things to alter our internal states, but our control over them is indirect. We can count sheep in order to fall asleep, recall pleasant experiences to alleviate sadness, and distract ourselves in various ways to diminish the experience of pain. Still, we may find ourselves wide awake, in tears, and in pain. Nonvolitional responses are experienced as outcomes of acts and can only be controlled indirectly—that is, by voluntary acts that might bring about those outcomes.

Nonvolitional Responses as Expected Outcomes

The outcomes that have been considered most frequently by expectancy theorists are external objects or events, such as money, grades, social acceptance, and so on. Therefore, our expectancies about their occurrence can be termed *stimulus expectancies.*

Yet we also have expectancies about our own nonvolitional reactions to events. We expect to feel guilty when we lie, to laugh hysterically when being tickled, and to feel intoxicated after consuming a certain quantity of alcohol. Although these *response expectancies* have been given little attention in most theories, they too are important determinants of behavior. We drink coffee in the morning in anticipation of feeling more alert and may put off going to the dentist in order to delay the anticipated discomfort. In fact, the value of a reinforcing stimulus is ultimately linked to the pleasure we expect it to bring and to the discomfort we think it will avoid or end. In other words, nonvolitional responses are primary reinforcers. Even the value of food to a starving person is a function of its ability to prevent the occurrence of a nonvolitional response (death).

As anticipated outcomes, response expectancies are among the most important determinants of phobic avoidance and substance abuse. Agoraphobics are not afraid of the supermarkets, shopping malls, elevators, and city streets that they avoid; they know full well that these situations are not dangerous. However, they do expect to experience panic attacks in these places. Their avoidance is due to their fear of these anticipated panic attacks (Goldstein & Chambless, 1978).

Similarly, the extent to which people drink alcohol is largely determined by their beliefs about the effects that alcohol will have on them (Goldman, Brown, & Christiansen, in press). People who abuse alcohol have different alcohol-related expectancies than nonabusers. They expect that alcohol will transform their experience of the world by enhancing social and physical pleasure, sexual arousal, and power. These expectations are formed before people first begin drinking and are better than parental drinking habits or demographic variables at predicting alcohol use. Thus, an understanding of the effects of response expectancies should have important implications for the prevention and treatment of agoraphobia and alcohol abuse.

Response Expectancies as Self-Fulfilling Prophesies

Response expectancies affect experience and behavior in two ways. First, they are a form of outcome expectancy. We do things to bring about positively valued nonvolitional responses and to avoid those that are negatively valued. Second, response expectancies tend to be self-confirming. When we expect to experience something strongly enough, we find ourselves actually experiencing it. Response expectancies can alter our experiences of pain, nausea, tension, anxiety, depression, sexual arousal, and relaxation. They also affect the physiological processes with which these subjective experiences are associated (for example, pulse rate, blood pressure, gastric motility, penile tumescence, and the release of endorphins in the brain).

The role of response expectancies in generating nonvolitional responses is similar to the role of intentions in generating voluntary actions. In reasoned action theory, *intention* is defined as the subjective probability that one will behave in a particular way. Similarly, response expectancy is a subjective probability that a response will occur. Thus, the distinction between intention and expectancy depends on whether the response is volitional or nonvolitional. Because nonvolitional responses are outcomes rather than actions, they are expected rather than intended. Thus, we *intend* to see a movie, but we *expect* to be amused by it. Despite this difference, in both cases the response is generated by the subjective probability of its occurrence.

Response expectancies and intentions are not mirror images of each other, and they do not play identical roles in determining behavior. Intentions are hypothesized to be the only immediate determinants of voluntary acts. In contrast, response expectancies are seen as only one of a number of factors that produce nonvolitional responses. For example, although fear can be produced by the expectancy of its occurrence, it can also be elicited by the perception of danger (Reiss & McNally, 1985). Also, when a response is not fully under volitional

10

control, a person can intend and therefore attempt to bring it about, yet not expect to be able to do so.[1] For example, a man who experiences erectile dysfunction may intend to become sexually aroused and may engage in various strategic, goal-directed acts and cognitions in order to gain an erection. He might take a drink, tell himself that he will become aroused, or fantasize an especially exciting sexual encounter. However, because sexual arousal is not subject to direct voluntary control, he may expect to fail in his efforts to gain an erection. As a nonvolitional response, sexual arousal is more directly affected by response expectancies than by intentions.

The capacity of response expectancies to affect subjective experiences and their physiological concomitants is not difficult to understand. It is frightening to think that one is about to experience a panic attack; the thought that depression might last forever is very sad; and the anticipation of excitement is in itself exciting. Our hearts beat faster when we are excited or frightened and more slowly when we are relaxed. However, the self-confirming effects of response expectancies on physiology do not appear to be limited to the substrates of subjective experience. As documented in Chapter 2, response expectancies can cure warts and produce or inhibit contact dermatitis (for example, poison ivy). They may even be capable of affecting the immune system, thereby altering the course of such serious physical conditions as cancer (Klopfer, 1957).

Response expectancy is not the only type of self-confirming expectation. A similar discovery about interpersonal expectancies led to the concept of the "self-fulfilling prophesy" (Merton, 1948). The behavior of students may be affected by the expectancies of their teachers, the behavior of experimental subjects by the expectancies of experimenters, and the behavior of clients by the expectancies of their therapists (Rosenthal & Rubin, 1978). Because these expectancies pertain to the behavior of other people, their effects are necessarily less direct than response expectancy effects and therefore may be less reliable. Before an expectancy about a client, student, or experimental subject can affect that person's behavior, it has to affect the behavior of the therapist, teacher, or experimenter. Next, the target of the expectation must perceive the difference in the other person's behavior and, finally, that perception must somehow generate behavior that is consistent with the expectation.

Because response expectancies are anticipations about one's own responses, the means by which they affect behavior are more direct. In fact, response expectancies may mediate some of the effects of interpersonal expectancies. A therapist expects her client to improve and acts in a manner that is consistent with that expectation. The client interprets his therapist's behavior as an indication that she thinks he will improve. This heightens his own expectations for improvement, which in turn enhances his response to treatment. This sequence of events is suggested by a study in which both client expectancies and therapist expectancies

---

[1]One implication of this is that the definition of the term *intention* as a person's subjective estimate of the likelihood of a response applies only to responses that are fully under voluntary control. If the response is under our control, then our expectancy of its occurrence is identical to our intention. But because we can intend to emit responses that are not fully controllable (for example, crying, sleeping, and so on), a broader definition of the term *intention* would be useful.

were assessed immediately after intake interviews at a university mental health center (Phelps, 1986). Client and therapist expectancies were correlated significantly, but the clients were much better than their therapists at predicting their response to treatment.

From Artifact to Main Effect

Although the idea of response expectancy is not new, it has only recently been distinguished from other kinds of expectations. Furthermore, even when recognized, response expectancies generally have been treated as unwanted artifacts—contaminating factors that require control, and impediments that could even lead to the abandonment of entire areas of investigation if not removed. The discovery of placebo effects in the 1950s, for example, changed the way in which new medications were tested and led people to question whether psychotherapy might be no more than a placebo, but it produced relatively little information about the placebo effect itself.

McGuire (1969) has described "three stages in the life of an artifact" (p. 15). The artifact is first ignored, then it is controlled, and finally it is investigated as an important phenomenon in its own right. The history of response expectancy provides a good illustration of this three-stage development. Initially, expectancy effects were not clearly recognized. Placebos were widely thought to be incapable of generating genuine curative effects, and expectancy effects in psychotherapy, when considered at all, were quickly dismissed. When it was finally recognized that expectancy could mimic the effects of drugs, attention was devoted to devising procedures that would reduce its contaminating influence. More recently, expectancy has been recognized as a factor that should be treated as a main effect, rather than as an artifact (Fish, 1973; Frank, 1973; Kirsch, 1978; Lick & Bootzin, 1975; Wilkins, 1986). It is, after all, a psychological variable, differing from other psychological variables in no essential way, but being perhaps more potent and ubiquitous than most.

In the chapters that follow, it is shown that response expectancies can have substantial effects on subjective mood, behavior, and physiology. They are important causal factors in the etiology of many of the problems that lead people to seek treatment—such problems as anxiety disorders, depression, substance abuse, sexual dysfunction, insomnia, and conversion and dissociative disorders. They also play an essential role in the treatment of these disorders.

The collected data suggest that we are on the wrong track when we attempt to control for expectancy effects and focus on what remains when it is removed. Instead, we should investigate the so-called placebo effect as an important psychological mechanism. Rather than eliminating expectancy effects, we should uncover the laws governing their operation and devise means of maximizing their impact. This book is a step in that direction. It is an effort to understand response expectancy in order to exploit it as a therapeutic mechanism. After all, few, if any, psychological factors can lay claim to such a wide range of effects.

THE POWER OF PLACEBOS

The preceding chapter claimed that response expectancies can affect a very wide variety of responses, including sensations and emotions, as well as their physiological substrates. If this claim is true, response expectancy may be one of the most potent psychological variables yet uncovered, one that must certainly have important implications for the practice of psychotherapy. However, is this claim really warranted? To what extent have the effects of response expectancy been documented?

This chapter examines the experimental literature on placebo effects, the best known and most extensively studied class of response expectancy effects. What has already been learned from the study of placebos has important implications, not only for clinical practice, but also for the methods by which new medications are evaluated.

The Discovery of Placebo Effects

Before the 20th century, most medical treatments were either inert or harmful. Patients were "purged, puked, poisoned, punctured, cut, cupped, blistered, bled, leached, heated, frozen, sweated, and shocked" (Shapiro & Morris, 1978, p. 370), and were made to consume almost every known ingestible (and often indigestible) substance. Among the medications prescribed by physicians of old were lizard's blood, crocodile dung, pig's teeth, putrid meat, fly specks, frog's sperm, powdered stone, human sweat, worms, spiders, furs, and feathers (Honigfeld, 1964). Because these treatments have been shown to have no physically curative properties, the history of medicine has been characterized as largely the history of the placebo effect (Shapiro, 1960).

Though physically inert, placebos may not be therapeutically inert. Throughout history, some healers suspected that belief might have curative properties. The Greek physician Galen, for example, noted that "he cures most in whom most are confident," and a famous aphorism of disputed origin admonishes doctors to "treat as many patients as possible with the new drugs while they still have the power to heal" (Shapiro, 1960). Charcot (1893), whose demonstrations of hypnosis convinced Freud of the power of unconscious processes, argued that faith could produce actual physical cures in suggestible individuals, though only in disorders that were psychologically caused.

Nevertheless, until recently the placebo effect went largely unrecognized. The term *placebo* is Latin for "I shall please" and was originally used to denote a treatment intended to please patients, but not to benefit them in other ways. The common assumption was that inactive medicines might mollify a patient, but they could not cause therapeutic change.

During the 1940s and 1950s, the possibility that placebo treatment might have genuine effects became more widely recognized, and the use of placebo controls in medical research became common. In case after case, medicines and treatment procedures that had been "proven" effective in clinical trials were found to be no more effective than treatment by placebo. Though the mechanism of placebo-induced change was a mystery, medical researchers began to suspect that many effects previously attributed to specific treatments were in fact placebo effects. It was suggested that placebos could reduce the frequency of asthma attacks, relieve hay fever, suppress coughs, alleviate tension and anxiety, cure headaches, reduce pain, prevent colds and alleviate cold symptoms, cure ulcers, inhibit symptoms of withdrawal from narcotics, alter gastric function, control the blood sugar levels of diabetics, reduce enuresis, lessen the severity of arthritis, reduce the frequency and severity of angina attacks, and reverse the growth of malignant tumors (Beecher, 1961; Honigfeld, 1964; Klopfer, 1957; Volgyesi, 1954).

Not all the effects attributed to placebos are beneficial. Placebos have also been reported to produce symptoms that mimic the unwanted side effects of active medications. Among the side effects that have been attributed to placebo treatment are drowsiness, weakness, confusion, headache, nervousness, insomnia, nausea, constipation, dizziness, dry mouth, cramps, anorexia, vomiting, delirium, diarrhea, nightmares, tremors, skin rash, sweating, fatigue, and constriction of the pupils (Beecher, 1955; Pogge, 1963). There have even been reports of addiction to placebo medication, replete with the withdrawal symptoms commonly associated with addiction to opiates (Vinar, 1978).

Experimental Studies of Placebo Effects

Current medical and pharmacological research practice implies a puzzling contradiction. The use of placebo controls in testing every medicine from experimental cold remedies to proposed cures of cancer or AIDS implies a belief that placebos may produce significant effects on a remarkably wide range of physical and psychological disorders. After all, if these conditions could not be affected by psychological manipulations, there would be no reason for a placebo control group. "Treatment-as-usual" or no-treatment controls would serve as well, be less costly in time and effort, and avoid the ethical issues that are raised by placebo use.[1]

---

[1]Treatment-as-usual groups receive the same treatment that they would have received had they not been part of an experimental study. When this is used as a control, the experimental group should receive the experimental drug in addition to whatever treatments are administered to subjects in the treatment-as-usual condition.

On the other hand, if there is a reasonable possibility that placebos can affect all manner of disorder (including life-threatening illnesses for which no cure is known), and if that possibility is great enough to warrant the routine use of placebo controls, then shouldn't a high priority be placed on intensive investigations of the scope and mechanisms of placebo effects? Where placebo effects can be substantiated, new vistas would be opened for the development of psychological treatments with few, if any, side effects. Where they are not found, medical research could be simplified and its cost reduced.

Nevertheless, despite thousands of medical and pharmacological studies that have included placebo controls, we know relatively little about their effects. The reason for our relative ignorance is that most of these studies were designed to test the effectiveness of a drug or of some other treatment, rather than to determine the effectiveness of placebos. Typically, one group of subjects receives the experimental treatment and a second group receives placebo treatment. Alternately, the same subjects might be given the experimental treatment at one point in time and placebo treatment at another time. In either case, the effectiveness of the treatment is gauged by comparing it to the effects observed in the placebo condition.

But how are the effects of administering a placebo to be assessed? When the efficacy of particular drugs are being investigated, placebo effects are unwanted artifacts. The purpose of using placebos is to establish the pharmacological effect of a drug by controlling for the psychological effect of its administration. However, when the purpose of an investigation is to learn about the power of placebos, then placebo effects are main effects rather than artifacts. A different set of controls are needed to ensure that what appears to be a placebo effect is genuine rather than artifactual.

Changes observed in a placebo control group *might* be due to subjects' beliefs that they are receiving efficacious treatment, but they might also be due to the mere passage of time or to naturally occurring fluctuations in the condition being treated (Ross & Olson, 1982). In order to be sure that an effect was due to a placebo, we need some way of estimating what would have happened had nothing been administered. Ideally, we would want to compare the changes in a placebo group to those in a no-treatment control group—a rarity in medical research.

By definition, the effects of placebos are not due to the physical properties of a treatment, but rather to its psychological properties. Therefore, they exemplify the self-confirming power of response expectancies. This chapter is devoted to assessing what we already know about the power of placebos to produce genuine changes in experience, behavior, and physiology. Although most of the studies that have included placebo controls can tell us nothing about the power of placebos, drug-related expectancy effects have been evaluated in a much smaller body of research. Some of these studies have included untreated control groups. Others have controlled for the effects of spontaneous change by using active medications that produce pharmacological effects opposite to those being suggested. Still others have examined variables that might influence the magnitude of the placebo effect—varying the apparent dose of the "medication," for example. Taken together, these studies indicate areas in which credible expectancy manipulations are likely to be effective.

Placebo Analgesia

Placebos are best known for their ability to reduce pain. Compared to untreated controls, subjects given placebo analgesia report less pain at similar levels of stimulation, tolerate more intense levels of stimulation, and have a higher threshold for reporting that a stimulus is painful (Camatte, Gerolami, & Searles, 1969; Gelfand, Ullmann, & Krasner, 1963; Kirsch & Baker, 1987; Liberman, 1964). Some recent studies have indicated that placebo pain reduction may be associated with the release of endorphins in the brain (Grevert, Albert, & Goldstein, 1983; Levine, Gordon, & Fields, 1978). Other studies, however, have produced conflicting results (Gracely, Dubner, Wolskee, & Deeter, 1983; Posner & Burke, 1985).

Not all placebos are equally effective in reducing pain. Placebo morphine is considerably more effective than placebo Darvon, which in turn is more effective than placebo aspirin (Evans, 1974). In each case, the placebo is about half as effective as the pharmacologically active drug. Similarly, placebos produce more pain relief when given after a more potent drug than they do when given after a less potent drug (Kantor, Sunshine, Laska, Meisner, & Hopper, 1966). Thus, the effectiveness of a placebo pain reliever varies as a function of its believed effectiveness.

Early estimates suggested that placebos reduce pain in about one-third of all patients (Beecher, 1955), but procedures that enhance the credibility of a placebo also enhance its effectiveness. For example, Traut and Passarelli (1957) reported an improvement rate of 50% following the administration of placebo tablets to patients suffering from rheumatoid arthritis. Those showing no improvement were then given placebo injections. Sixty-four percent of them reported improvement, half of whom complained that the effects wore off after three days and were therefore given injections twice a week. Thus there was an overall improvement rate of 82% from either the tablet or the injection. Patients reported greater relief when the placebo was injected near the affected part of the body, and continued placebo treatment was reported to be effective for as long as 30 months.

B*ckman, Kalliola, and Östling (1960) reported similar results for placebo treatment of pain produced by peptic ulcers and other gastroduodenal disorders. Instead of administering one or two pills, the patients in this study were instructed to take six tablets, four times a day, over a two-week period. Symptom improvement was reported for 92% of the patients.

These studies have important implications both for research and practice. First, they reveal that all placebos are not alike. Rather, some are more effective than others. Therefore, if a study has shown a psychotherapy to be more effective than a placebo therapy, we need to find out the contents of the placebo. What the study has demonstrated is that the treatment was more effective than the particular placebo that was used as a control. A more persuasive placebo might have been

16

as effective or possibly even more effective than the treatment under investigation.

Clinically, the finding of different degrees of effectiveness for different placebos suggests that in presenting treatment to clients, we should communicate a high degree of confidence in the treatment's effectiveness. Also, when an intervention fails to produce an intended result, abandoning it for some other therapeutic approach may not be the wisest course of action. An alternative is to increase gradually the apparent "dose" of the treatment. For example, if relaxation practice for 15 minutes, two times a day, has little or no effect, an increase to 25 minutes, four times a day, might make a difference.

Similarly, the packaging of the treatment can make a difference in its effectiveness. Just as an injected placebo may be more effective than an orally-administered placebo, for some clients relaxation training, desensitization, and other treatments can be made more effective by presenting them in the guise of "hypnosis."

Is There Less Pain or Does It Just Hurt Less?

There is some question as to whether placebos actually reduce the intensity of sensation produced by a painful stimulus or whether they alter the way in which the sensation is experienced. Placebo administration has been seen by some writers as producing the reaction: "My pain is the same, but it doesn't hurt me now" (Beecher, 1956, p. 111; also see Barber, 1959).

This explanation has considerable intuitive appeal. In a number of situations, the same sensation elicits markedly different reactions in different people. For example, spicy foods contain irritants that produce a sensation of burning heat, a feeling that small children avoid. As they grow older, however, some youngsters begin to like the effect and develop a craving for spicy food. Similarly, some people experience cold as painful, whereas others learn to experience the same sensation as bracing and refreshing. A similar phenomenon is indicated by the fact that some people are ticklish, whereas others are not.

The similarity of these phenomena to placebo pain reduction is illustrated by the fact that people's reactions to spice, cold, and being tickled can be changed by altering their expectations (as described in the Preface). For example, a variety of persuasive procedures can be used to change people from being uncontrollably ticklish to not being ticklish at all in a matter of minutes. Having people imagine themselves as no longer ticklish is a frequently effective procedure. Some people may be more successful if this procedure is preceded by a hypnotic induction. For many, a very persuasive verbal communication indicating that ticklishness can be altered by deciding and believing that one is no longer ticklish will suffice. Typically, people are able to predict whether or not they are still ticklish prior to being tested, and the effect appears to be stable and long lasting.

It is usually assumed that active pain medications are unlike placebos in that they decrease the sensation of pain as well as affecting the person's reaction to that sensation. However, Beecher (1956, 1957) has suggested that morphine and other analgesics operate in much the same way as placebos: "Narcotics really alter pain perception very little but do produce a bemused state, comparable to distraction" (Beecher, 1957, p.152). From this perspective, placebos and active analgesics operate via similar mechanisms. According to Beecher, placebos reduce the anxiety associated with clinical pain, thereby making the pain more tolerable. In addition to reducing anxiety, active medications generate an altered state of consciousness that distracts the person from attending to the pain. But neither active nor placebo medication affect the sensation itself.

Beecher's hypothesis was based in part on the erroneous belief that the effects of placebos—and of opiates as well—were limited to clinical pain. He argued that because subjects in an experimental situation had no reason to be anxious about the meaning of their pain (for example, it was clearly not an indication of serious disease), there was no pain-related anxiety to reduce—hence the failure of placebos and general anesthetics to relieve experimental pain. In fact, numerous early studies appeared to show that neither placebos nor opiates had any effect on experimentally induced pain. However, the failure of these studies to find an effect was at least partly due to the absence of no-treatment control groups in experimental designs. Subsequent studies indicated that repeated administration of experimental pain stimuli can produce increases in pain, which can mask the pain-relieving effects of treatment. Studies that include no-treatment control groups show reliable placebo effects on both clinical and experimental pain (Camatte et al., 1969; Gelfand et al., 1963; Kirsch & Baker, 1987; Liberman, 1964).

General Anesthetics as "Active" Placebos

The results of two recent studies suggest that Beecher may have been correct in hypothesizing that placebo and pharmacological pain reduction are due to similar mechanisms (Dworkin, Chen, LeResche, & Clark, 1983; Dworkin, Chen, Schubert, & Clark, 1984), though they also suggest that his theory needs to be modified. The studies indicate that the altered states of consciousness produced by active drugs do not automatically reduce pain. Instead, the pain-relieving effects of some active drugs may be entirely due to expectancy. Rather than reduce pain, altered states of consciousness may confirm people's expectations for reduced pain. These studies also suggest that whether induced by placebos or by active drugs, expectancies can affect the sensation of pain as well as a person's reaction to that sensation.

Like other general anesthetics, nitrous oxide (N_2O), an analgesic gas that is frequently used in dentistry, produces global alterations in consciousness, which Beecher refers to as a "bemused state." However, Dworkin et al. (1983) demonstrated that this bemused state can either decrease or *increase* sensitivity to painful stimulation, depending on people's expectations. In that study, one group of subjects was given a rationale that described the common use of nitrous oxide as a pain reliever in dentistry. A second group was told that the altered state of consciousness produced by nitrous oxide can increase sensitivity to physical sensations, creating "a kind of exquisite awareness of what's going on in the body" (p. 1075). The authors reported that whereas nitrous oxide decreased pain in the first group, it led to increased pain in the second.

The effect of this expectancy manipulation was not limited to reports of pain. Besides assessing pain threshold and tolerance, Dworkin et al. (1983) measured the effects of nitrous oxide on their subjects' absolute sensation threshold, a measure of sensitivity to nonpainful stimulation. Their results on this measure were similar to those reported for pain. With expectations for pain relief, subjects were less sensitive to nonpainful levels of stimulation with nitrous oxide. Conversely, nitrous oxide increased sensitivity to stimulation when subjects were led to believe that this would be its effect.

Placebos are generally inert substances, but the use of "active" or "impure" placebos have also been recommended (Blumenthal, Burke, & Shapiro, 1974). Active placebos are substances that produce pharmacological effects, but not for the condition being treated or investigated. They may mimic the side effects of other drugs, for example, and so are more likely to convince recipients that they are receiving effective medication. The data reported by Dworkin et al. (1983) suggest that general anesthetics can function as "active" placebos and that their pain-relieving effects may—in some cases—be entirely due to expectancy. The superiority of these drugs to inactive placebos may be due to the convincing character of their side effects. The bemused state acts to confirm the potency of the drug, thereby confirming subjects' expectations of decreased pain. Most drugs that produce an altered state of consciousness have analgesic effects as well. Furthermore, the degree of pain relief that is brought about by these drugs appears to be proportional to the intensity of the altered states of consciousness that they elicit.

In a follow-up to their earlier study, Dworkin et al. (1984) tested the hypothesis that the mood-altering effect of active medication enhances expectancy by confirming that the drug is working as intended. In this study, the analgesic effects of nitrous oxide were tested with and without information intended to highlight the connection between pain reduction and the mood alterations and other side effects produced by the drug. Subjects in the "high" information condition (the pun appears to have been unintended) were told that:

> Nitrous oxide works as a sedative or tranquilizer. It lowers the brain's level of consciousness about anxiety and pain, making people feel good. Actually, the first signs that nitrous oxide is changing how your brain is processing information comes from changes you can readily experience with the lowest dosages of nitrous oxide—your toes, maybe your hands, may begin tingling and a kind of warm glow may come over you, a feeling of relaxation of muscle tension. *These signs from your body,* which some compare with drinking a good glass of wine or even smoking marijuana, *indicate that the nitrous oxide has reached physiologically active levels. The drug is now working.* [italics added] (p. 343)

As predicted, this information increased the effectiveness of nitrous oxide as a pain reliever. Furthermore, as in their earlier study, this effect was obtained for absolute sensitivity to sensation as well as for pain threshold.

Taken together, these two studies suggest that active analgesic medication may function via the same mechanism as placebos; that is, by altering pain

19

expectancies. The pharmacologically active components of these drugs enhance their effectiveness by strengthening the expectancy for pain reduction. These studies also show that the effects of expectancy are not limited to people's classification of sensations as painful or nonpainful. Instead, expectancies can affect absolute sensitivity to sensation.[2]

Additional evidence that placebos can affect the sensation of pain, rather than just the reaction to that sensation, is provided by data indicating that expectancies can generate pain, as well as alleviate it. For example, headaches are a frequently reported side effect of lumbar puncture, a clinical procedure used to administer anesthetics or to extract spinal fluid for diagnostic purposes. Daniels and Sallie (1981) performed lumbar punctures on two groups of subjects, only one of which was warned of the possibility of headaches. Seven of the 15 subjects who were forewarned subsequently reported headaches, as compared to only one of the 13 control subjects, suggesting that this commonly reported consequence of lumbar puncture is a placebo effect.

Placebo Tranquilizers and Stimulants

Of the relatively small body of research devoted expressly to investigating placebo effects, the largest number of studies have involved the use of placebo stimulants and tranquilizers, mostly with healthy volunteer subjects. In one of the first of these studies, two placebos—one labeled a stimulant and the other a tranquilizer—were administered to a single group of subjects in separate sessions (Frankenhaeuser, Jarpe, Svan, & Wrangsjö, 1963). The "stimulant" placebo produced significant increases in pulse rate, systolic and diastolic blood pressure, actual and perceived reaction speed, and reports of feeling happier, more alert, less sleepy, and less depressed. The "depressant" placebo produced significant effects in the opposite direction.

These effects of placebo stimulants and tranquilizers have since been replicated enough times to be considered well-established (Blackwell, Bloomfield, & Buncher, 1972; Brodeur, 1965; Buckalew, 1972; Frankenhaeuser, Post, Hagdahl, & Wrangsjö, 1964; Kirsch & Weixel, 1988; Lyerly, Ross, Krugman, & Clyde, 1964; Morris & O'Neal, 1974; Ross, Krugman, Lyerly, & Clyde, 1962). The effects of placebos on subjective mood are particularly important for psychotherapists because mood disturbances (especially anxiety and depression) are among the most common targets of psychotherapeutic intervention.

In two studies of placebo stimulants, the effects of verbal feedback have also been investigated. Buckalew (1972) reported that reinforcing subjects' perception of the placebo effect, by telling them that their reaction time was faster after each of three practice trials, tended to enhance the significant effect of taking the pill. In a similar study, Morris and O'Neal (1974) provided half of their subjects with

---

[2]Signal detection analysis has also been used to evaluate whether given instances of pain reduction are due to decreased sensitivity or to changes in subjects' criterion for reporting a sensation as painful. These studies have yielded inconsistent results. More importantly, it has been shown that signal detection analyses are, in principle, incapable of discriminating between changes in sensitivity and changes in pain criteria (Coppola & Gracely, 1983).

bogus feedback of improved manual dexterity following "practice trials" at a pursuit rotor task. On subsequent trials, the feedback had significant effects on perceived dexterity and on self-reported mood.

It is likely that feedback indicating improvement has facilitative effects on psychotherapeutic outcome as well. False feedback has been used as a component of effective treatments designed to be "placebo controls" in studies of psychotherapy (for example, see Lick, 1975; Marcia, Rubin, & Efran, 1969). In clinical practice, however, there is no reason for feedback to be bogus, nor should it be limited to verbal communication, as it has been demonstrated that attitudes and expectancies based on direct experience have a greater impact on behavior (Fazio & Zanna, 1981; Wickless & Kirsch, in press). Providing opportunities for clients to observe their own improvement is a built-in feature of many effective psychotherapies. In desensitization treatments for phobic disorders, for example, clients are directed to repeatedly confront feared stimuli. In this way, they are able to observe that their fear is gradually decreasing.

Double-Blind versus Deceptive Administration

In the studies cited in the previous section, subjects were led to believe that they were taking an active drug. Similarly, when drugs are taken in real-life settings, people have no reason to suspect that they might be taking a placebo. However, this is not generally the case in double-blind studies. Typically, subjects in double-blind studies are aware that they may be receiving a placebo rather than the active drug. Both subjects and experimenters are told that the study involves a placebo group and an active drug group, but none of the participants are told to which group they have been assigned until after the study has been completed.[3]

Presumably, the placebo and drug effects that are observed in double-blind situations are comparable to those produced in clinical practice. But are they? Kirsch and Weixel (1988) conducted a study that was designed, in part, to address this issue. In our study, we gave college students varying doses of placebo caffeine (decaffeinated coffee). Half of the students were given the placebo under "double-blind" conditions; that is, they were told that the coffee might or might not be caffeinated. The remaining students were led to believe that they were receiving caffeinated coffee. We anticipated that effects would be associated with the amount of caffeine that students thought they were ingesting, and also with how sure they were that the beverage they had consumed actually contained caffeine.

Specifically, we expected to find a greater placebo effect with deceptive administration than with double-blind administration. We also hypothesized that

---

[3]At least, this is how double-blind studies are *supposed* to be conducted. I have heard of instances of studies sponsored by pharmaceutical companies that were ostensibly double-blind, but in which experimenters were aware of the status of various subjects and chose to inform control subjects that they *were in fact* receiving a placebo (L. McClenney, personal communication, November 27, 1986). I do not know how widespread this practice is, but its implications are disturbing. Informing control subjects of their status defeats the purpose of their inclusion in double-blind studies and may lead to inflated estimates of drug effectiveness. Brodeur (1965), for example, found that informing subjects that the drug they had taken was a placebo produced pulse rates between those produced by a "stimulant" placebo and those produced by a "tranquilizer" placebo.

with low to moderate dosage, the effects of the placebo would increase as a function of the amount of caffeine that subjects believed they were consuming. At extremely high doses (the apparent equivalent of eight cups of coffee), we thought that the placebo manipulation might become unbelievable, especially for subjects in the double-blind condition. We saw this situation as analogous to "overselling" a treatment by promising far more than it actually could deliver. At these high doses, we predicted a "backlash," which would be shown by less of a placebo effect than had been obtained at moderate apparent dose levels.

As shown in Figure 2–1, for the deceptive administration group the predicted response curve was found on scales measuring alertness and tension, and on systolic blood pressure. This curvilinear effect was also found regarding subjects' judgements about whether their beverage had in fact contained caffeine.[4] Subjects receiving moderate doses had higher blood pressures and were more alert, tense, and certain that they had been given a caffeinated beverage than those who had received low or extremely high doses of the placebo. In contrast to deceptive administration, double-blind administration (in which the students were aware that they might be given a placebo) produced response curves in the opposite direction. Placebo effects on each of these variables were more pronounced at low and high doses than at moderate doses.[5]

This study shows that two aspects of response expectancy can be identified and experimentally isolated. One of these is the amount of change that is expected, which we manipulated by varying the apparent dose of the placebo caffeine. The second is the strength of the expectancy—that is, the person's subjective probability that the anticipated response will in fact occur—which we manipulated by administering the placebo with either double-blind or deceptive instructions.

This distinction between the level of an expectation and the strength or certainty with which it is held has important implications about the kind of information that might best facilitate therapeutic change. In many situations, the degree of change that is expected and the strength of the expectancy are closely associated. People who find a particular treatment believable are likely to have greater confidence that it will produce an effect *and* to expect that the effect will be large. However, this is not always the case. For example, when a treatment is touted as having nearly miraculous effects, many people will be skeptical of the claims, but they may not be ready to dismiss those claims altogether without first testing to see whether they might not in fact be true. These people have weak expectancies for great amounts of change, a situation in which expectancies should be most easily altered. Conversely, a treatment that is convincingly presented as producing reliable but moderate change ought to generate expectancies that are relatively immune from disconfirmation (Kirsch, 1985a).

---

[4] So as not to induce an element of doubt to subjects who were told that their beverage was caffeinated, these ratings were obtained after all other measures were taken.

[5] A significant placebo effect on pulse rate was also found, but only in subjects to whom the beverage had been deceptively administered as containing caffeine, not in those given double-blind instructions. This suggests that double-blind studies underestimate placebo effects and possibly drug effects as well.

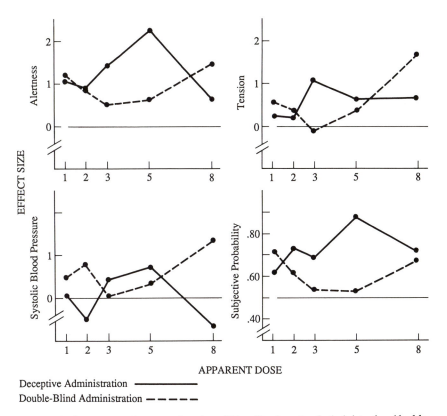

Deceptive Administration ————————
Double-Blind Administration ——————

FIGURE 2–1 Placebo effects as a function of "dose" and mode of administration (double-blind or deceptive). SOURCE: Reprinted from Kirsch & Weixel, 1988.

A second important issue that is raised by our study of placebo caffeine relates to the validity and generalizability of drug evaluation studies using double-blind methods. When drugs are administered in experimental settings, subjects are generally informed that they may receive a placebo. Yet drug-taking in real life more closely resembles deceptive administration of a placebo; that is, people taking a drug in nonexperimental settings typically have no reason to doubt that the drug is real. Our data suggest that results based on double-blind administration may not be generalizable to clinical situations, leaving open the possibility that by relying on double-blind studies, we may be reaching spurious conclusions about the effects of various drugs.

The Balanced Placebo Design

The Kirsch and Weixel (1988) study reveals a potentially serious problem with the double-blind design that is currently the norm in drug evaluation studies. This problem could be ameliorated by retiring the double-blind paradigm and replacing it with the "balanced placebo design." The balanced placebo design was first introduced in 1962 (Ross et al., 1962) and then neglected for many years, until it

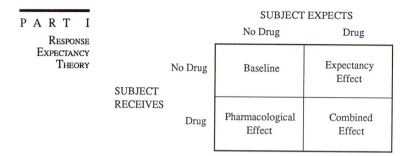

SUBJECT EXPECTS

		No Drug	Drug
SUBJECT RECEIVES	No Drug	Baseline	Expectancy Effect
	Drug	Pharmacological Effect	Combined Effect

FIGURE 2–2 The balanced placebo design.

was revived and used extensively to separate expectancy effects and pharmacological effects associated with alcohol use (Marlatt & Rohsenow, 1980). It is an elegant experimental design that allows independent evaluation of pharmacological and expectancy effects, as well as providing information about how those effects interact when active medications are given.

The balanced placebo design involves four groups of subjects (Figure 2–2). One group (lower-right) knowingly receives a drug. A second group (upper-right) is given a placebo. These conditions are similar to those in many drug-placebo studies, except that they are not double-blind; none of the subjects are given reason to doubt that they are receiving active medication.

The most innovative aspects of the balanced placebo design are represented on the left side of the figure. To the more traditional drug and placebo conditions, baseline (upper-left) and disguised drug or "antiplacebo" (lower-left) groups are added. In the disguised drug condition, the drug is administered without the subjects' knowledge.[6] Differences between baseline and antiplacebo conditions can be attributed to the pharmacological properties of the drug and, in fact, provide a more direct estimate of that effect than can be obtained from traditional drug versus placebo comparisons. Differences between baseline and placebo conditions are due to expectancy, and the effects observed in the nonblind drug condition reflect the combined effects of expectancy and pharmacology.

In the Ross et al. (1962) study, in which the balanced placebo design was first introduced, one group of subjects was given an amphetamine pill and another group was given a placebo to be taken with orange juice. The disguised drug group received amphetamine dissolved in orange juice, and the control group was given plain orange juice. This study reveals what can happen when people expect mood changes that are opposite to those produced pharmacologically by the drug. Mood ratings for the undisguised drug group and the control group were virtually identical. In contrast, mood scores for the disguised drug and the placebo groups were significantly different from those of the control group, but in opposite directions. Subjects given the placebo reported significantly greater comfort, whereas subjects given amphetamine in disguised form reported significantly more discomfort than control subjects. The authors comment that "these two

[6]Informed consent is obtained prior to assignment to condition, with all subjects agreeing to participate in a study in which they might or might not receive an active drug.

effects cancel each other in such a way that *Ss* who knew that they had received the drug reported a mean index score approximately equal to that of the control group, which received nothing" (p. 390).

The Ross et al. study has important implications for the way in which medications are evaluated. Suppose only two groups of subjects, an active drug group and a placebo group, had participated in the study. The failure to find a significant difference between these groups would have led to the conclusion that the drug had no effect on mood. But this conclusion would have been erroneous. The addition of the disguised drug group and the baseline control group revealed that amphetamine had a negative pharmacological effect on mood ratings, an effect that was masked by the opposite effect of the subjects' positive expectations.

In a subsequent study (Lyerly et al., 1964), the investigators expanded the balanced placebo design to include two medications, a stimulant and a sedative. The stimulant produced independent pharmacological and expectancy effects on self-reported mood. These effects were additive and of approximately equal magnitude, so that subjects who knowingly received the stimulant reported the greatest change in mood.

Using a design similar to the balanced placebo design (though not as elegant), Frankenhaeuser et al. (1964) tested subjects under three conditions: (1) pentobarbitone administered as a depressant, (2) pentobarbitone administered with ambiguous information about its effects, and (3) a placebo administered as a depressant. When the active drug was administered as a depressant, it produced greater alterations in reaction time and in subjective state than it did when it was administered with ambiguous information. No differences were found between the effects of the placebo and the effects of the active drug administered in the ambiguous information condition.

These three studies provide further evidence of the power of placebos to affect subjective mood and motor performance. They also provide information about the ways in which psychological and pharmacological factors interact. In all three studies, the effects of expectancy were as strong as the pharmacological effects of the active drugs. Also, these effects were additive. When expectancies were consistent with the pharmacological effects of the drug, they enhanced the drug's effectiveness. When people expected effects that were opposite to those produced by the drug, the pharmacological effects were effectively canceled. It is likely that clients' expectations can enhance or inhibit psychotherapeutic change in a similar manner, although the Kirsch and Weixel (1988) study suggests that *unrealistically* high expectancies might also inhibit positive change.

Placebo Alcohol

The balanced placebo design has been used most extensively in investigating the contributions of expectancy and pharmacology to the effects of alcohol consumption. These studies have shown that many of the effects commonly attributed to alcohol can be produced by a placebo. They also show that, at moderate doses, these effects are not produced by the pharmacological properties of alcohol, suggesting that at least some of them might be entirely due to expectancy.

One of the pharmacological effects of alcohol is that it inhibits sexual arousal in both men and women (Farkas & Rosen, 1976; Rubin & Henson, 1976). However, most people are not aware of this and in fact believe the opposite (Brown, Goldman, Inn, & Anderson, 1980). Because alcohol-related expectancies about sexual arousal stand in marked contradiction to pharmacological reality, the results of balanced placebo studies on this topic are particularly interesting. When exposed to erotic stimuli, both men and women report greater sexual arousal when they believe that they have consumed small doses of alcohol, doses that have no significant pharmacological effect on arousal (Briddell et al., 1978; Lang, Searles, Lauerman, & Adesso, 1980; Lansky & Wilson, 1981; Wilson & Lawson, 1976, 1978). Among males, these reports of increased arousal have been substantiated by increases in penile tumescence, heart rate, and skin temperature. In contrast, women's reports of enhanced arousal following real or placebo alcohol are not reliably accompanied by vaginal engorgement.

Another belief that many people have about alcohol is that it reduces inhibitions, thereby allowing freer expression of sexual and aggressive impulses. If this were a pharmacological effect, we would expect to find it constant across cultures, but in fact, the effect of alcohol on sexual and aggressive behavior varies from culture to culture (MacAndrew & Edgerton, 1969).

The idea that the apparent disinhibitory effects of alcohol are culturally learned phenomena is also supported by experimental data. One of my colleagues at the University of Connecticut (Mosher, 1966) has developed an inventory that measures the degree to which people have guilty feelings associated with sexuality. Lang et al. (1980) administered Mosher's sex guilt scale to a group of male college students, gave them alcoholic or nonalcoholic beverages with balanced placebo instructions, and then had them look at erotic slides while unobtrusively recording how long they looked at each slide. For men who were low in sex guilt, the more pornographic the picture, the longer they spent looking at it. This was true regardless of the actual or believed content of their beverages. In contrast, subjects who were high in sex guilt spent more time viewing the more pornographic slides only if they thought they had consumed alcohol. Once again, only subjects' beliefs mattered; the actual content of the beverage had no effect.

Similar results have been found with measures of aggressiveness (Lang, Goeckner, Adesso, & Marlatt, 1975). After administering beverages with balanced placebo instructions, the researchers had their subjects administer bogus electric shocks to a confederate who had insulted them. Not knowing that the shocks were in actuality not real, those who thought they had consumed alcohol delivered stronger "shocks" for longer periods of time. However, a fairly high dose of alcohol (the amount for determining legal intoxication in most states) did not affect this measure of aggresiveness unless subjects were informed that the beverage was alcoholic. Pihl, Zeichner, Niaura, Nagy, and Zacchia (1981) reported similar results.

In contrast to these effects on measures of physically aggressive behavior, Rohsenow and Bachorowski (1984) reported that subjects who thought they had consumed alcohol were *less* verbally aggressive after being provoked. In this study, actual alcohol increased aggressiveness, but only in women and only at a relatively low dose.

In our culture, one of the most widely held beliefs about alcohol is that it produces in alcoholics an irresistible craving for more alcohol. Total abstinence is therefore seen as their only recourse. However, balanced placebo research suggests that increased craving and loss of control are at least partially due to expectancy. In two of these studies, alcoholics who thought that they had been given alcoholic beverages rated their alcohol craving as higher than did those who thought that their beverages were nonalcoholic (Engle & Williams, 1972; Merry, 1966). In contrast, there was no difference in craving as a function of whether subjects had in fact consumed alcohol. In another balanced placebo study, nonabstinent alcoholics and social drinkers were given an opportunity to drink as much as they wanted as part of a supposed "taste rating task" (Marlatt, Demming, & Reid, 1973). Among both groups of subjects, those who thought that the beverages contained alcohol drank more, whereas actual alcohol content had no effect.

Although alcohol is often thought of as a drug that reduces social anxiety, the belief and the resulting effects may depend on the person's sex and the nature of the situation. Wilson and Abrams conducted two virtually identical balanced placebo studies on the effects of alcohol on social anxiety in men and women (Abrams & Wilson, 1979; Wilson & Abrams, 1977). After drinking real or placebo alcohol, subjects were asked to make a good impression on a confederate of the opposite sex. Males who thought they had consumed alcohol were less anxious as a result of that belief, but women in an analogous situation reported a need to monitor their behavior more closely and were therefore more anxious than those who did not think that they had drunk alcohol. The genuineness of these self-reported effects was corroborated by measures of heart rate and skin conductance and by objective ratings of behavior.

In sum, balanced placebo studies demonstrate that response expectancies can affect aggressiveness, sexual arousal, social anxiety, and alcohol craving. In contrast, moderate doses of alcohol do *not* affect these responses *unless the subject is aware* that he or she has consumed alcohol. Furthermore, placebo alcohol enhances sexual arousal despite the fact that it is inhibited by larger doses of real alcohol. Thus it is possible that many of the effects of alcohol are in fact placebo effects, a possibility that has important implications for the development of treatments for substance abuse (Goldman, Brown, & Christiansen, in press).

Nausea, Vomiting, and Gastric Function

The effects of placebos on gastric function were first demonstrated in a seminal report by Stewart Wolf (1950). A pioneer in the investigation of placebo effects, Wolf reported three successful experimental attempts at reversing the effects of active medications that typically induce abdominal discomfort. In each case the reversal was brought about by misinforming the subject about the nature of the drug being administered, and in each case the subjective changes were verified by physiological assessment.

One of Wolf's subjects was a 28-year-old pregnant woman who was suffering from nausea and vomiting. Wolf gave her ipecac, a drug that interrupts normal gastric contractions, thereby inducing nausea and vomiting. Although ipecac is commonly used to induce vomiting when toxic substances have been swallowed, Wolf misinformed his patient that it was a medicine that would alleviate her nausea. Prior to taking ipecac, the patient displayed an absence of gastric contractions. Within 20 minutes after ingesting the drug, normal gastric contractions resumed and the nausea ended.

Wolf conducted a similar experiment on another patient suffering from nausea associated with recurrent interruptions of gastric contractions. When administered orally without counteracting instructions, ipecac predictably induced nausea and vomiting. However, when the same dosage was administered in disguised form and was accompanied by misinformation about its effects, it produced a resumption of normal contractile activity and the nausea disappeared.

The best known of Wolf's demonstrations of placebo effects on gastric function involved "Tom," whose enlarged gastric fistula made it possible to directly observe his gastric mucous membrane. Because of his condition, Tom was the subject of more than 100 experiments on the effects of various drugs. One of these was prostigmine, a drug that produces gastric hyperfunction, abdominal cramps, and diarrhea. These effects were later reproduced by inert placebos and also by atropine sulfate, which typically inhibits gastric function (Wolf, 1950). In another experiment, Tom was observed following 13 administrations of a placebo and during 13 control trials in which no substance was given to him (Abbot, Mack, & Wolf, 1952). Placebo administration resulted in a 33% decrease in gastric acid secretion, as compared to an 18% decrease during control trials.

The importance of informational cues is highlighted by a later report in which Wolf (1962) described two investigators in his clinic who frequently measured gastric acid secretion in patients following placebo administration. One investigator found an increase in gastric acid secretion in "almost every patient," whereas the other reported equally reliable decreases in secretion following placebo administration. Presumably, this difference was due to different cues being provided to subjects by the two experimenters.

In contrast to Wolf's reports, which are either anecdotal or based on very few subjects, one study of the effects of a placebo on seasickness among military personnel was well controlled (Tyler, 1946). The placebo in this study, compared to untreated controls, was ineffective in preventing signs of motion sickness. Taking into account these conflicting results, additional research is needed to determine the circumstances under which placebos affect gastric function.

Warts and Other Skin Conditions

The physiological changes produced by placebo alcohol, stimulants, and tranquilizers are associated with corresponding changes in subjective experience.

However, placebos have been reported to produce some rather startling effects on skin conditions that are not as closely linked to experiential changes.

The most impressive of these reports involves the suggestion-related production and inhibition of contact dermatitis (Ikemi & Nakagawa, 1962), a skin condition produced by chemical substances to which people have become sensitized. In this study, 13 students were touched on one arm with leaves from a harmless tree, but were told that the leaves were from a lacquer or wax tree (Japanese trees that produce effects similar to poison ivy and to which the boys had reported being hypersensitive). On the other arm, the subjects were touched with irritant leaves, which they were led to believe were from a harmless tree. All 13 subjects displayed a skin reaction to the harmless leaves (the placebo), but only two reacted to the irritant leaves. Five of the students were hypnotized before being touched with the leaves, but the results were virtually identical for hypnotized and nonhypnotized subjects.

In 1927, Bloch (cited in Allington, 1952) followed 179 patients whose warts had been treated with an elaborate placebo procedure. The warts were painted with various colored dyes and exposed to an impressive electrical machine, which was then turned on. After treatment, the patients were instructed not to touch the warts until the color had faded completely, at which time, they were assured, the warts would be cured. Bloch reported success rates of 44 to 88%, depending on the type of wart, with most of the warts disappearing within one month. Although this study used no control group, the results can be compared with data from other studies indicating a rate of spontaneous remission of about 25% over a six-month period (Allington, 1952).

Four years after Bloch's data were reported, Memmesheimer and Eisenlohr (cited in Allington, 1952) observed changes in warts among 70 patients to whom placebo treatment was provided and another 70 patients in a no-treatment control condition. Their treatment was not as impressive as that used by Bloch (only a few of their patients were exposed to the electrical apparatus), and their results were not as impressive. After six months, only 17 of the treated patients were cured of their warts, as compared to 20 of the untreated patients. However, the treated patients were cured more rapidly: 11 within one month (as compared to only two in the untreated group) and 14 within three months (as compared to five in the untreated group).

Johnston and Stenstrum (1986) compared the effects of hypnosis, placebo, and no-treatment on warts. Within six weeks, 50% of the hypnosis subjects had lost warts, compared to 25% of placebo subjects and 11% of untreated controls. The difference between the hypnosis and the untreated group was statistically significant, but the proportion of subjects losing warts in the placebo group did not differ significantly from that found in either of the other conditions. The fact that success in the hypnosis group was unrelated to subjects' hypnotizability levels suggests that these results were not due to hypnosis per se. In some situations, hypnosis can be a more credible expectancy manipulation than medical placebos, and this may be responsible for its greater efficacy in the Johnston and Stenstrum study.

What We Know and What We Suspect

Studies of placebo analgesia, tranquilizers, stimulants, and alcohol have produced clear-cut data about the self-confirming power of response expectancies. Placebo-induced expectancies can create or reduce pain and can increase or decrease sensitivity to nonpainful levels of stimulation. They can also alter mood states, the direction of change depending on people's beliefs about the nature of the substance they are taking. When given placebo tranquilizers, people describe themselves as being less alert and more relaxed, tired, drowsy, sluggish, sleepy, and depressed. Placebo stimulants elicit reports of greater alertness, happiness, and tension, and of being less sleepy and depressed. Placebo alcohol can enhance sexual arousal, counteract inhibitions associated with guilty feelings about sex, produce a craving for alcohol, increase or reduce aggressiveness, and either increase or decrease social anxiety, depending on the person's gender and the nature of the situation. Placebos also appear to be capable of producing or inhibiting nausea and producing changes in skin conditions, although these effects are not as well established as the others.

Though elicited by expectancy, these placebo-induced changes are not just imaginary. In many instances, their reality has been corroborated by corresponding changes in heart or pulse rate, systolic and diastolic blood pressure, penile tumescence (but not vaginal engorgement), skin temperature, gastric motility, vomiting, reaction speed, manual dexterity, and objective ratings of behavior by independent observers.

Even if placebos could do nothing else, these effects would indicate that response expectancy is an extremely powerful psychological mechanism with important implications for psychological treatment. Yet what about the other effects that have at times been attributed to placebos? Can placebos affect ulcers, symptoms of drug withdrawal, asthma, hay fever, coughs, diabetes, angina, cancer, and the common cold? There are data suggesting that placebos can affect many of these conditions. For example, Hillis (1952) reported that a placebo was more effective than no-treatment and as effective as codeine in inhibiting artificially induced coughs in a single subject. Volgyesi (1954) reported that 70% of patients with bleeding ventricular and duodenal ulcers were completely cured by placebo treatment, as verified by gastroscopic and X-ray examination. In contrast, among patients who were told that they were serving as experimental controls, the same procedures resulted in a cure rate of only 25%.

Although it is often assumed that the effects of placebos are transitory, some data suggests that this might not always be the case. Boissel et al. (1986), for example, reported that "long-term" (six months) placebo therapy for angina pectoris resulted in a success rate of 77%. More impressively, Thomsen, Bretlau, Tos, and Johnsen (1983) reported a 77% success rate at a three-year follow-up of patients treated for Meniere's disease with placebo surgery.[7] By comparison, the success rate among patients who had received the supposedly active surgical procedure was only 70%.

---

[7] The placebo surgery was a mastoidectomy, instead of the regular endolymphatic sac mastoid shunt.

30

Perhaps the most provocative report of placebo power is a case in which placebo treatment appeared to have profound effects on the course of a terminally ill cancer patient (Klopfer, 1957). The patient had a generalized advanced malignancy with huge tumor masses (the size of oranges) in the neck, armpits, groin, chest, and abdomen, and a prognosis of less than two weeks. Having read about a new experimental drug that was to be tested at the hospital, he pleaded with, and ultimately persuaded, his physician to include him in the experimental group. Three days later, "the tumor masses had melted like snow balls on a hot stove, and in only these few days, they were half their original size" (p. 338). Within ten days, practically all signs of the disease had vanished.

About two months later, reports began appearing in the press indicating that the experimental drug had been proven ineffective. Reading these reports, the patient lost faith in the treatment that had benefited him so greatly and relapsed to his pretreatment condition. However, at this point, his physician managed to persuade him that the negative results were due to a deterioration of the drug and that a new, refined, double-strength product was due to arrive shortly. A couple of days later, treatment with an inert placebo was begun.

The effects of this inactive placebo treatment were even more dramatic than those obtained with the experimental drug. Once again the tumor masses "melted" and the patient became ambulatory. He remained symptom-free for an additional two months, following which he read an AMA announcement in the press concluding that the drug he thought he was getting was "worthless." He died a few days later.

A Nondeceptive Placebo

Given the known and suspected power of placebos to effect improvement in a large variety of conditions, one might expect clinicians to be eager to take advantage of their therapeutic potential. Not wanting to deceive their patients, however, most clinicians are justifiably reluctant to use placebos knowingly. After all, how powerful would a placebo be if the patient knew it was a placebo?

That question is typically asked rhetorically. It is assumed that the answer is "not powerful at all." However, in one of the most tantalizing, frustrating, and inexplicably neglected studies in the placebo literature, Park and Covi (1965) sought to answer the question empirically. Based on their research, they reached the surprising conclusion that placebos can be used without deception and still be effective.

Park and Covi gave placebo pills to 15 psychiatric outpatients and *told them that the pills were placebos.* Specifically, the patients were told:

> Many people with your kind of condition have . . . been helped by what are sometimes called "sugar pills," and we feel that a so-called sugar pill may help you, too. Do you know what a sugar pill is? A sugar pill is a pill with no medicine in it at all. I think this pill will help you as it has helped so many others. Are you willing to try this pill? (p. 337)

Under these circumstances, one might expect patients to become angry or insulted, to refuse to take the pills, or at least to feel skeptical, even if reluctant to express their skepticism. We would certainly not expect them to improve. Nevertheless, all but one of the patients agreed to take the pills. Further, a count of the pills that remained the following week indicated that the subjects had taken them as prescribed, and symptomatic improvement was reported for all 14 compliant subjects.

On post-hoc questioning, six of the subjects reported that they suspected that the pills contained active medication. Three of these patients reported side effects that may have encouraged their suspicion. Another concluded that the pills could not have been placebos because they worked better than the medications she had taken previously. In other words, the effects of the pills were not necessarily due to the belief that they contained real medication. Rather, some patients concluded that the pills contained medication because they seemed to work.

Most impressively, substantial improvement was found in subjects who reported being certain that the pills were in fact placebos, as well as those who had come to suspect that they contained active medication. Fearing addiction to active medication, one patient expressed relief at having been given a placebo and asked to be allowed to continue taking her sugar pills after the experiment was over.

The Park and Covi study has, of course, a serious flaw: The experiment contained no control group against which the ratings of improvement could be compared; these patients might have improved just as much even had they not been given the placebo. This alternate explanation is especially salient given the fact that the nondeceptive placebo was administered at the intake session, and follow-up treatment was promised. Psychiatric outpatients typically show considerable improvement immediately after an intake interview, improvement that is presumably due to the promise of treatment (Frank, Nash, Stone, & Imber, 1963; Friedman, 1963; Goldstein, 1960; Kellner & Sheffield, 1971; Piper & Wogan, 1970; Shapiro, Struening, & Shapiro, 1980).

Surprisingly, the Park and Covi study has not been replicated with the addition of a control group that is not given the placebo. Nevertheless, the fact that most of the patients complied with the nondeceptive placebo treatment instructions and that some later attributed their improvement to having taken a "sugar pill" suggests that placebos need not be deceptive in order to be effective.

Despite the impressive results of this study, the prescription of "sugar pills" to patients cannot be recommended. In a study of "tranquilizer" and "stimulant" placebos among nonpatient volunteers, Brodeur (1965) obtained placebo effects only when the pills were administered deceptively. No effect was obtained among control subjects, who were given a pill described as "an inactive lactose placebo." Thus, the Park and Covi results may not be generalizable beyond the particular population from which it was obtained. Also, both psychotropic medication and placebos were relatively new in 1965. More experienced and sophisticated patients may not accept the "sugar pill" rationale so readily.

Still, the study has important implications for psychotherapists. If some of our most effective treatments achieve their effects by changing clients' expectations, would we then be faced with the undesirable alternatives of either deceiving our clients or withholding an effective treatment? As shown in subsequent chapters, this is not merely an academic question. The data indicate that the effects of some very effective treatments may be due to expectancy. Fortunately, it is possible to administer these treatments with rationales that are both credible and true, rationales that include a discussion of the role of expectancy, though in a more sophisticated manner than in the placebo rationale used by Park and Covi.

Implications for Medical Research

Many of the effects of placebo analgesia, tranquilizers, stimulants, and alcohol are well-established by reliable data. In contrast, the evidence for placebo effects on cancer, coughs, ulcers, and many other clinical conditions is provocative, but not convincing. In some articles, case studies are reported anecdotally; others are based on data from a single subject. Some are reports of effects that have not yet been replicated; others have been replicated many times, but without untreated controls. At this point, all that we can say is that expectancy *might* affect these conditions, but that the data needed to provide definitive answers have not yet been collected.

How can those data be obtained? It would be relatively easy to do so. The double-blind design, as already noted, should be replaced. Its use is predicated on the assumption that placebos may have real effects on the disorder for which a treatment is being tested, but it fails to provide a way to verify that assumption. In addition, the double-blind design may produce erroneous information about the pharmacological effects of drugs. Double-blind instructions can inhibit the effects of the placebo against which a drug is being evaluated and can also produce unpredictable dose-related effects (Kirsch & Weixel, 1988). A proper comparison of drug and placebo effects would be one in which both groups of subjects believe that they are receiving the active drug.

This modification of research design will not, however, in and of itself, provide much information about expectancy effects. To do this, a no-treatment or treatment-as-usual control group must be added. The routine addition of control groups of this sort would, in short order, reveal volumes of information about possible psychological effects on a variety of conditions. The combination of untreated controls and deceptively administered placebos has potential for revealing placebo effects where none have been observed before, as it did in the case of experimentally induced pain. Conversely, it may reveal that some of the effects that have been attributed to placebos are actually spontaneous remissions. Finally, this three-group design (drug, deceptive placebo, and no-treatment) would allow us to establish the kinds of conditions for which placebos may be ineffective.

Although this design would produce more definitive data about placebo effects, it might still generate some inaccurate estimates of pharmacological effects. This can occur when people expect effects that are opposite to those produced by the drug. In these cases, the placebo effect may cancel the pharmacological effect of the drug, leaving no difference between drug and no-treatment conditions (as in the Ross et al., 1962 study). This pitfall can be avoided by

33

adding a disguised drug condition. Unlike other experimental designs, the balanced placebo design permits direct evaluation of the pharmacological effects of the drug being tested—effects that we currently infer indirectly and perhaps inaccurately by comparison to placebo controls given double-blind instructions.

Though it is a considerable improvement over the double-blind design, the balanced placebo design is not without shortcomings. Knight, Barbaree, and Boland (1986) reported that when subjects were informed about the nature of the experimental design during debriefing, and when sufficiently large doses of alcohol were used, most subjects were able to figure out whether or not their beverage contained alcohol (see Collins & Searles, 1988, however, for a cogent critique of the Knight et al. study). This may lead to an underestimation of expectancy effects and an overestimation of pharmacological effects in studies using relatively high doses of a potent drug. However, this problem is not confined to balanced placebo studies. Many subjects in double-blind studies are able to correctly identify whether or not they have been assigned to the placebo control group (Ney, Collins, & Spensor, 1986; Moscucci, Byrne, Weintraub, & Cox, 1987). This presents a challenge to researchers to develop even more effective experimental methods. Until this is done, however, the balanced placebo design appears to be the best experimental paradigm that we have for drug research.

Clinical Implications

Much of psychotherapy is concerned with altering responses—such as dysphoric mood states (especially anxiety and depression), sexual dysfunction, substance abuse, and lack of control over aggressiveness—that have been shown to be affected by placebos. Also, the development of behavioral medicine (health psychology) as one of the most rapidly growing new specialty areas in psychology suggests that all of the conditions that are affected by placebos are potential areas for psychological intervention; wherever we find a significant placebo effect, we have a condition that can be treated psychologically. Psychological treatment might enhance the effectiveness of physical interventions, provide aid for conditions for which an effective medical treatment has not been established, or provide an alternative that avoids some of the unwanted side effects of drug treatment.

Cognitive and behavior therapists have developed a number of effective interventions for many of these psychological and physical disorders. Psychotherapeutic interventions include combinations of relaxation training, hypnosis, imagery, *in vivo* exposure, activity scheduling, role-playing, and cognitive restructuring. Subsequent chapters present data on the degree to which the effectiveness of these treatments are mediated by response expectancy, but for the moment, let us assume that their effects are due to other mechanisms. If this is the case, what bearing does the literature on placebo effects have for clinical practice?

The situation that we are supposing is analogous to that in much of the research that we have examined in this chapter. In both cases, effects can be due to expectancy, as well as to other mechanisms. Changes in mood, for example, can be brought about by *either* the pharmacological characteristics of a drug *or* the belief that one has consumed a mood-altering medication. More importantly, in many cases these two factors interact in an additive fashion. Positive expectations can enhance the effects of medication, whereas negative expectations can inhibit those effects.

Recent data suggest a similar additive relationship between placebo effects and the effects of potent psychological treatments. Mavissakalian (1987) compared the effects of *in vivo* behavioral treatment in two groups of agoraphobic clients. Clients in one of these groups were given placebo pills in addition to real-life exposure to the situations they feared. The clients in this group showed more improvement than those who were not given pills. In fact, on two common measures of agoraphobic fear, the difference between the groups after eight weeks of treatment amounted to a full standard deviation, meaning that the average subject in the placebo group was better off at this point in time than 94% of the subjects in the control group.

This suggests that we need to be concerned about our clients' expectations before we begin administering a treatment. At the very least, the purpose of the intervention and the way in which it will produce change should be carefully explained. The more certain clients are that a treatment will be effective, the more effective that treatment is likely to be. On the other hand, one needs to be cautious of the pitfall of overselling a treatment. As shown in the decaffeinated coffee study (Kirsch & Weixel, 1988), expectations for unrealistically extreme effects are likely to backfire. Clients should do best if they expect initial changes of a relatively small magnitude, while at the same time holding those expectations with a high degree of certainty. In describing a treatment plan to clients, the therapist should therefore display a high degree of confidence in its effectiveness. On the other hand, clients should be cautioned not to expect a "quick fix." Instead, they should be led to expect a realistically moderate rate of change.

Inevitably, some clients fail to respond, regardless of the therapist or the therapeutic technique. In some cases, a change in therapeutic strategy may be the wisest course. But sometimes a less substantive change will suffice. Simply increasing the "dose" of the treatment may produce a therapeutic effect where none was obtained before. Similarly, repackaging may vitalize a failing intervention. If "imagery" and "relaxation" are not working, "hypnosis" might. If "hypnosis" is mystical nonsense to the client, "classical conditioning" might be tried instead. Some therapies, such as systematic desensitization, could be given any of these labels with little or no change in actual procedure, and the change in label might be enough to produce a substantial difference in outcome.

An important part of any effective treatment is the inclusion of some means by which therapeutic change will be apparent to the client. It does not matter whether the initial change is due to the treatment itself, to expectancies generated by the treatment, or simply to random fluctuations. The important thing is that it be noticed by the client and interpreted as a sign of improvement. Feedback, especially experiential feedback, strengthens the effects of positive expectations.

These treatment suggestions are based on the notion that psychotherapy is analogous to active medication, in that its effects are due to a combination of expectancy and nonexpectancy factors. In later chapters, it is shown that much of the effectiveness of psychotherapy is due to its effects on clients' beliefs and expectations, the same mechanism by which placebos produce their effects. Hypnotherapists, behavior therapists, and cognitive therapists have developed specific, nondeceptive techniques for therapeutically altering expectancies, often without being aware that this is what they were doing. These developments point the way for the nondeceptive utilization of the mechanism underlying placebo effects—the self-confirming action of response expectancies.

PSYCHOTHERAPY AND THE PLACEBO EFFECT

First [the Dodo] marked out a race-course, in a sort of circle, ("the exact shape doesn't matter," it said,) and then all the party were placed along the course, here and there. There was no "One, two, three, and away!" but they began running when they liked and left off when they liked, so that it was not easy to know when the race was over. However, when they had been running half-an-hour or so, and were quite dry again, the Dodo suddenly called out, "The race is over!" and they all crowded round it, panting, and asking, "But who has won?"

This question the Dodo could not answer without a great deal of thought, and it stood for a long time with one finger pressed upon its forehead, (the position in which you usually see Shakespeare, in the pictures of him) while the rest waited in silence. At last the Dodo said *"Everybody* has won, and *all* must have prizes. (From Lewis Carroll, *Alice's Adventures in Wonderland.*)

Hundreds of psychotherapies, based on different psychological theories and using different treatment procedures, are now available to prospective clients. The proponents of each therapy believe that its benefits are due to the mechanisms specified by the underlying theory, but it is unlikely that all of these theories are true. Indeed, many of them directly conflict with each other.

It is generally assumed that therapies based on valid theories are more effective than those based on incorrect theories. Thus, the proponents of each therapy believe their treatment method to be superior. However, most reviewers of psychotherapy outcome studies have reached a different conclusion. In general, psychological treatment produces better outcomes than no treatment at all, but the differences between types of treatment are thought to be small (Luborsky, Singer, & Luborsky, 1975; Shapiro & Shapiro, 1982; Smith, Glass, & Miller, 1980). In comparing the effects of different treatments, the Dodo bird's verdict is widely believed to apply: "Everybody has won, and all must have prizes."

Effects that can be produced by many different drugs with different chemical compositions are generally presumed to be placebo effects. Therefore, the perception that all psychotherapies are equivalent made it inevitable that the placebo concept would be applied to psychotherapy. Placebos, after all, are purely psychological treatments, and although they produce physiological as well as psychological effects, their effects on psychological states are more reliable and more pronounced.

Once this issue was raised, hundreds of studies compared the effects of a recognized psychotherapy to those of a control treatment given the label "placebo." These placebo treatments were quite diverse, ranging from complex techniques resembling bona fide therapies (for example, Kirsch, Tennen, Wickless, Saccone, & Cody, 1983) to such innocuous procedures as listening to stories, reading books, attending language classes, viewing films, participating in "bull" sessions, playing with puzzles, sitting quietly with a silent therapist, and discussing current events (see Prioleau, Murdock, & Brody, 1983). In some studies, simply being placed on a waiting list has been labeled a placebo (Sloane, Staples, Cristol, Yorkston, & Whipple, 1975). It was hoped that the results of these studies would demonstrate that psychotherapy is an effective treatment for psychological disturbance and not merely a placebo.

The results of these experiments have been evaluated by means of meta-analyses, a relatively new statistical procedure for combining the results of different studies. In a meta-analysis, an "effect size" is calculated for each measure of therapeutic effectiveness in each study.[1] Because effect sizes provide a common standard of measurement, they can be averaged across studies to provide a numerical estimate of the effectiveness of treatment, an estimate that takes into account the results of all included studies.

These meta-analyses have revealed that (1) both psychotherapy and placebo treatment are more effective than no treatment at all and (2) psychotherapies that are actually used in treatment settings are more effective than treatments designed as placebos in therapy outcome studies (Andrews & Harvey, 1981; Landman & Dawes, 1982; Priorleau et al., 1983; Smith, Glass, & Miller, 1980). More specifically, the average effect size for psychotherapy ranges from .85 to .93 of a standard deviation, depending on the criteria used for including studies in the meta-analysis. These effect sizes have been interpreted as meaning that the average person who receives therapy is better off at the end of therapy than 80 to 82% of those who do not receive therapy, depending on which effect size we accept. However, the average effect size for placebo treatment ranges from .56 to .71 standard deviations, indicating that the average person who receives placebo treatment is better off than 71 to 76% of the people who do not receive treatment. This suggests that a substantial proportion of the effects of psychotherapy are also produced by placebo treatment.

These data have been interpreted in various ways (see Prioleau et al., 1983). Some see the results of placebo-controlled psychotherapy research as a vindication of the effectiveness of established therapies. Others argue that the difference between psychotherapy and placebo treatment is small enough to constitute a challenge to the hypothesis that psychotherapy is effective. However, both arguments are based on a common assumption. The use of placebo control groups in psychotherapy research was based on the use of placebos in drug evaluation studies. It was assumed that just as inert pills had been used as placebos to test

---

[1]Effect size is typically calculated as the mean score of the treatment group minus the mean score of the control group divided by the standard deviation of the control group.

the effectiveness of medications, inert psychological treatments could be developed to test the effectiveness of psychotherapy. This chapter argues that this assumption is unwarranted; it is based on an inaccurate analogy between chemotherapy and psychotherapy and on some misleading definitions of the term *placebo*.

Differences Between Pharmacological and Psychological Research

Just as placebos are used in pharmacological studies to determine the effectiveness of various drugs, therapy outcome studies are ostensibly used to establish the effectiveness of psychotherapy. However, fundamental differences exist between double-blind pharmacological studies and the psychotherapy studies that have been modeled after them. Despite the deficiencies described in Chapter 2, double-blind studies provide information about the effectiveness of particular drugs. In contrast, comparisons of psychotherapy with placebo control procedures cannot tell us whether psychotherapies are effective (Horvath, 1987).

In drug research, placebos are used to control for the psychological effects of administering a treatment so that its pharmacological effects can be studied. The placebo and the active drug are chemically different but psychologically the same. Care is taken to ensure that the placebo is identical to the pharmacologically active treatment in all ways except for its chemical action. It is made to look the same, taste the same, and feel the same, and the patient is given the exact same explanation about its effects. Therefore, any difference between them will be due only to differences in their chemical composition. If no difference is found between the effects of the drug and the effects of the placebo, it is concluded that the drug is not pharmacologically effective. Instead, whatever effects were observed are interpreted as psychological effects.

In psychotherapy research, the situation is reversed. Placebos and psychotherapies are chemically the same—they are inert—but they are psychologically different. Although treatments and placebos can be made to *appear* the same in pharmacological research, in psychotherapy research the control treatment is always very different from the experimental treatment. That is because in psychotherapy, the package *is* the treatment. If control treatments were made to look, sound, and feel the same as the psychotherapies to which they were being compared, they would *be* the same. Unlike chemotherapy research, in which a chemical treatment is compared to a psychological treatment—a placebo—in psychotherapy research two psychological treatments are compared.

What can we learn from studies in which a psychological treatment labeled "therapy" is compared to a psychological treatment labeled "placebo"? Because psychotherapies are chemically inert, we already know that their effects are due to psychological mechanisms. Similarly, if treatments labeled "placebos" produce change, then *they too are psychologically active.* Because placebo drug studies are used to test the effectiveness of medication, it is often assumed that a placebo-controlled psychotherapy study is a test of the effectiveness of psychotherapy. However, finding that two psychological treatments are equally effective does not render either of them less effective, regardless of whether one happens to be labeled a "placebo."

The effectiveness of psychotherapy is more accurately evaluated by comparisons with no-treatment or delayed-treatment controls, and the results of those comparisons are clear and convincing. Psychotherapy works! Rather than providing information about the effectiveness of psychotherapy, comparisons between treatments called "treatments" and treatments called "placebos" can provide information about *why* a treatment works. Further, because both treatments are psychological, the "why" must be more specific than the obvious fact that the mechanism is psychological rather than chemical.

Placebo: A Treatment by Another Name

Presumably, the finding that psychotherapy is more effective than placebo control treatments indicates that it is not a placebo and that its effects are not placebo effects. But what does that mean? When we say that a drug is not a placebo, we mean that its effects are pharmacological rather than psychological. But the effects of psychotherapy are psychological regardless of whether they can be duplicated by placebo treatment. To make sense of the results of the studies in which the effects of psychotherapies have been compared to those of placebo control procedures, we need to examine the meaning of the term *placebo* when used in the context of psychotherapy.

As long as we restrict ourselves to physical medicine, the term *placebo* is easy to define. Placebos are substances and procedures presented in the guise of physically active treatments, but that are not physically active for the condition being studied. This definition is perfectly adequate for somatic medicine, but we immediately encounter problems when attempting to apply it to psychotherapy because *all* psychotherapies are physically inactive and would therefore be termed *placebos* by definition. Of course, if all psychological treatments are defined as placebos, the idea of comparing psychotherapy to a placebo is meaningless. Placebo-controlled psychotherapy outcome research would be interpreted as comparative studies of the effectiveness of different placebos, and the results obtained would be interpreted as indicating that some placebos are more effective than others.

Placebos as Nonspecific Treatments

Recognizing that a standard medical definition of *placebo* could not be applied to psychotherapy, Shapiro and Morris (1978) proposed the following influential definition:

> A *placebo* is defined as any therapy or component of therapy that is deliberately used for its nonspecific, psychological, or psychophysiological effect, or that is used for its presumed specific effect, but is without specific activity for the condition being treated.
>
> A *placebo*, when used as a control in experimental studies, is defined as a substance or procedure that is without specific activity for the condition being evaluated. (p. 371)

40

Unfortunately, this definition introduces a new term as ambiguous as the one being defined. What does it mean to say that an effect or activity is either *specific* or *nonspecific*? The effects of placebos can be specified as precisely as those of other treatments. Depending on how they are labeled, they can reduce pain, alleviate tension, increase alertness, alter pulse rate and blood pressure, enhance sexual arousal, and so on. These effects are as specific when produced by placebos as when they are produced by active drugs.

Traditionally, the term *specific* has been used to indicate a substance or procedure that affects a condition by virtue of its physical properties. In the 17th century, for example, it was claimed that garlic was a "specific" for the treatment of gout, and elder tree a "specific" for the cure of dropsy (see examples in the *Oxford English Dictionary*). More recently, Wolf (1959) defined the placebo effect as one that is due to the administration of a pill, potion, or procedure, but not to its "pharmacodynamic or specific properties" (p. 689). In other words, *specific* means pharmacologically active. With this use of the term, placebos are certainly not specifics, but then neither are psychotherapies. In fact, this definition merely returns us to the traditional somatic definition of *placebo*, according to which all psychotherapies are necessarily placebos.

The term *specific* has also been used to denote a treatment that is especially indicated for a particular disease. Thus, the term *nonspecific* would describe a treatment that is equally effective for many different disorders, rather than for a small number of specific conditions with similar characteristics. However, many psychotherapies use the same treatment procedures for a wide variety of psychological disorders. For example, regardless of their client's diagnosis, Rogerian therapists listen empathically and reflect the clients' thoughts and feelings. In this sense, client-centered therapy is not specific to the problem being treated and might therefore be regarded as a placebo. Conversely, many treatments used as placebos in psychotherapy research were designed to be specific for a particular target disorder. For example, Gordon Paul's (1966) "placebo" treatment for phobic anxiety would not be very credible as a treatment for most other disorders. Thus, in this sense of the term, many placebos are specific treatments, whereas many psychotherapies are nonspecific.

Recognizing that all effects are produced by specific means, some writers have suggested that the term *nonspecific* should be interpreted as meaning "not currently understood." According to this line of reasoning, someday we will discover the specific mechanisms by which particular placebos work, and at that point they will be called therapies. However, this assumes that we currently understand the mode of action of existing therapies; otherwise we would be forced to call them placebos. If "understanding" is to be judged by some degree of professional consensus, we must then concede that as of today, all of our methods of treatment are placebos, since there is no general agreement as to how any therapeutic procedure works. Expectancy modification, for example, can be regarded as an important mechanism in many therapeutic procedures and possibly the only active ingredient in some. It would be nice to think that there was general agreement on this issue, but there is not.

Placebos as Common Factors

In a more general sense, *specific* means "particular" and refers to things possessing properties that distinguish them from other things. Thus, a placebo would be a treatment that lacks any distinguishing characteristics. Of course, all treatments have characteristics that distinguish them from other therapies. The question is whether their effects are due to those distinguishing characteristics or to factors that all therapies share in common (Critelli & Neumann, 1984).

But what do all treatments and all placebos have in common? For one thing, regardless of their theoretical differences, most therapists respond to their clients with empathy and positive regard. For another, even the most nondirective therapist reinforces clients when they act in ways that should lead to improvement (Truax, 1966). According to Rogerian theory, empathy and positive regard are two of the most important factors producing therapeutic change. Similarly, contingent reinforcement is believed to be the "active ingredient" of behavior modification. Do we really want a definition that would lead us to classify these two forms of treatment as placebos precisely because their effects are due to the theoretical mechanisms on which they are based?

Another problem with the "common factor" definition of placebo is that the effects of some placebos may be partly due to specific characteristics not shared with other treatments. In psychotherapy research, treatments used as "placebo controls" typically contain components not shared by other therapies, including the therapies for which they are serving as controls (Horvath, 1988). Because these control treatments are composed of unique ingredients, the "common factor" definition would lead us to conclude that they are not placebos. Thus, this definition leads us to label some recognized treatments as placebos, while denying the label to most treatments that have been devised to serve as placebo control procedures.

Placebos as Incidental Treatment Components

In place of the common factor definition, Adolf Grünbaum (1985) has proposed a definition of *placebo* in which the status of a treatment depends on the theory on which it was based. Treatments contain some features that are theoretically designated as essential and others that are regarded as incidental. For example, in psychoanalytic theory, the uncovering of unconscious motivation is regarded as a defining characteristic of therapy. In contrast, the therapist's warmth and caring is seen as incidental. According to Grünbaum, a treatment is not a placebo if its observed effects are due to the mechanisms specified by the theory as essential. However, if the effects of treatment are in fact due to other factors, the treatment is a placebo. Thus, psychoanalysis would be a placebo if its effects of treatment turned out to be due to the genuine, empathic warmth of the therapist, rather than to the uncovering of repressed conflict. Similarly, client-centered therapy would be a placebo if its effects were due to the unintentional delivery of contingent reinforcement, rather than to noncontingent positive regard.

What happens when we apply Grünbaum's definition to treatments that are intentionally used as placebos? The essential ingredient of a placebo is its capacity to generate the belief that one is receiving effective treatment. But if this factor produces a therapeutic effect, then by Grünbaum's definition, the placebo is not a placebo. Thus, Grünbaum's definition leads us to conclude that when the inert pills used in drug research produce an effect, they are not placebos and their effects are not placebo effects.

Placebos as Expectancy Manipulations

One factor that is common to most treatments and placebos is the belief by recipients that they are receiving treatment, and the subsequent anticipation that some effect will occur. This anticipation is frequently referred to as an expectancy for improvement, but the use of placebos in research with healthy volunteers indicates that placebo-generated expectancies are not always expectancies for improvement. Healthy volunteers may expect various effects, but because they are not suffering from any disorder, these effects would not be regarded as improvement.

Even the placebo-generated expectancies of clinical subjects are not limited to expectancies for improvement. Besides expecting improvement in the condition for which they are being treated, some subjects also anticipate and subsequently experience various side effects from placebos (for example, Pogge, 1963). Rather than producing expectancies for improvement, placebos generate very specific expectancies that depend on the information presented when they are administered. Some of these expected changes can be categorized as beneficial, but others are neutral or even deleterious.

This suggests a definition that might be used in both somatic and psychological treatment contexts. A placebo effect could be defined as any effect that is brought about by the alteration of people's expectancies. A placebo would then be defined as a treatment or a component of a treatment that produces an effect by altering people's expectations.

Although this definition is consistent with how we commonly use the term placebo, it has three problems. First, in order to qualify as a placebo, a treatment would have to produce an effect. Many drug placebos may not affect the conditions for which they are used, but this should not automatically disqualify them as placebos. The question of whether placebos are effective should remain an empirical question.[2] A second objection to defining placebos in terms of expectancy is that it is not universally agreed that the effects of placebo pills are due to expectancy. Finally, a growing number of psychological theories, including the one presented in this book, views expectancy as a specific therapeutic mechanism (for example, Bandura, 1977; Frank, 1973; Kirsch, 1985a). Why should this mechanism be singled out with the derogatory label placebo? Expec-

---

[2]We could alter our definition of placebo to be any treatment or treatment component that alters expectations, regardless of whether the altered expectancies produce any subsequent effect. However, all treatments alter expectations and would therefore need to be classified as placebos.

tancy is no different from any other psychological mechanism, except perhaps that it is more potent than most.

Placebos as Treatments With a Different Label

Are the effects of psychotherapy placebo effects? It should now be clear that this question cannot be answered empirically. Instead, the answer depends on how one chooses to define the term *placebo*. If we use a traditional pharmacological definition, then the answer is "yes," but this answer is not based on the data produced by psychotherapy research. Instead, it is merely a logical deduction from our definition of the term *placebo*. Other proposed definitions that we have considered lead to different answers to the question "Are the effects of psychotherapy placebo effects?" But in each case, the answer can be deduced from the definition and is independent of the data produced by psychotherapy research.

What, then, can we learn from placebo-controlled psychotherapy research? There is one definition of *placebo* that provides a basis for interpreting these studies: *A placebo is a control treatment that has been labeled as such by the investigators.* This definition is conceptually empty but may be the only reasonable one in psychotherapeutic contexts. In fact, it is the implied operational definition used in reviews of psychotherapy outcome studies (for instance, Prioleau, et al., 1983).

Interpreting Placebo-Controlled Outcome Studies

If a placebo is nothing more than a label, the conclusions to be drawn from placebo-controlled outcome studies depend on the specific nature of the treatments that have been given the label *placebo*; and the meaning of these studies depends on what all of the placebo treatments have in common. Unfortunately, they appear to have very little in common. Some could be presented plausibly to subjects as effective psychological treatments, but many others are completely unbelievable. Taken together, these studies demonstrate only that the activities typically selected by researchers as control procedures are less effective than those considered to be bona fide therapies. However, the control procedures are also viewed as less efficacious by clients (Borkovec & Nau, 1972), and treatments that are *believed* to be less effective tend to *be* less effective (Shapiro, 1981). Therefore, the effect sizes calculated from meta-analyses of most placebo-controlled psychotherapy outcome studies have probably underestimated the potency of expectancy modification as a mechanism of therapeutic change.

Although comparisons between psychotherapies and placebo control procedures cannot tell us whether psychotherapy is effective, they might tell us something about how psychotherapies produce their effects. In particular, they could test the hypothesis that the effects of psychotherapy are due to expectancy, but only if certain conditions are satisfied. Medical placebos induce the belief that one has received a treatment and that certain changes will occur. The nature of these changes varies as a function of the condition being treated and the information administered along with the placebo. Consequently, the effects of placebos also vary: They reduce pain when administered as analgesics, enhance arousal when administered as stimulants, decrease arousal when administered as tranquilizers, and so on. Different placebos not only produce different effects but produce those effects to different degrees, and placebos that are more credible and convincing are also more effective (for example, Traut & Passarelli, 1957).

To test the hypothesis that psychotherapy and placebos operate via a common mechanism, the two procedures must be equated in terms of the expectations that they engender (see Rosenthal & Frank, 1956). If control treatments that are as credible as psychotherapy and that generate equivalent expectancies can be shown to produce equivalent effects, then expectancy modification remains a viable explanation for those effects. Conversely, if particular psychotherapies are shown to be reliably more effective than equally credible alternative procedures, then mechanisms other than expectancy modification are probably involved.

To control adequately for expectancy effects, one must use placebos as credible as the therapies against which they are being compared. A few of the placebo treatments that have been used in psychotherapy research satisfy this criterion (for instance, Kirsch et al., 1983). Most, however, do not. Playing with puzzles, sitting quietly with a silent therapist, or discussing current events are hardly credible controls for the effects of therapeutic expectancies. In fact, the finding that such procedures have a substantial therapeutic effect is rather surprising.

It is unlikely that expectancy modification is the only mechanism by which psychotherapy produces therapeutic effects. Although many people come into therapy because of problematic nonvolitional responses such as anxiety and depression, many others enter therapy for different reasons (for example, problems in their relationships with friends and family members). If therapeutic outcome expectancies affect these latter conditions, it could only be through enhancing clients' compliance with treatment. Clients take a more active role in the treatment process if they expect the treatment to be effective (Phelps, 1986). However, being more actively involved in the process of treatment would lead to greater improvement only if the treatment was effective.

There is a second reason for suspecting that the outcome of psychotherapy is not entirely due to altered expectancies. Response expectancy is only one of the determinants of nonvolitional responses. Although people can generate feelings of anxiety by expecting to be anxious, keep themselves depressed by expecting to remain depressed, inhibit their sexual arousal by anticipating not being aroused, and keep themselves awake by expecting to be unable to fall asleep, these expectancies are not the only causes of anxiety, depression, inhibited sexual arousal, and insomnia. People also become anxious and depressed when they anticipate negative events; are sexually dysfunctional when they have consumed too much alcohol; and are unable to sleep if they have napped too much during the day.

For both of these reasons—that people enter therapy for reasons other than problematic nonvolitional responses, and that response expectancy is only one determinant of those kinds of responses—expectancy ought to be only one factor in producing psychotherapeutic improvement. The results of comparing therapy to not very credible control treatments should be the results found when therapy is compared to credible placebo controls. We would expect the control procedures to be more effective than no treatment at all, but we would expect other therapies to be even more effective.

In fact, these are exactly the results found by Barker, Funk, and Houston (1988) in their meta-analysis of psychotherapy outcome studies. Unlike other meta-analytic researchers, Barker et al. (1988) limited their analysis to studies using control procedures as credible and believable as the bona fide therapies against which they were being compared, a total of 17 studies out of the hundreds of therapy outcome studies that have been published. Compared to no treatment at all, the psychotherapies used in these studies (primarily behavior therapies) produced an average effect size of 1.06, indicating that the average person who received one of those treatments was better off than 85% of those who had not been treated at all. In contrast, the effect size produced by equally credible expectancy control treatments was only .47.

These data indicate that psychotherapy (or at least behavior therapy) has effects over and above those that can be attributed to the credibility of the treatment rationale.[3] On the other hand, they also confirm that treatments aimed solely at modifying subjects' expectancies about a problematic condition produced substantial improvement, almost half that produced by the psychotherapies under investigation.

The results described above were based on assessments made immediately after the conclusion of treatment. However, in some of these studies, subjects' conditions were reassessed some time later to establish whether the changes produced by treatment were lasting. These follow-up data are among the most interesting reported by Barker et al. (1988). Not only had the effects of treatment remained largely intact (the mean effect size was .96), but the effectiveness of "placebo" treatment relative to no treatment at all had increased dramatically, from .47 immediately after treatment to .73 at follow-up. This suggests that the effects of expectancy modification are not ephemeral. Rather than dissipating

---

[3]Although the Barker et al. (1988) study summarizes the best data currently available, it might also represent an underestimate of the role response expectancy in treatment outcome. The usual means of establishing that two treatments are equal in the degree to which they engender therapeutic expectancies is to have subjects rate how believable the treatments are based on a brief verbal description of them. However, these ratings are not a very sensitive measure of degree to which treatments produce alterations in response expectancies. First, credibility ratings are a composite of subjects' answers to a number of questions (for example, "How logical does the treatment seem to you?"), some of which may relate to characteristics of the treatment other than its perceived effectiveness. Ratings of expected outcome have been shown to be substantially better than these credibility ratings at predicting actual outcome (Kirsch et al., 1983). Second, because credibility ratings are evaluations of brief verbal descriptions of the treatment, rather than of the treatment itself, their validity depends on the accuracy and comprehensiveness of those descriptions. As shown in later chapters, effective psychotherapies contain a variety of methods for changing expectations that are not typically described in the rationales with which the treatments are presented. Finally, psychotherapy outcome studies are rarely double-blind. The therapists are almost always aware of which procedure is the "treatment" and which is the "placebo." It is likely that most therapists expect the treatment to be more effective than the placebo, and this expectation might inadvertently be communicated to subjects, thus biasing the results in favor of the treatment.

over time, they may set into motion a benign cycle leading to further improvement.

Placebo Therapy

The perceived lack of differences in effectiveness between different psychotherapies led Jerome Frank (1973) to examine their shared features in order to establish their mechanisms of effectiveness. He identified four common factors:

1. A therapeutic relationship between a client and a socially sanctioned help-giver. The therapist is perceived as having special training, by means of which he or she has mastered special therapeutic techniques, a perception that enhances faith in the help-giver's competence.

2. The provision of treatment in a specially designated location, such as a hospital, clinic, university health center, or office. According to Frank, the setting itself arouses expectancies for improvement.

3. A rationale upon which the therapy is based. There are different rationales for different therapies. Psychodynamic therapies are based on the idea of unconscious conflicts, for example, whereas behavioral therapies are based on principles of learning. Nevertheless, each therapy has *some* rationale, and the rationale includes the presumption that treatment of a specific sort should lead to improvement.

4. The use of a therapeutic ritual or procedure. These also vary from therapy to therapy, but are consistent with the rationale of the therapy.

Based on this analysis, Frank (1971) hypothesized that most psychotherapy clients suffer from a sense of helplessness, hopelessness, and demoralization. According to Frank, effective therapies enhance clients' positive expectations, restore their faith in the future, and foster a sense of mastery and competence. From this point of view, the effectiveness of therapeutic techniques and their associated rationales may not lie in their specific contents. Although the specific procedures involved in different therapies may be dissimilar, all of them may function via a common mechanism: the restoration of faith.

In 1973, Jefferson Fish transformed Frank's description of the common features of psychotherapy into a prescription for what—with tongue firmly planted in cheek—he called "placebo therapy." First, the therapist assesses the client's beliefs and the problems for which he or she is seeking help. Next a therapeutic contract is negotiated that specifies the goals of treatment. On the basis of this contract and the therapist's assessment of the client's problems, the therapist develops a therapeutic ritual that will be believable to the client. True to Frank's description of therapy, Fish is unconcerned with the details of the therapeutic ritual and rationale.

> Suffice it to say that, if what the patient does is actually helpful, so much the better. The important point is that the patient must be persuaded that it is what *he* does, not what the therapist does, which results in his being cured. This belief

is crucial because it implies that the patient is the master of his behavior rather than its servant. [Fish, 1973, p. 17]

The treatment rationale is then explained to the client, and the healing ritual is begun. When change takes place, it is used as proof that improvement is possible, thus setting a benign cycle into effect.

Are Different Psychotherapies Really Equivalent?

The suspicion that psychotherapy might be a placebo was based on the Dodo bird's verdict, the perception that all psychotherapies are more or less equivalent. But is that verdict justified? Is it true that all psychotherapies are equally effective? Most of the meta-analytic reviewers appear to believe that the answer is "yes." But a closer examination of the results of these studies suggests a different answer.

Table 3–1 shows the effect sizes reported for different therapies by Smith et al. (1980) in the first and most comprehensive meta-analysis of psychotherapy outcome studies. It is clear from these data that different therapies produced different effect sizes, ranging from 1.82 for hypnotherapy to a meager .28 for counseling. Cognitive and behavior therapies were more effective than the more traditional, insight-oriented therapies, and counseling was substantially less effective than placebo treatment, which is particularly surprising given the nature of some of the procedures used as placebo controls.

TABLE 3–1 Differential Effects of Various Psychotherapies

Type of therapy	Effect size
Hypnotherapy	1.82
Cognitive therapy	1.58
Behavior therapy	1.02
Psychodynamic therapy	.76
Humanistic therapy	.63
Placebo therapy	.56
Undifferentiated counseling	.28

NOTE: This list was formed by regrouping the therapies listed by Smith et al. (1980, pp. 70–73) into broader categories. Cognitive therapy as used here includes those classified by Smith et al. as rational emotive therapy and "other cognitive therapies." Behavior therapy includes systematic desensitization, cognitive-behavior therapy, and "eclectic-behavioral therapies." Psychodynamic therapy includes psychodynamic therapies, "dynamic-eclectic therapies," Adlerian therapy, and transactional analysis. Humanistic therapy consists of client-centered therapy and gestalt therapy.

The studies from which these average effect sizes were calculated include some conducted with real clients as subjects and others in which the subjects were students who were recruited for participation in an experiment. It is possible that the results of studies with student volunteers (generally referred to as analogue studies) are not generalizable to more typical psychotherapy situations. To control for this possibility, Andrews and Harvey (1981) restricted their meta-analysis to studies involving real clients with diagnoses of neurosis, phobic disorder, depression, and psychosomatic disorder, "the type of patients who usually seek psychotherapy" (p. 1204). The results of their analysis are presented in Table 3–2. Once again, the top-ranked treatments were the behavior and cognitive-behavior therapies; counseling and client-centered therapy were the least effective forms of treatment; and psychodynamic therapy and placebo treatment fell between these extremes.

TABLE 3–2 Differential Effects of Various Psychotherapies on Typical Client Populations

Type of therapy	Effect size
Cognitive and gestalt therapies	1.20
Behavior and cognitive-behavior therapies	.97
Psychodynamic therapy	.72
Placebo therapies	.55
Client-centered therapy	.39
Counseling	.31

NOTE: Adapted from Andrews and Harvey (1981).

One of the criticisms leveled against these meta-analyses is their reliance on data from disparate studies. Effect sizes can be influenced by factors other than the type of treatment evaluated. For example, different effect sizes might be produced by differences in client population, presenting problems, outcome measures, and so on. Perhaps the larger effect sizes obtained for cognitive and behavior therapies are due to these differences in experimental design, rather than to differences in the effectiveness of the treatments.

To control for this possibility, Shapiro and Shapiro (1982) restricted their meta-analysis to published reports in which two or more treatments were compared simultaneously. Because different therapies were evaluated in the same study, differences in outcome could not have been due to differences in experimental design. Nevertheless, the results of this meta-analysis were similar to others we have examined (see Table 3–3). Behavior therapy and cognitive behavior therapy were more effective than placebo treatment, which, in turn, was more effective than psychodynamic and humanistic therapy.

In summary, despite differences in the criteria for selecting or excluding studies, the results of meta-analyses are fairly consistent. They indicate that not all therapies are alike. Behavior therapy and cognitive therapy show a distinct advantage over more traditional methods of treatment. Though less effective than these newer therapies, psychodynamic psychotherapy is more effective than typical control procedures. In contrast, client-centered therapy is less effective than the treatments designed as placebos.

TABLE 3–3 Differential Effects of Various Psychotherapies in Studies Including Simultaneous Comparisons

Type of therapy	Effect size
Mixed (mainly behavioral)	1.42
Behavioral	1.06
Cognitive	1.00
Placebo	.71
Psychodynamic and humanistic	.40

NOTE: Adapted from Shapiro and Shapiro (1982). Therapies designated as "mixed" contain elements of more than one type of treatment. For example, they might contain both modeling and behavioral rehearsal. According to Shapiro and Shapiro (1982), most of these treatment components are behavioral in nature.

Beyond the Placebo Effect

At this point, a summary may be helpful. Over the last 40 years, medical research has revealed a powerful psychological variable that affects a remarkably wide range of subjective, behavioral, and physiological responses. This variable has been termed *response expectancy,* and it has been shown how this type of expectancy fits in with concepts contained in other expectancy theories, particularly social learning theory.

Though first discovered as placebo effects in medical research, the effects of response expectancies are not limited to pharmacological treatment; they play a substantial role in psychological treatment as well. Meta-analyses reveal that expectancy can account for at least half of the effectiveness of psychotherapy. Further, both medical and psychological research indicate that expectancy effects can be substantial and long-lasting. In fact, there is some evidence that highly credible expectancy manipulations produce therapeutic effects that continue to strengthen after treatment has ended (Barker et al., 1988).

These findings suggest that the effects of psychotherapy can be enhanced by attending to the therapeutic potential of our clients' expectations. Some of the methods by which this can be done have been suggested by Frank (1971) and Fish (1973). The therapist assesses the client's beliefs about the problem that has led to therapy, devises a healing ritual, and presents it in a manner as consistent as possible with the client's belief system.[4]

Additional hints for maximizing therapeutic expectancies have been drawn from the literature on medical placebos described in Chapter 2. These data suggest

[4]Fish (1973) is unconcerned with the truth of the rationale with which the treatment plan is presented. His stance is that "lying to a client is desirable if the lie furthers the therapeutic goals, is unlikely to be discovered (and hence backfire), and is likely to be more effective than any other strategy" (p. 39). I have a far less casual attitude toward this issue, believing that the effectiveness of therapeutic interventions often depends on clients' trust. This trust is fostered by our own honesty, which is often communicated to clients by nonverbal messages over which we do not have full control. Betraying this trust may cause considerable damage. In any case, it is not necessary. Therapeutic expectancies can be created and enhanced without resort to dishonesty.

that the rationales accompanying treatments should not promise too great an initial change. Instead, the aim should be to support a high degree of confidence that *some* change in the desired direction will be experienced, so that relatively small fluctuations in a client's condition can be interpreted as evidence of improvement. This provides the client with experiential feedback indicating therapeutic effectiveness, feedback that is likely to promote greater change. Finally, the effectiveness of a healing ritual can be enhanced by increasing its "dose" or by delivering it in a manner that conveys greater therapeutic potency to the client. For example, just as multiple injections can be more effective than a single pill, frequent applications of "hypnosis" may be more effective than less frequent practice of "progressive relaxation."

Getting Specific About Psychotherapy and Expectancy

Although therapy outcome data have substantiated the relevance of the placebo effect as a component of effective psychological treatment, they have also revealed that there is more to psychotherapy than a simple, undifferentiated placebo effect. Different psychotherapies are not equally effective. In particular, cognitive behavior therapies have been consistently found to be superior to other forms of treatment, and in one meta-analysis, hypnotherapy was found to be the most effective treatment of all. If we are to move beyond the lowest common denominators of the various psychotherapies, we should look at those treatments found to be most effective.

How do the behavior and cognitive-behavior therapies differ from more traditional forms of psychological treatment? One difference is that they are designed to be effective for particular problems. Systematic desensitization, for example, was designed as a treatment for irrational fear. It is specifically intended for phobic disorders, although it can also be used to treat other conditions in which unwarranted anxiety is attached to particular situational cues (for example, erectile dysfunction and insomnia). However, it would not be the treatment of choice for depression. Behavior therapists treat depression by scheduling activities to produce pleasure and a sense of mastery, rehearsing difficult anticipated tasks, teaching assertiveness, and challenging depressive cognitions. In other words, behavioral and cognitive therapies are directed toward very specific therapeutic goals that vary with the presenting problem.

Much psychotherapy research has been devoted to answering some very general questions, such as "Does psychotherapy work?" In contrast, studies of cognitive and behavioral treatments pose more specific questions. The question is not whether psychotherapy works, but which specific therapy procedures work best for which clients with what kind of specific problems (Paul, 1967a). In fact, when behavior therapy and psychodynamic therapy were compared for clients with different presenting problems, using global, undifferentiated outcome measures that are not geared to those specific problems, the difference in effectiveness between the two forms of treatment vanished (Sloane et al., 1975). It is only when the effects of therapy on the specific problem for which the client has sought treatment is evaluated that the superiority of behavior therapy becomes evident.

Kiesler (1966) has complained that the myth of uniformity has hampered psychotherapy research. When different methods of therapy used with clients who have different psychological problems are treated as equivalent, not much can be learned. The question "Is psychotherapy effective?" is too broad to be answered meaningfully. Meaningful answers can be found only when more specific questions are addressed, such as those typically posed in studies of cognitive and behavior therapy.

Questions about expectancy effects have been plagued by the same lack of specificity as questions about psychotherapy: Is psychotherapy a placebo? Are its effects greater than those of placebos? Are its effects due to expectancy? When questions are posed in this manner, all placebo control procedures, as well as all therapies, are treated as if they were the same. Yet there are even more differences among different placebo control procedures than there are among different types of psychotherapy. Procedures used as placebos range from placing clients on a waiting list (Sloane et al., 1975) to making surgical incisions (Beecher, 1961). Just as we need to ask more specific questions about therapeutic procedures, so too must we ask more specific questions about the effects of expectancy.

Part Two examines some of the specific procedures found to be particularly effective in treating specific problems: systematic desensitization and other treatments of phobic anxiety, cognitive-behavioral treatments of depression, and hypnosis. The focus in each case is on the role of response expectancies, not only in producing treatment effects, but also as contributing causes of the problems for which treatment is sought. Our questions: What are the specific dysfunctional expectancies that contribute to particular problems? What kinds of interventions can alter those expectancies? And what happens when dysfunctional expectancies are changed?

SPECIFIC TREATMENTS FOR SPECIFIC PROBLEMS

SYSTEMATIC DESENSITIZATION 4

The First Specific Psychotherapy

As discussed in Chapter 3, placebos are sometimes defined as nonspecific treatments. In medical contexts, one connotation of the term *nonspecific* is that the treatment is not specific to a particular disease. One can use the same inert ingredient as a placebo treatment regardless of the patient's disorder.

In this sense of the term, traditional psychotherapies are largely nonspecific. One might enter psychoanalytic treatment for any number of problems—depression, compulsions, sexual dysfunction, phobias, a mid-life crisis, or others. But whatever the presenting problem, the treatment is likely to be more or less the same—free association aided by interpretation to uncover the unconscious roots of one's symptoms. Similarly, the work of a Rogerian therapist does not depend on the client's presenting problem. Whatever the problem, Rogerian therapists listen empathically and reflect their clients' feelings back to them.

In his 1958 book, *Psychotherapy by Reciprocal Inhibition,* Joseph Wolpe proposed a radical innovation in treatment strategy. At the same time that medical researchers were discovering the importance of nonspecific factors in medical treatment, Wolpe developed *specific* psychological treatments for emotional and behavioral disorders. Based on behaviorist conditioning theories, Wolpe argued convincingly that psychological disorders could be treated directly and relatively briefly by therapeutic procedures designed for specific problems. Submissiveness would be treated by assertiveness training; maladaptive habits by aversion therapy; unwarranted anxiety by systematic desensitization; and so on.

Psychotherapy by Reciprocal Inhibition is the cornerstone of behavior therapy, but its importance transcends the boundaries of behavior modification. Besides inaugurating the behavior therapy movement, Wolpe's work paved the way for subsequent approaches—such as cognitive therapies and therapies based loosely on systems theory—all of which share a commitment to producing rapid change via strategic, problem-focused interventions. In addition, these new problem-oriented therapies are amenable to systematic evaluation. Because treatments like desensitization clearly specify the problematic emotions and behaviors at which they are aimed, and because they specify with equal clarity the treatment procedures with which those problems will be addressed, they prompted the kind of outcome research that is typical in the evaluation of medical treatments, but that had not previously been possible in the field of psychotherapy. For the first time, researchers were able to evaluate the effects of specific therapeutic procedures on particular psychological problems.

The most influential of the treatment techniques introduced by Wolpe was systematic desensitization, a procedure specifically designed for treating unwarranted anxiety. Treatment by systematic desensitization proceeds as follows. First, patients are taught progressive relaxation (Jacobson, 1929), an exercise designed to induce deep muscular relaxation through alternate tensing and relaxing of various muscle groups. Concurrent with practice in progressive relaxation, clients and therapists work together to construct a hierarchy of anxiety-related scenes, each involving closer approach to the feared stimulus-situation. Once the hierarchy has been constructed and deep relaxation has been learned, desensitization proper may begin. Patients are instructed to relax, close their eyes, and imagine the first scene on their hierarchy. They imagine this scene until they begin to feel anxious, at which point they are instructed to stop visualizing and to focus instead on relaxing their muscles. Once relaxation is regained, the imagery is resumed. This is repeated until the patient can tolerate the imagery comfortably, at which point the entire process is repeated with the next scene on the hierarchy. Desensitization is complete when clients can tolerate the last scene of their hierarchies without discomfort.

The Efficacy of Systematic Desensitization

The subject of hundreds of controlled experiments, systematic desensitization has been more thoroughly investigated than any other psychological procedure. One of the earliest and most influential controlled evaluations of desensitization was reported by Gordon Paul in 1966. Paul's well-designed study has become a model not only for research on systematic desensitization, but for research on psychological treatments in general.

Paul assigned college students suffering from public-speaking anxiety (stage-fright) to one of four conditions: systematic desensitization, traditional insight-oriented psychotherapy, an "attention-placebo" expectancy modification treatment, and a no-treatment control condition. After five treatment sessions, systematic desensitization was found to have produced substantial reductions in fear, significantly more so than either traditional psychotherapy or the expectancy modification control procedure. Paul also reported that although both were more effective than no treatment at all, traditional therapy was no more effective than the expectancy control treatment. A follow-up evaluation two years later indicated that these effects were durable.

Since 1966, hundreds of experimental studies have confirmed the effectiveness of desensitization as a treatment for phobic anxiety, with no indication that eliminating the phobia leads to "symptom substitution" (the development of a new symptom to replace the one that was removed). Reports have also described the use of desensitization for other problems in which anxiety is thought to be a factor. Besides phobias, desensitization has been applied to the treatment of insomnia, auditory hallucinations, compulsions, recurring nightmares, chronic diarrhea, anorexia, stuttering, excessive urination, and sexual dysfunction (Kazdin & Wilcoxon, 1976).

The success of systematic desensitization led to the development of a number of related and procedurally overlapping fear-reduction treatments, treatments bearing such names as *in vivo* desensitization, anxiety management training, flooding, cue-controlled relaxation, applied relaxation, self-control desensitization, successive approximation, covert modeling, participant modeling, and implosive therapy. Each of these variants of desensitization has been experimentally demonstrated to be successful in reducing anxiety, and some of them—particularly those involving real-life exposure to the feared situation—are somewhat more effective than desensitization in its original form. Because of the well-documented effectiveness of this type of treatment, it can be argued that it would be irresponsible for a therapist not to at least inform phobic patients of specific therapy as a treatment option.

The Mechanism of Change

Because systematic desensitization has been more extensively investigated than any other psychological treatment, it has been viewed as an exemplar of psychotherapy in general (Bootzin & Lick, 1979; Wilkins, 1979b). This research contains a wealth of information about the cause of irrational fears and how they can be eliminated. It also provides important clues about the mechanisms by which other forms of psychotherapy may be effective.

In psychodynamic theories, phobias are viewed as symptoms of unconscious intrapsychic conflict. According to these theories, attempts to remove the phobia without resolving the underlying conflicts should either fail or result in symptom substitution, neither of which occurs when desensitization is used. In developing systematic desensitization, Wolpe abandoned psychodynamic formulations of phobias in favor of a conditioning model. According to this model, phobic stimuli can be thought of as conditioned stimuli that have come to elicit fear (the conditioned response) as a result of prior association with aversive consequences (unconditioned stimuli).

The clearest demonstration of the conditioning model of human fear is the famous experiment reported in 1920 by John B. Watson, the founder of behaviorism, and his graduate student, Rosalie Rayner. At the beginning of their study, little Albert (the "Little Hans" of behaviorism) was a normal 11-month-old baby. Like all normal infants, little Albert could be frightened by sudden loud noises. Watson and Rayner produced a conditioned fear response in Albert by pairing a loud noise (the unconditioned stimulus) with presentations of a white rat (the conditioned stimulus), which the boy had not previously feared. According to conditioning models of fear acquisition, phobias are acquired when similar sequences of events occur naturally in the environment. For example, a child may come to fear dogs after fortuitously being bitten.

The idea behind systematic desensitization is to recondition the phobic stimulus to a response that is incompatible with fear. The first demonstration of this procedure was reported in 1924 in a study conducted under the guidance of John Watson. Mary Cover Jones (1924) successfully eliminated a 3-year-old child's fear of rabbits by gradually bringing a rabbit closer to him while he was eating food that he liked. Wolpe's procedure is essentially similar. Food is replaced by relaxation, and the gradual approach of the stimulus is replaced by the anxiety hierarchy. According to the reciprocal inhibition or counterconditioning model, the use of a graduated hierarchy is necessary for desensitization to be successful. Too intense an anxiety stimulus presented to the patient would inhibit the relaxation and thereby render the treatment unsuccessful. Conversely, when relatively mild fear stimuli are presented, the anxiety normally elicited is inhibited by relaxation. In theory, the repeated pairing of relaxation with the phobic stimulus weakens the conditioned association between that stimulus and fear, thereby gradually eliminating the phobia.[1]

By 1970 the effectiveness of systematic desensitization was no longer in doubt (Wilkins, 1971), but the reason for its effectiveness was controversial. The very research that had so ably established its efficacy also demonstrated that one could modify the procedure in any number of ways without decreasing its effectiveness. Various studies indicated that patients need not be instructed to relax in order for desensitization to be effective (Emmelkamp, 1982); in fact, relaxation can be replaced with instructions to tense one's muscles while imagining the phobic stimulus, with no apparent reduction in treatment effectiveness (Sue, 1972). Similarly, it is not necessary to use a graduated hierarchy when desensitizing people to phobic stimuli. A single, highly fear-evoking scene can be imagined, with or without relaxation. One can even have patients imagine horrible consequences as a function of approaching the situations they fear (Morganstern, 1973). Clearly these data are inconsistent with the counterconditioning hypothesis. The discovery that neither relaxation nor a graduated hierarchy are necessary for successful desensitization rendered the counterconditioning model untenable.

The Extinction Hypothesis

Some procedural variations of desensitization therapy were developed as experimental controls; others were christened with their own names and proposed as alternatives to desensitization. However, their procedures overlap so much that

---

[1] Although Wolpe (1958) used the terms *reciprocal inhibition* and *counterconditioning* interchangeably, Gerald Davison (1968) has pointed out that there is a subtle but important distinction between the two models. The reciprocal inhibition model assumes specific neurological processes by which one response (relaxation) inhibits another (fear). The counterconditioning model does not contain any inferences about underlying neural processes but is otherwise identical to the reciprocal inhibition model.

these therapies are more reasonably viewed as examples of a single type of treatment that can be varied along a number of dimensions. The phobic stimulus can be presented in imagination or in real life; presentations may or may not be discontinued when anxiety is experienced; a graduated hierarchy might or might not be used; patients can be instructed to relax, to tense their muscles, or to do neither; they can imagine themselves or imagine someone else approaching the feared situation. The one factor common to most of these variations of systematic desensitization is that they involve exposing the patient to the phobic stimulus, either in real life or in imagination.

Many comparative outcome studies have found no difference between desensitization in its original form and any of its variants; differences that were obtained were typically small and often inconsistent across studies. The most consistent and substantial finding was that treatments involving real-life exposure to the phobic stimulus are more effective than treatments based on imagery. Yet most desensitization treatments produce reductions in self-reported anxiety and increases in approach to the feared stimulus. It is *possible* that each of these variations on a theme is effective for different reasons, but given the degree of overlap in their procedures and the similarity in their effects, it is more likely that they share a common causal mechanism.

When it became clear that the counterconditioning hypotheses was untenable, the idea of extinction was proposed as an alternative (O'Leary & Wilson, 1975). In classical conditioning, the unconditioned stimulus (aversive consequences in the case of conditioned fear) is said to reinforce the conditioned response (fear). If the conditioned stimulus (the phobic stimulus or situation) is repeatedly presented and the conditioned response is not reinforced (by aversive consequences), the response gradually extinguishes; that is, it becomes weaker and weaker until it disappears entirely. Because desensitization and similar treatments involve nonreinforced exposure to the phobic stimulus, extinction became the preferred explanation for its effects.

An interesting test of the extinction hypothesis was reported by Marvin and Anita Goldfried in 1977. Their study compared two forms of desensitization. In one treatment condition, relaxation was paired with imagery related to subjects' fears of speaking in public. In the other condition, subjects were instructed to imagine anxiety-arousing scenes unrelated to their stage-fright. The latter procedure was made credible by couching treatment in a rationale that stressed self-control of anxiety. Subjects were told they were learning how to use relaxation to control anxiety; that the purpose of the imaginary scenes was to provide practice in relaxing away tension; and that the exact content of the scenes was unimportant. Both treatments were equally effective in reducing public-speaking fear. Because both treatments were absolutely identical except for the content of the imagery, their effects were probably due to the same causal mechanism. Yet students in the second treatment condition were not exposed to any representation of a public-speaking situation, so the reduction in their fear could not have been due to extinction.

According to the extinction hypothesis, a necessary condition for successful desensitization is that exposure to the phobic stimulus not be followed by aversive consequences. However, in one variant of desensitization, called "implosive therapy," clients are instructed to vividly imagine detailed horrifying consequences of encounters with the phobic stimulus. For example, people fearful of snakes might be asked to imagine snakes biting them, wrapping around their necks, and slowly strangling them (Hogan and Kirchner, 1968). The implosive therapy procedure is virtually identical to a procedure called "covert sensitization" (Cautela, 1967); in both procedures, the patient imagines adverse consequences to an encounter with a targeted stimulus. However, the aims and outcomes of the two procedures are exactly opposite. The purpose of implosive therapy is to reduce fear and avoidance, while the purpose of covert sensitization is to promote avoidance of such behaviors as smoking, drinking, or undesirable sexual practices. Clients are instructed to imagine engaging in the behavior, and then to imagine negative consequences, such as choking, vomiting, or being caught in the act. The fact that the same procedure can have opposite effects, depending on the stated reasons for its use, suggests that those effects are due to cognitive factors, rather than to some automatic conditioning or extinction process. In other words, it is not the *procedures* that are producing change, but clients' *interpretation of the meaning* of those procedures.

In implosive therapy the aversive consequences are imagined, rather than actually experienced, and the stated purpose of these imagined consequences is to maximize the client's anxiety so that it will extinguish completely. In a control procedure called "operant desensitization," Dave Henry and I paired imagined scenes from an anxiety hierarchy with *actual* aversive consequences, rather than instructing people to imagine negative consequences (Kirsch and Henry, 1977). In this way, we hoped to provide a definitive test of the extinction hypothesis and of other theories of desensitization based on conditioning principles. The operant desensitization procedure was identical to systematic desensitization, with which it was compared, except for the addition of one feature: visualizations of scenes on the anxiety hierarchy were paired with painful electric shocks.

The use of electric shock was made plausible to the students by telling them that its purpose was to punish their anxiety. Although the students accepted this rationale as believable, in terms of psychological theory it made no sense at all. Pairing a stimulus with aversive consequences is the means by which conditioned fear responses are produced, not the way in which they are eliminated. According to classical conditioning theories, our operant desensitization treatment should have made people more, rather than less, fearful. In fact, operant desensitization is very similar to aversion therapy (Wolpe, 1958), a treatment intended to produce conditioned aversion responses. The relation between operant desensitization and aversion therapy is analogous to that between implosive therapy and covert sensitization. The procedures are very similar, but their intended and actual outcomes are exactly opposite.

Contrary to the predictions generated by conditioning theory, operant desensitization produced substantial reductions in fear, as great as that produced by standard systematic desensitization. Because the students' fears were systematically reinforced by aversive consequences (the painful electric shocks), these results could not have been due to extinction, nor to any other conditioning process. Yet except for the addition of the shocks, the operant desensitization procedure was identical to systematic desensitization. It is therefore reasonable to assume that whatever mechanism led to fear reduction in the operant desensitization condition is also responsible for the therapeutic effects of systematic desensitization.

The Search for Effective Procedural Components

One strategy for uncovering the causal mechanism of desensitization is to identify procedural components and establish which of them contribute to treatment effectiveness. In standard desensitization, patients encounter a therapist, form a therapeutic relationship, and receive instruction in deep muscular relaxation as a competing response. They are then instructed to imagine encounters with the phobic stimulus, during which no aversive consequences are experienced.

TABLE 4–1 Components of Treatments
Demonstrated to Be as Effective as Systematic Desensitization

	Component			
Treatment	Therapeutic relationship	Competing response (relaxation)	Imagined stimulus exposure	Absence of aversive consequences
Systematic desensitization	x	x	x	x
Automated desensitization		x	x	x
Imaginal flooding	x		x	x
Cue-controlled relaxation	x	x		x
Operant desensitization	x	x	x	

The components of systematic desensitization are shown in Table 4–1. Also shown are treatment variations missing one of the components. In automated desensitization, the therapist is replaced by a programmed mechanical apparatus containing tape-recorded treatment instructions. In imaginal flooding, the client, without training or instructions for relaxation, imagines encountering the feared stimulus. In cue-controlled relaxation, visualization of the feared situation is dispensed with; relaxation is instead associated with a cue word that can be used in anxiety-arousing situations. The use of electric shock as an aversive consequence in operant desensitization was described above. Research comparing each of these procedures to standard systematic desensitization reveals them to be equivalent in their ability to reduce fear, thereby indicating that none of the specific procedural components of systematic desensitization are necessary to its effectiveness (Emmelkamp, 1982; Grimm, 1980; Kirsch & Henry, 1977; Lang, Melamed, & Hart, 1970).

Importance of the Treatment Context

Not represented in Table 4–1 is one factor common to all of these treatments: the awareness of patients that they are being treated. Some researchers have attempted to disguise the nature of systematic desensitization so that subjects would be unaware that it was intended to reduce their fear. Although this strategy has not been successful in all cases, most studies have shown that disguising the therapeutic intent of systematic desensitization—by presenting it as an experimental investigation of visualization, for example—can significantly lower its effectiveness, in some cases rendering it no more effective than no treatment at all (Lick & Bootzin, 1975).

The mixed results of these studies are not difficult to understand. Systematic desensitization is a very convincing procedure. Even without being explicitly told that this is the case, subjects might realize that pairing relaxation with phobic imagery is intended to produce a reduction in fear, especially since progressing to the next scene is contingent on the absence of an anxiety response to the previous scene. In other words, the treatment procedures themselves suggest the experimenter's therapeutic intent to the intelligent subject (Kazdin & Wilcoxon, 1976; Lick & Bootzin, 1975). Evidence for this hypothesis has been reported by Miller (1972), who coupled desensitization with therapeutic instructions, misleading instructions, or no instructions at all about the purpose of the treatment. Although misleading instructions inhibited the therapeutic effects of desensitization, the absence of instructions did not. These subjects were able to figure out the therapeutic intent of the treatment and therefore attributed their improvement to it. In contrast, subjects given misleading instructions did not attribute therapeutic effectiveness to desensitization.

Another factor makes it difficult to disguise the therapeutic intent of desensitization: The experimenters administering the treatment are aware of its purpose and its previously established effectiveness. Medical treatment studies indicate that the enthusiasm of the physician can greatly enhance treatment outcome (Shapiro & Morris, 1978). Similarly, psychological researchers have found that the expectations of experimenters can produce self-confirming results (Rosenthal, 1969). For that reason, double-blind treatment studies produce fewer positive results than single-blind studies, in which the experimenter is aware of the experimental hypothesis and each subject's treatment condition. Unfortunately, most desensitization studies are single-blind at best. The experimenters understand the fear-reducing purpose of the procedure, and as was all too common prior to the implementation of double-blind strategies in medical research, they may inadvertently convey their enthusiasm to subjects. Nevertheless, some researchers have been so successful in disguising the purpose of the procedure that they have canceled its effectiveness.

The Credibility of Control Treatments

Although none of the specific components of systematic desensitization are necessary for successful treatment of phobic anxiety, its fear-reducing effects can be inhibited or even completely eliminated when it is disguised as a nontherapeutic procedure. Ordinarily, this would lead us to conclude that the effects of treatment are due to expectancy, but there are a number of studies—Gordon Paul's, for instance—that appear to contradict that conclusion. Those studies showed that desensitization was more effective than a variety of treatments designed to control for the effects of expectancy.

Researchers at the University of Iowa took the first step toward solving this apparent paradox when they began to assess the credibility of various experimental and expectancy control treatments for phobic anxiety (Borkovec & Nau, 1972). College students were asked to read descriptions of systematic desensitization, Paul's (1966) "attention-placebo" treatment, and other experimental and control treatments used in experimental tests of fear reduction. Based on these descriptions, the students were asked to rate how logical the treatment seemed, how effective they thought it would be, whether they would recommend the treatment to a friend, how easy it would be, and whether they would be willing to undergo it themselves. Borkovec and Nau (1972) reported that systematic desensitization was rated as more credible than any of the control procedures, including Paul's (1966) "attention-placebo" treatment, on the basis of which it had been concluded that desensitization was more effective than an expectancy manipulation. In other words, systematic desensitization is more believable that many control treatments, and its superior effectiveness might be due to its greater believability.

"A rose is a rose is a rose," wrote Gertrude Stein. We all know that no two roses are exactly alike, but we often think that things bearing the same label are equivalent. Chapter 3 noted that not all placebos are equally effective. Placebo morphine, for example, is more potent than placebo codeine, which in turn is more effective than placebo aspirin. Each of these produces a different expectancy for pain relief and therefore a different degree of experienced pain relief. The Borkovec and Nau (1972) study suggests this might also be true of treatment procedures used to control for expectancy effects in psychotherapy outcome research.

Borkovec and Nau's (1972) study demonstrated that some psychological treatments are more credible than others, but it left open the question of whether those differences in credibility produce differences in treatment outcome. The beginning of an answer to that question was reported the following year in a study by McReynolds, Barnes, Brooks, and Rehagen (1973). McReynolds et al. compared desensitization to two different expectancy modification treatments. One of the control treatments was Paul's "attention-placebo" treatment; the other was a more credible treatment that they called "dissonance enhancement." As in Gordon Paul's study, systematic desensitization was found to be significantly more effective than the "attention-placebo" treatment. However, "dissonance enhancement," which was also designed to have no effects other than those associated with changes in expectancy, was as effective as desensitization in reducing fear.

Systematic desensitization has been compared to highly credible expectancy control treatments in at least 15 studies. In 13 of these experiments,[2] expectancy modification and desensitization were reported to be equally effective. In a 14th study (Tori & Worell, 1973), the expectancy modification treatment was *more* effective than desensitization. Tori and Worell achieved these results by informing control subjects, but not desensitization subjects, that they were receiving an effective treatment.

A reliable advantage for desensitization over the control treatment was reported in only one of these 15 studies (Gelder, Bancroft, Gath, Johnston, Mathews, & Shaw, 1973). In that study, the superiority of desensitization was limited to a single self-report measure, and even on that one scale, it was limited to only certain types of fears. Furthermore, the expectancy modification treatment used by Gelder et al. was less effective than desensitization in modifying subjects' expectancies, which may explain why it was slightly less effective in reducing fear. In summary, the results of these 15 studies lead to the conclusion that the effects of desensitization can be duplicated by expectancy modification. These results are all the more impressive since the experimenters in these studies were not "blind." This factor should have increased the effectiveness of desensitization relative to the control treatments.

Expectancy and *In Vivo* Exposure in the Treatment of Anxiety

The 15 studies reported in the previous section involved comparisons between expectancy modification and standard systematic desensitization. Though other treatments for unwarranted fear have not been studied as thoroughly, there is evidence that expectancy plays an important role in their effectiveness as well. For example, although people can gain a degree of control over their heart rate by means of biofeedback, the effects of heart rate biofeedback on fear and avoidance can be duplicated by expectancy modification treatments. Similarly, expectancy modification has been reported to reduce fear as effectively as cue-controlled relaxation (Gatchel, Hatch, Maynard, Turns, & Taunton-Blackwood, 1979; Gatchel, Hatch, Watson, Smith, & Gass, 1977; Grimm, 1980).

---

[2] Allen, 1971; Gatchel, Hatch, Maynard, Turns, & Taunton-Blackwood, 1979; Holroyd, 1976; Kirsch & Henry, 1977; Kirsch, Tennen, Wickless, Saccone, & Cody, 1983; Lick, 1975; Maleski, 1971; Marcia, Rubin, & Efran, 1969; Marks, Gelder, & Edwards, 1968; McGlynn, Gaynor, & Puhr, 1972; McGlynn, Reynolds, & Linder, 1971; McReynolds & Grizzard, 1971; McReynolds et al., 1973.

Additional evidence of a relationship between treatment credibility and treatment outcome was reported by David Shapiro (1981). Prior studies had shown that systematic desensitization reduces fear more effectively than either client-centered therapy or rational emotive therapy, and that desensitization with real-life exposure is more effective than treatments based on visualization. Shapiro found that these differences in treatment effectiveness were paralleled by expectancy ratings based on simple descriptions of each of these treatments. In other words, desensitization is a more believable treatment for phobias than either client-centered therapy or rational emotive therapy, and real-life exposure is more credible than visualization.

The discovery that real-life exposure is more effective than imagery procedures in treating anxiety established exposure-based therapies as the treatment of choice for phobic disorders. It also diverted the attention of many researchers away from the topic of expectancy. However, two recent studies suggest that the effects of *in vivo* exposure might also be mediated by expectancy (Gauthier, Laberge, Freve, & Dufour, 1987; Southworth & Kirsch, 1988).

Both of these studies capitalized on the similarities between exposure-based treatments of phobias and frequently used measures of the severity of phobic avoidance. Behavioral measures of phobic avoidance involve asking subjects to approach the phobic stimulus as closely as possible or to remain in the feared situation as long as possible. *In vivo* treatment of phobic anxiety also involves asking subjects to approach the phobic stimulus or to remain in the feared situation. The major difference between treatment and assessment is the person's understanding of the purpose of the requested behavior—in one case it is to assess fear; in the other it is to reduce fear.

In an assessment of the importance of therapeutic expectations using *in vivo* exposure to feared situations, two groups of severely agoraphobic clients were instructed to walk away from their homes until they became anxious and then to return (Southworth & Kirsch, 1988). This procedure was repeated for ten sessions over a two-week period. Half of the subjects were informed that this was the beginning of their treatment. The others were told that the purpose of the walks was to obtain an accurate assessment of their fear and that treatment would not begin until after the assessment period. A third group of agoraphobic subjects served as a no-treatment control group. They were assessed at the beginning and end of the two weeks, but received no treatment in the intervening period.

Compared to the control group, subjects in both exposure groups were able to stay outside longer and reported less fear at the end of the two-week period. However, the degree of improvement was substantially greater for those given therapeutic instructions. The effect of the expectancy manipulation over the ten sessions of real-life exposure is shown in Figure 4–1. As you can see, the effects of exposure without therapeutic expectancies were minor, but when exposure was coupled with the expectancy that fear would be reduced, steady improvement ensued.

These data clearly demonstrate that expectancies for improvement are necessary to the success of *in vivo* exposure treatments. But how do these differences

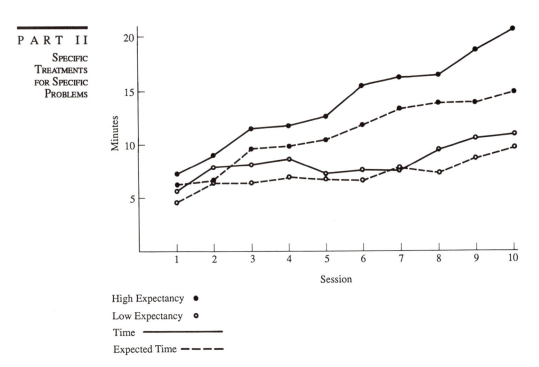

High Expectancy ●
Low Expectancy ○
Time ——————
Expected Time — — — —

FIGURE 4–1 Changes in expectancy and behavior as a function of therapeutic or non-therapeutic instructions. SOURCE: Reprinted from Southworth & Kirsch, 1988.

in expectancy produce differences in outcomes? By the end of treatment, the high-expectancy group had received a significantly greater amount of total exposure time than the low expectancy group. Perhaps people who believe that their excursions are part of treatment are more motivated to exert themselves by tolerating greater anxiety in order to stay out longer during each session. Maybe exposure has an automatic fear-reducing effect, and the effect of expectancy is merely to increase exposure so that the anxiety can be extinguished.

In order to control for this possibility, Southworth and Kirsch examined the amount of time that high-expectancy subjects spent walking away from home during the seventh treatment session. By the end of the sixth treatment session, high-expectancy clients had spent as much time walking away from their homes as had low-expectancy clients by the end of the ten-session treatment. Therefore, the seventh session scores of high-expectancy subjects were compared to the amount of time that low-expectancy subjects were able to spend outside during the last assessment session. Thus, in this reanalysis of the data, the two groups were equated for the total amount of time that they had spent on their walks. The results of this analysis indicated that high-expectancy subjects were able to travel significantly farther from home after six sessions of *in vivo* practice than low-expectancy subjects were after nine sessions, despite the fact that the comparison was based on equal amounts of prior *in vivo* exposure. This result indicates that the capacity of positive expectations to enhance the effects of treatment is not due to greater amounts of exposure to the feared situation.

These results have been replicated in a very similar study on dental phobics (Gauthier et al., 1987). In that study, one group of dental phobics received *in vivo* exposure in the guise of treatment, and another group received identical treatment, but with instructions indicating that the procedures were for the purpose of assessment, rather than for treatment. As in the Southworth and Kirsch study, subjects who thought they were receiving treatment improved significantly more than those who believed that they were undergoing an assessment procedure. Gauthier et al. also reanalyzed their data controlling for differences in exposure time, and just as in the Southworth and Kirsch study, the superiority of the high-expectancy over the low-expectancy group was maintained in the more stringent reanalysis.

Taken together, these two studies suggest that *in vivo* exposure treatments and systematic desensitization operate via similar mechanisms. Both are credible treatments that convince clients they are no longer phobic. *In vivo* exposure is the more credible of the two, and it is also more effective. Once its credibility is effectively countered, however, its effectiveness as a treatment all but vanishes.

There is one more reason to conclude that the effects of exposure are cognitively mediated, rather than automatic. Agoraphobic and nonagoraphobic panic disorders have similar diagnostic criteria. Both involve the occurrence of panic attacks in a wide range of situations, such as being alone outside the home, being in a crowd, standing in line, driving a car, crossing a bridge, and so forth. The distinction between the two disorders depends on whether the person fears and avoids the situations in which the panic attacks occur.

Agoraphobia is almost always preceded by a nonagoraphobic panic disorder. People with nonagoraphobic panic disorders experience unanticipated panic attacks in the same situations that are avoided by agoraphobics; however, the former do not avoid these situations. In fact, many agoraphobics experience panic attacks for nine years or longer before they begin to avoid such situations (Thyer & Himle, 1985). Only when they interpret the situations as causes of their anxiety do they begin to limit their activities as a way of warding off the anticipated panic.

If *in vivo* exposure was sufficient to reduce fear, nonagoraphobic panic disorders would be self-correcting. Repeated exposure to the situations in which panic most frequently occurs would lead to extinction of the anxiety and remission of the disorder. In fact, the reverse occurs. Some people continue to suffer panic attacks even though they do not avoid agoraphobic situations. These people do not become agoraphobic; instead, they retain the "panic disorder without agoraphobia" diagnosis. They are continually subjecting themselves to *in vivo* exposure, but because the exposure is not accompanied by therapeutic expectations, their condition does not improve. More commonly, people suffering from panic disorder without agoraphobia begin to avoid the situations in which their panic occurs. These people become agoraphobic after considerable *in vivo* exposure to the situations in which panic is likely. Effective treatment of agoraphobia involves the same exposure by which the disorder was generated, but with the addition of therapeutic expectancies.

The Reason for Improvement: Credibility or Expectancy?

Occasional studies indicate that a particular treatment procedure is more effective in reducing fear than an equally credible control (for example, Lent, Russell, & Zamostny, 1981). However, none of these studies have used double-blind methods, so these results may arise from the impact of the experimenters' expectancies. Another reason may lie in the nature of the measures used to assess credibility—typically very short scales of three to six items, only one of which asks people to predict the effect of treatment on their targeted fear.[3] Other items ask them to rate how logical the treatment description is, how willing they are to undergo the treatment, how easy it would be, how confident they would be in recommending it to a friend, and how effective they think it would be as a treatment for some other fear.

Even if the effects of a treatment were entirely due to expectancy, most of these scale items might be unrelated to treatment outcome. A treatment rationale can be logical, yet fail to convince someone that the treatment would be effective for some particular purpose. Nor is the perceived easiness of undergoing a treatment any indication of its effectiveness. Another problem with the scale is that outcome expectancy is only one of the factors that might influence a person's willingness to undergo a particular treatment. One might believe that a treatment would be effective, for example, yet decide not to undergo it because of the discomfort it would entail. One might even feel that the treatment would be worse than the disorder. In fact, these items are related to treatment outcome in different ways (Shapiro, 1981), and scales that ask people to rate the degree of fear they expect to experience after treatment are more accurate than typical credibility measures as predictors of improvement (Kirsch et al., 1983).

Fear is produced by the expectancy of its occurrence, not by the credibility of a treatment rationale. The relationship between expectancy and fear reduction in systematic desensitization is most clearly demonstrated in a study of 46 severely snake-phobic patients who applied to the University of Connecticut hospital for treatment after reading a newspaper story about the treatment program (Kirsch et al., 1983). Besides feeling unable to touch a live snake during the pretreatment assessment, these patients indicated that their fear of snakes caused them considerable difficulty. Many reported that their fear interfered with their reading habits, causing them to avoid the "S" volume of encyclopedias, for example, lest they come across a picture of a snake. Virtually all of these patients

---

[3] A third reason is related to the timing of credibility assessments. When treatment is described to patients, the description influences their expectancies for improvement and their expected posttreatment fear levels, but these expectancies are not etched in stone. They can be changed, for better or worse, by people's experiences during treatment, including so-called placebo treatment (Lent, 1983). For that reason, credibility and expectancy are more accurate predictors of improvement when they are assessed later in treatment (Kirsch et al., 1983; Lick, 1975). When treatment includes real-life exposure to the phobic stimulus, these changes in expectancy may be based on patients' observations of the degree to which they have in fact improved (Wilkins, 1986b). When treatment does not include exposure, however, subjects have no opportunity to judge their actual improvement. In these cases, the association between expectancy and improvement can more clearly be interpreted as evidence of a causal relationship.

found their recreational activities inhibited—they felt unable to walk in the woods, jog in the country, camp, swim in lakes, visit zoos, parks, or natural history museums, or relax in their own backyards. Five suffered from recurrent nightmares about snakes, and three reported that their phobia interfered with their jobs.

These patients were randomly assigned to three groups: systematic desensitization treatment, an expectancy modification treatment called "systematic ventilation," or a waiting list control condition. In systematic ventilation, patients were asked to relive in their imagination a series of discomforting childhood events. They were told that clinical research had established these particular events as being related to the fear of snakes. In fact, the events they were asked to remember were ones that all children experience—their first day at school, for example—events that are not, in all probability, in any way related to snakes. The therapists encouraged expressions of emotion while these memories were relived, but diverted their patients' attention away from any incidents that involved contact with snakes. Regardless of what the client experienced, the therapist interpreted that experience as an indication that the treatment was working as intended. This "systematic ventilation" procedure proved as effective as desensitization, in reducing patients' fears, and substantially more effective than no-treatment.

Immediately after the treatment was described, but before it was begun, subjects in both treatment conditions were asked to rate the credibility of their particular treatment procedure. In addition, they were asked to estimate how closely they would be able to approach the snake after being treated and how much fear they would experience as they approached the snake. Although traditional credibility ratings were not significantly correlated with treatment outcome, pretreatment predictions of posttreatment fear and behavior were, with correlations for desensitized subjects ranging from .48 to .84.

As in most fear-reduction studies, subjects' fears were assessed before and after treatment by asking them to approach a live snake as closely as possible. Immediately before attempting this task, they were asked to predict how close they would be able to get to the snake (their "self-efficacy" expectancies) and how much fear they would experience in the process. These measures of expected fear were highly correlated with their ability to approach the snake and with their levels of reported fear, both before and after treatment. The effect of treatment was to substantially reduce expected fear as well as actual fear. Similar results have since been reported for other fears and different treatment procedures (Bandura, 1977; Kirsch, 1986c; Southworth & Kirsch, 1987).

Are Behavioral Treatments Placebos?

Systematic desensitization and related treatments reduce fear by modifying patients' expectancies. The effects of desensitization do not depend on any of its specific procedural components; they can be canceled by disguising the procedure as something other than treatment; they can be duplicated by a variety of expectancy modification control treatments; and individual differences in effectiveness are very highly correlated with clients' expectancies. The effects of other fear-reduction treatments are similarly related to the expectancies that they generate.

Ironically, the effects of desensitization—the prototype of specific psychotherapy—are brought about by the same mechanism that is responsible for placebo effects in medical research. Both placebos and desensitization produce their effects by changing peoples' expectancies about their own internal reactions, but this does not mean that desensitization is "merely" a placebo. After all, windmills are not called sailboats, despite the fact that they both operate via the same causal mechanism.

Sugar pills are physical substances that are deceptively presented as working for physical reasons. Systematic desensitization fails to meet the criteria of that definition on a number of counts. First, it is a psychological treatment rather than a physical substance. Second, its effectiveness does not depend on deception, and its effects are not due to physical causes. Finally, desensitization is a specific treatment for unwarranted fear. Chapter 5 presents evidence that most fears are caused by one or another kind of expectancy and that a particular type of expectancy—expected fear—is the cause of phobic anxiety. Rather than being a placebo, systematic desensitization is a genuine psychological treatment with known causal mechanisms. It has specific activity for the treatment of anxiety precisely because its effectiveness is due to expectancy modification.

WHEN THERE IS NOTHING TO FEAR BUT FEAR ITSELF

Two conclusions can be drawn from the large body of research on the behavioral treatment of phobic anxiety. First, these treatment procedures are capable of producing a substantial reduction in fear and avoidance, considerably more than is produced by traditional, nonbehavioral treatment. Second, the effects of behavioral treatments are not due to the conditioning mechanisms on which they were based. Instead, expectancy modification appears to be their mode of operation. Treatments that include real-life exposure to the phobic stimulus situation are more effective than imagery treatments, but treatment effectiveness is not greatly affected by other variations in procedure. As long as the treatment remains believable, the inclusion of relaxation, a graduated hierarchy, imagery instructions, or a therapeutic relationship are optional. Even the effects of *in vivo* treatments appear to depend on clients' beliefs and expectations. When exposure is disguised as a method of assessment, its effectiveness all but vanishes (Gauthier et al., 1987; Southworth & Kirsch, 1988).

Why is treatment effectiveness so closely linked to therapeutic expectancies? How do these expectations reduce fear and avoidance? The answer to these questions begins with discussion of agoraphobia, which is not the most common phobic disorder but is the most incapacitating and the one for which treatment is most frequently sought.

Agoraphobia comes from the Greek words *agora,* meaning public square, market, or place of assembly, and *phobia,* meaning fear. Thus *agoraphobia* literally means a fear of open spaces and market places. Yet agoraphobics fear much more than public places and open spaces; they fear bridges, tunnels, public transportation, city streets, country roads, elevators, restaurants, heights, crowds, being alone, driving, and much more. Not every agoraphobic person fears each of these situations, and no single situation is feared by all agoraphobics, but all agoraphobics fear many different situations (Williams, 1985).

How does one come to fear so many different situations? The traditional learning theory view of phobias is based on classical conditioning. Phobic anxiety is seen as a conditioned response that is due to the pairing of the phobic stimulus with aversive consequences. This is at least plausible for simple phobias involving discrete stimuli, such as fears of dogs, snakes, and heights. The phobic individual may have fallen from a ladder or been bitten by a dog or snake, thereby developing a conditioned fear response. By invoking the idea of stimulus generalization, we can even use a conditioning model to account for fears of broad classes of stimuli (for example, animals in general). However, it is difficult to comprehend how a conditioned fear could generalize to the wide range of situations feared by agoraphobics. Furthermore, studies of the etiology of agoraphobia indicate that precipitating traumatic events can be identified in only a small number of agoraphobics (Emmelkamp, 1982). Despite the fact that agoraphobia typically develops in adulthood, most people who suffer from the disorder cannot recall any event that would typically be regarded as an instance of classical conditioning.[1]

A major breakthrough in our understanding of agoraphobia occurred when it was recognized that agoraphobia is not really a fear of public places, but rather a fear of fear. Freud (1895/1959) may have been the first to realize this when he wrote, "In the case of agoraphobia etc., we often find the recollection of a state of *panic*; and what the patient actually fears is a repetition of such an attack under those special conditions in which he believes he cannot escape it" (p. 136). Freud's conception of agoraphobia as a fear of fear was ignored for many years, until the idea was rediscovered in a very influential paper by Goldstein and Chambless (1978). It is now commonly accepted that agoraphobics are not afraid of the various situations that they come to avoid, but of the feeling of panic that they expect might occur in these situations. Agoraphobia is thus exemplary of a response expectancy disorder. It is a condition defined by the presence of a stable expectancy for the nonvolitional response of intense fear or panic.

As a result of this new way of understanding agoraphobia, it is often regarded as fundamentally different from other phobic disorders. Other phobias are treated as fears of specific stimuli and situations. In contrast, agoraphobia is seen as a fear of fear. In this chapter, the view of agoraphobia as a fear of fear is extended to other phobias as well. There are a number of differences between agoraphobics and people with specific, circumscribed phobias. For example, specific phobias typically develop early in childhood (McNally & Steketee, 1985), while agoraphobia most frequently develops in adolescence or adulthood (Breier, Charney, & Heninger, 1986). Agoraphobia is also a more pervasive disorder in that it involves a large number of feared situations. But both types of disorder can be better understood as a fear of fear, rather than as a fear of the situations that are avoided.

---

[1] Some writers (for example, Goldstein & Chambless) have treated the occurrence of fear as the conditioned stimulus, as well as the conditioned and unconditioned response, thus allowing the first experience of a panic attack, no matter how it was generated, to be interpreted as a conditioning trial. This hypothesis has been criticized by Reiss (1987) for allowing too many roles for the same event (fear). It also renders the conditioning model irrefutable and therefore untestable.

The Structure of Human Fear

People fear and avoid situations that are dangerous—in other words, fear is produced by the expectation of harm. The extent of our fear depends on the amount of harm that we expect and on the likelihood of that harm occurring. We are usually more afraid of bears than of spiders because they can do more damage to us. The presence of a barrier between us and the bear reduces our fear because it reduces the likelihood that the bear will be able to harm us.

Phobic disorders appear paradoxical because phobics are afraid of situations that harbor little or no danger. In fact, it is the absence of a perceptible threat that distinguishes phobic anxiety from a normal fear (American Psychiatric Association, 1987). Phobics know that the situation is not dangerous, but they are afraid nevertheless.

Given that phobics do not expect harm, why are they afraid? Aaron Beck has suggested that phobics' beliefs about the dangerousness of feared situations depend on their proximity to those situations (Beck, 1976; Beck & Emery, 1985). When far removed from the situation, they are aware that it is benign, but as they get closer, their beliefs begin to change. The closer they get, the greater the perceived danger.

Some support for this hypothesis was presented by Williams and Watson (1985). Before and after providing a single session of *in vivo* behavioral treatment to subjects with a fear of heights (acrophobia), Williams and Watson conducted multiple assessments of their subjects' perceptions of danger. The first of these assessments was made at ground level, the others at increasing heights. Subjects were brought to a ten-story building with a balcony on each floor. While still on the ground, they were asked to rate the likelihood that they would fall if they were to stand at the railing of each floor. They were then asked to proceed from one floor to the next, pausing at each floor to look down from the railing of each balcony. At each floor, they were again asked to rate the probability of falling. As predicted in Beck's theory, danger ratings made at the balconies were higher than those made on the ground.

Still, the riddle of phobic anxiety cannot be fully explained by perceptions of danger. As Williams and Watson (1985) note, phobic avoidance typically occurs when people are far removed from the situations they fear:

> Height phobics typically refrain from taking part in skiing activities long before they are standing in line for the chair lift; social phobics decline invitations to future social events from the safety of their living rooms; and bridge phobics plan vacation routes precisely to insure that they will not be confronted with an intimidating span. [p. 138]

In other words, phobics decide to avoid particular situations long before they occur, at a point in time during which they perceive the situation as not being very dangerous.

There is yet another reason for doubting that anticipated harm fully explains phobic avoidance. Some of the situations avoided by phobics cannot be thought of as dangerous by any stretch of the imagination—for example, avoidance of certain National Geographic television programs by people with extreme fears of snakes. These are not psychotic people. Other than their circumscribed fears, many show no evidence of psychopathology. They do not believe that the photographed snake will somehow come to life, spring from the screen, and bite them. Their expectancies of being harmed by the picture are zero, regardless of when those expectancies are measured. Nevertheless, they take measures to avoid the possibility of seeing a television program of snakes or spiders, sometimes at considerable inconvenience to themselves, and they experience discomfort when they do happen to see one.

Expecting to Be Afraid

Being bitten is not the only consequence expected by snake phobics; height phobics anticipate more than the possibility of falling; and claustrophobics fear more than a lack of air. These people also expect to become anxious when in phobic situations. They expect to experience heart palpitations, tremors, nausea, cold sweat, shortness of breath, and/or dizziness. They think that they might vomit, faint, lose control over their behavior, or otherwise humiliate themselves. In other words, they expect to be afraid.

The idea that fear is frightening is common enough to have become a colloquialism. It has been suggested that Franklin Delano Roosevelt should be credited with first formulating the response expectancy interpretation of phobias. In fact, the credit may belong to Henry David Thoreau, who noted in his journal that "nothing is so much to be feared as fear." Extreme fear is a terrifying feeling, and it is therefore no wonder that people attempt to avoid its occurrence. Further, it seems intuitively obvious that the anticipation of terror should produce a feeling of apprehension. In this way, fear is no different than any other aversive consequence.

Fear is due to a combination of two factors: expected harm and expected anxiety (Reiss & McNally, 1985). The former is a stimulus expectancy; the latter a response expectancy. Normal fear is due largely to expected harm, but when people expect to experience intense fear unrelated to their perceptions of the dangerousness of the stimulus situation, the fear is diagnosed as phobic.

The roles of expected harm and expected anxiety as predictors of fear and avoidance were assessed by Williams, Turner, and Peer (1985). Height phobics were asked to rate the likelihood of falling and the degree of fear they thought they would experience at each floor of an eight-story building. These assessments of expected harm and expected fear were made at the ground floor of the building, just before subjects were asked to try to ascend as high as they could and were instructed to stop at each floor to stand at the edge of the building and look down. Also, at each floor that they succeeded in reaching, subjects were asked to rate how anxious they felt. These assessments were conducted at three points in time: before brief behavioral treatment was administered, immediately after treatment, and one month after the treatment had been completed.

As is typical of outcome studies of *in vivo* behavioral treatments for phobic anxiety, substantial gains were made. Despite the brevity of treatment (three hours), after the most effective of these therapies, most subjects were able to ascend to the top (eighth) floor of the building and look down. Prior to treatment, the fourth floor was as high as any subject was able to go.

More important to the issue at hand are the relations between danger expectancies, anxiety expectancies, behavior, and self-reported fear. Before treatment was administered, expected harm (perceived danger) did not predict the number of floors to which subjects were able to ascend or the average degree of fear they experienced at each floor. In contrast, expected fear was highly correlated with both behavior ($r = -.51$) and reported fear ($r = .51$). After treatment had been administered, the predictive power of danger expectancies increased substantially, but so too did the predictive power of anxiety expectancies, rising to $r = -.88$ between anticipated anxiety and behavior, and $r = .86$ between anticipated anxiety and self-reported fear.[2] Therefore, regardless of when the assessments were made, fear and avoidance were more closely related to anxiety expectancies than to perceived danger.

On the other hand, these correlations may provide an inflated estimate of the degree to which anxiety expectancy causes fear. The following example illustrates why this is so. Suppose you were asked to enter the lion cage at a zoo. Presumably you would refuse this request because of the danger involved. Moreover, if you were asked to rate how fearful you would be upon entering the lion cage, your rating of expected fear would probably be similar to your estimate of the danger involved. In other words, the anticipation of harm not only produces fear; it also leads us to *expect* to be fearful. For that reason, anxiety expectancy ought to be highly correlated with fear and avoidance even if it is not their cause. In fact, Williams et al. (1985) reported substantial correlations, ranging from $r = .26$ to $r = .61$, between perceived danger and anticipated anxiety.

If anxiety expectancies cause fear, they should have an association with fear that is independent of their correlation with anticipated harm. By statistically controlling for differences in danger expectancies, Williams et al. (1985) assessed the *independent* contribution of anxiety expectancy to the prediction of their behavioral measure of fear (the number of floors ascended). At each assessment period, anxiety expectancies predicted behavior to a substantial degree, even with differences in perceived danger held constant. Although Williams et al. did not report partial correlations with self-reported anxiety as the dependent variable, these can be calculated from the data that they did report, and both sets of partial correlations are presented in Table 5–1.

These data demonstrate a substantial association between anxiety expectancies and both behavioral and self-report measures of fear, an association that is independent of the perceived danger of the feared situation. They are consistent

---

[2] The increase in the magnitude of the correlations at posttreatment is at least partly due to the fact that some of the subjects received treatment, whereas others (the control group subjects) did not. As a result, across experimental groups, there was greater variance in posttreatment scores, thereby allowing for larger and more reliable correlations.

with the hypothesis that the anticipation of fear is not just an epiphenomenon. Rather, the anticipation of fear produces fear and avoidance.

TABLE 5–1 Correlations Between Anxiety Expectancy and Fear with Danger Expectancies Held Constant

	Assessment period		
Fear measure	Pretreatment	Posttreatment	Follow-up
Self-report	.49*	.68**	.77**
Behavior	−.51**	−.76**	−.82**

*p < .01.
**p < .001.
SOURCE: Adapted from Williams et al. (1985).

Self-Efficacy and Fear

Albert Bandura's (1977) theory of fear and avoidance is closely related to response expectancy theory. According to Bandura's *self-efficacy theory,* people fear and avoid potentially aversive situations when they believe themselves unable to cope with them. They are afraid that they will lose control, have ruminative thoughts about the situation, or be unable to prevent various aversive outcomes from occurring.

Unfortunately, to date there are no published data evaluating the relation between people's perceptions of their coping abilities and their levels of fear and avoidance. Instead, self-efficacy has been assessed by people's ratings of their ability to approach a feared stimulus. Typically, the tasks on a Behavioral Approach Test (BAT) are described, and subjects are asked to indicate which tasks they believe they will be able to accomplish. Depending on the phobia, the tasks might consist of approaching a harmless snake, ascending to various floors of a building, walking various distances from home, and so on. As operationally defined, self-efficacy consists of the number of tasks that the person believes he or she can perform.

Correlations between anxiety expectancy, self-efficacy, approach behavior, and self-reported fear have been reported in three published studies involving different phobic disorders (Kirsch et al., 1983; Williams, Dooseman, & Kleifield, 1984; Williams et al., 1985). The pattern and magnitude of the correlations are similar in all three studies, and the data presented in Table 5–2 are based on the mean correlations across the three studies. As you can see, anxiety expectancy and self-efficacy are both excellent predictors of fear and avoidance. At posttreatment assessment, anxiety expectancy may be somewhat more powerful than self-efficacy in predicting self-reported fear, but otherwise, the predictive power of the two variables are more or less equal.

These data indicate that self-efficacy and anxiety expectancies are closely related, which is best indicated by the correlations between the two variables. Not only are these correlations substantial, but they are also consistently higher than their association with fear and avoidance, the variables they are intended to predict. In fact, across 11 data sets from four independent studies, the average correlation between self-efficacy and anxiety expectancy is $r = -.89$ (Kirsch, 1986c). In other words, the relationship is almost perfect; all but 20% of the variance in one measure is accounted for by the other.

TABLE 5–2 Mean Pretreatment and Posttreatment Correlations Between Anxiety Expectancy, Self-Efficacy, Approach Behavior, and Self-Reported Fear Across Three Separate Studies.[3]

	Self-efficacy	Approach behavior	Reported fear
		Pretreatment	
Anxiety expectancy	−.68	−.63	.57
Self-efficacy		.62	−.52
		Posttreatment	
Anxiety expectancy	−.88	−.77	.72
Self-efficacy		.80	−.59

Why are the correlations between self-efficacy and anxiety expectancy so uniformly high, higher than the relation between either variable and fear? One possibility is that they are both, in essence, measures of the same variable. The correlation between self-efficacy and anxiety expectancy is similar in magnitude to the correlation between different intelligence tests, and their similarity in predicting fear parallels what is found when two measures of intelligence are used to predict academic performance.

Conceptual reasons also support the notion that self-efficacy scales and anxiety expectancy scales measure the same thing. Self-efficacy scales ask people to predict their performance on behavioral approach tests, which are behavioral measures of phobic anxiety. Anxiety expectancy scales ask people to predict the levels of fear they will experience during the test. Thus, both scales ask subjects to predict their fear levels. Self-efficacy scales require them to predict their scores on a behavioral measure of fear; anxiety expectancy scales require predictions of self-reported fear.

Differences Between Anxiety Expectancy and Self-Efficacy

Most of the existing data can be explained quite easily by the hypothesis that anxiety expectancy scales and self-efficacy scales are measures of the same

[3]Correlations between approach behavior and self-reported fear have been omitted because of a measurement artifact that renders them uninterpretable. In two of these studies (Williams et al., 1984; Williams et al., 1985), fear was measured at each step of the approach test and the sum of these ratings was divided by the subject's score on the behavioral approach test. Because the fear score was derived by dividing by the subject's behavioral approach score, any correlation between the two variables would be artifactually contaminated.

underlying variable—expected fear. However, this explanation may not be entirely valid. There may be an important difference between the two variables. Fear and avoidance are *not* the same thing, and neither are the expectations of their occurrence.

Self-efficacy scales ask subjects to predict how closely they will "be able" to approach a feared stimulus, but the actions required for approaching a feared stimulus are well within the capacities of phobic individuals. A person who is phobic has not forgotten how to stand, walk, grasp, look, or drive. What, then, do people mean when they report that they are "not able" to walk towards a caged snake, look down from the third floor of a building, stand still in an elevator, or drive across a bridge?

We sometimes say that we "cannot" do something, when we might more properly say that we "will not" do it. Substituting "cannot" for "will not" is a normal linguistic habit, but it also shifts responsibility away from us and makes change more difficult. It is for that reason that therapists often suggest that a client rephrase a statement, substituting "won't" for "can't." When people say "I couldn't kill a kitten," what they really mean is that they *wouldn't* kill a kitten because of the guilt that such an act would arouse. Similarly, when phobic individuals say that they *cannot* approach the feared stimulus, they are really telling us that they *would not* do so because of the intolerable level of fear it would produce. Because intense fear and panic are so aversive, phobics are telling us that they "will not" do something when they indicate on a self-efficacy scale that they "cannot" do something.

Approaching feared stimuli and killing kittens are voluntary acts and as such, they are controlled by our intentions. Ajzen and Fishbein (1980) define *intention* as the expectancy that one will perform a voluntary act. This is exactly what self-efficacy scales measure in phobic subjects. In other words, self-efficacy scales are measures of *intention,* as that term is defined in the theory of reasoned action. As such, self-efficacy should be determined by expected outcomes and their values.

In an evaluation of this interpretation of fear-related self-efficacy scales, 50 snake-fearful college students were asked to complete two self-efficacy scales (Kirsch, 1982). On one of these, they were asked to indicate how closely they would "be able" to approach a live snake. On the other, they were asked to indicate whether they would "be able" to toss a wad of paper into a basket from various distances. They were then asked whether they would be able to perform these tasks if various consequences, ranging from receiving five dollars to saving their lives, depended on their success. When offered these hypothetical incentives, all of the students altered their self-efficacy judgements for approaching the snake, many for as little as five dollars. In contrast, most subjects did not believe that inducements at any level, even saving their own lives, would improve their aim.

When asked why the offer of an incentive had changed their judgements of their ability to approach a snake, but not their judgements of their ability to hit a target, most responded by referring to the skill involved in the paper-tossing task. This task required an ability that they knew they did not have. In contrast, they knew that they *did* have the capacity to approach a snake, despite their fears.

78

Knowing that they *could* approach the snake if they had to, they had responded to the self-efficacy questionnaire by indicating how closely they *would* approach, given the amount of fear they expected. The more money involved, the more fear they were willing to tolerate.

When offered hypothetical incentives, people alter their judgements of their "ability" to tolerate fear. Are these people merely persuading themselves that they can do more than they really can, or are their self-efficacy judgements accurate even in light of these hypothetical incentives? The data support the latter interpretation, suggesting that the effects of hypothetical incentives on efficacy judgements are paralleled by the effects of actual incentives on behavior. Valins and Ray (1967), for example, recruited a sample of male college students who reported being very fearful of snakes, and asked them whether they would be able to touch a boa constrictor housed in a glass cage. If the subject refused to touch the snake, he was offered $1 to do so. If he still refused, the offer was increased to $2. Of the 17 subjects who initially were "unable" to touch the snake, all but four did so when offered these small incentives.

Approaching a feared stimulus is a voluntary act. Whether we do so or not depends on the consequences that we expect and on the value of those consequences. In contrast, anxiety is a nonvolitional response. We cannot directly control the degree of fear we feel in the same way that we can control our physical acts. For that reason, a nonvolitional response cannot be as easily influenced by incentives. Given some incentive, phobics can be persuaded to tolerate their anxiety and confront the situations that they fear. If this were not true, *in vivo* flooding therapies, which require people to remain in the phobic situation for extended periods of time, would not be feasible. But incentives will not make the fear go away. People with an extreme fear of heights, for example, might ascend to the top floor of a tall building in order to save someone's life, but they would experience extreme fear while doing so. People agree to tolerate the discomfort of *in vivo* flooding in order to overcome their fears, but the fears are reduced only after they have spent some time in treatment.

If self-efficacy and anxiety expectancy are not merely different measures of the same variable, why are they so highly correlated? One possible explanation is that they have been measured in situations in which the incentives for approach are more or less the same for all subjects. If all other anticipated consequences are held constant, self-efficacy will be determined entirely by the amount of fear that the person anticipates experiencing. In other words, self-efficacy and anxiety expectancy are functionally equivalent only when the incentives for approaching the feared stimulus are held constant. Incentives should affect self-efficacy, but not anxiety expectancy. Therefore, when different subjects have different incentives, the relationship between the two variables ought to be lower.

Figure 5–1 portrays a model of the interaction of anxiety expectancy and self-efficacy in generating phobic fear and avoidance. As a voluntary act, approach behavior depends on one's intention, which is measured by self-efficacy scales. In turn, self-efficacy is determined by anticipated outcomes. For phobics, anxiety is the most salient anticipated outcome of approach. Therefore, anxiety expectancy is a direct determinant of self-efficacy and an indirect determinant of

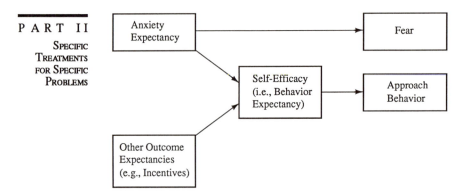

FIGURE 5–1 A hypothetical model of the causal relations between anxiety expectations, self-efficacy, approach behavior, and fear.

approach. Because anxiety expectancies are self-confirming, they are also direct determinants of the amount of fear experienced during approach.

The data for adequately evaluating this model have not yet been collected. The problem with the existing data is that they have been obtained with very little variance in the incentives for approach behavior. As a result, self-efficacy in these data is almost entirely a function of anxiety expectancy. In fact, the two are so closely related that they appear to be measures of the same thing. Testing this model would require varying the consequences of approach, so that the distinction between self-efficacy and anxiety expectancy could become empirically evident. One would then expect self-efficacy to be only moderately correlated with anxiety expectancy. Self-efficacy should be the better predictor of behavior, and anxiety expectancy the better predictor of experienced fear.

Anxiety Sensitivity

How does one acquire the expectancy that a failure to avoid certain situations or stimuli will lead to panic? Circumscribed, specific phobias are typically acquired quite early in life, so early that many people cannot recall the onset of their phobias, reporting that they have had their fears for as long as they can remember (McNally & Steketee, 1985). Most people who can remember the onset of their phobias report a frightening experience with the feared stimulus in early childhood, though it is typically an experience free of aversive consequences (other than the fear itself). Most snake phobics, for example, have never been bitten by a snake. A more commonly reported experience is being frightened by playmates who teased the person with a real or toy snake. A few people report becoming frightened as a result of being exposed to misinformation as a child, through hearing horrifying stories or watching frightening movies, for instance.

Agoraphobia generally develops later in life than simple phobias. It is almost always preceded by a history of panic attacks, which first occur during late adolescence or young adulthood. Numerous factors have been associated with the occurrence of these attacks, including stressful life events, hyperventilation, mitral valve prolapse syndrome (MVPS), and spontaneous fluctuations in physiological arousal accompanied by lower rates of habituation (Breier et al., 1986; Emmelkamp, 1982; Faravelli et al., 1985; Lader, 1967; Lader & Wing, 1969; Roy-Byrne, Geraci, & Uhde, 1985; Salkovskis, Warwick, Clark, & Wessels, 1986). However, none of these factors is sufficient to account for the development of panic disorder or agoraphobia. Most people do not develop these disorders following extremely stressful life events, and neither do most people with MVPS. The relationship between basal arousal levels and agoraphobia is only moderate, and people can hyperventilate without experiencing panic. In fact, underwater swimmers intentionally hyperventilate in order to stay under water longer (Ley, 1985).

Stress, hyperventilation, and MVPS produce physical sensations similar to those that occur during a panic attack. However, these sensations are not always experienced as panic. Furthermore, some people even enjoy the experience of fear as long as they know they are not really in danger. These people enjoy horror movies and the more terrifying amusement park rides, for example, whereas other people shun those activities.

In social learning theory, behavior is predicted on the basis of peoples' expectations that particular acts will lead to particular outcomes, and by the subjective value of those outcomes. Similarly, the experience of panic is brought about not only by the expectancy of its occurrence, but also by the extent to which it is experienced as aversive. To understand phobic disorders, we must recognize that people place different values on the experience of the sensations associated with fear and anxiety.

Steven Reiss and his associates have developed an Anxiety Sensitivity Index (ASI), designed to measure individual differences in the subjective value that people place on the experience of fear (Reiss, Peterson, Gursky, & McNally, 1986). The ASI asks people to rate the extent to which they are scared or upset by symptoms of anxiety, such as feeling faint, shaky, nauseous, short of breath, and so on. Agoraphobics have particularly high scores on the ASI, and people with other anxiety disorders—that is, simple phobias, obsessive-compulsive disorders, and psychophysiological disorders—achieve scores that fall between those of agoraphobics and people without anxiety disorders.

The role of anxiety sensitivity in producing fear has also been investigated experimentally. Holloway and McNally (1987) instructed two groups of subjects to hyperventilate. One group consisted of college students with high scores on the ASI, and the other was composed of low scorers. Subjects who were high in anxiety sensitivity reported more intense hyperventilation symptoms and greater anxiety than did those who had scored low on the ASI. In other words, people who find anxiety symptoms aversive experience those symptoms more intensely and are more frightened by them, even when the symptoms have been self-induced by intentional hyperventilation.

Why are some people more sensitive than others to anxiety sensations? In social learning theory, the value of an outcome or reinforcer depends on two factors: (1) the expectancy that it will lead to other reinforcements and (2) the value of those other reinforcements. This is the cognitive counterpart to the behaviorist concept of secondary reinforcement. We know what a ten-dollar bill can buy, and we expect increased referrals (as well as personal gratification) when our clients improve. These expectations determine the degree to which we value a ten dollar bill and our clients' improvement.

From this point of view, differences in anxiety sensitivity should be related to differences in the perceived consequences of the sensation of fear, and there is evidence that this is the case. Dianne Chambless and her colleagues have developed an Agoraphobic Cognitions Questionnaire (ACQ), on which people are asked to rate the frequency with which various thoughts occur during anxiety episodes. The scale includes such items as "I am going to pass out," "I will have a heart attack," and "I am going to go crazy." Agoraphobic subjects rate these thoughts as occurring substantially more frequently than do control subjects (Chambless, Caputo, Bright, & Gallagher, 1984). More germane to the present issue, research has yielded correlations ranging from $r = .62$ to $r = .70$ between the Anxiety Sensitivity Index and the Agoraphobic Cognitions Questionnaire (Southworth, 1986). From a social learning perspective, this association between the two measures exists because the fear of anxiety depends, at least in part, on the perception that it can lead to other aversive outcomes.

Other evidence of the role of these cognitions comes from an epidemiological study of agoraphobia (Breier et al., 1986). People who regard their first panic attacks as dangerous or even life-threatening events—heart attacks, "going crazy," brain tumors, strokes, etc.—tend to develop agoraphobia relatively quickly. They typically begin to avoid the situations in which panic occurs within a year and a half of their first attack. In contrast, among those who realize that their experiences are due to anxiety and not to some life-threatening condition, the average latency between the first panic attack and the onset of agoraphobia is more than five years.

A model of the cognitive factors that are involved in the development of agoraphobia can be constructed from these data, a model that includes social or biological stressors, misattributions, and expectancies. Initial panic attacks can be generated by physiological conditions—MVPS, for example—that produce sensations similar to those reported during panic attacks and heart attacks—chest pain, shortness of breath, and heart palpitations. If the person experiencing these sensations does not understand their real cause, the sensations may be interpreted as an anxiety attack. Worse yet, they might be interpreted as a heart attack or stroke, or as evidence of a brain tumor or psychosis, conditions that would produce intense fear in anyone.

Initial panic attacks can also be instigated by stressful life events. Most psychosocial stressors induce levels of anxiety far less intense than panic attacks, but if a person hyperventilates, moderate levels of anxiety can be transformed into extreme panic. Some people tend to breathe more rapidly or deeply when they are anxious. Overbreathing results in a depletion of carbon dioxide and produces light-headedness, heart palpitations, shortness of breath, perspiration, and tingling sensations. Feeling unable to breathe, the person may intentionally breathe even more deeply and rapidly, thereby intensifying these symptoms. If the person is not aware that these sensations are merely a function of the way in which he or she is breathing, the experience can be quite frightening.

Whatever the cause of the initial attack, the development of panic disorder and agoraphobia is heightened by the fear that it may recur. As a result of this fear, people may begin to monitor their internal sensations more closely. Moderate levels of anxiety may then be interpreted as an indication that another attack is beginning to occur. Naturally, this belief increases the person's level of anxiety, thereby initiating a vicious cycle. This is especially the case when anxiety attacks are misattributed to life-threatening, physical conditions, but even when understood as anxiety, the feelings may be distressing enough to produce a full-fledged panic attack. As described by Goldstein and Chambless (1978), "having suffered one or more panic attacks, these people become hyperalert to their sensations and interpret feelings of mild to moderate anxiety as signs of oncoming panic attacks and react with such anxiety that the dreaded episode is almost invariably induced" (p. 55).

The development of simple phobias in children may also involve misattribution. In most instances, when we say that we are frightened of something, we mean that we believe it might harm us. We are not really afraid of guns, bears, and lightning, for example, but rather of the harm they might cause in particular situations. That is why we do not fear guns displayed in a museum, bears caged in a zoo, or lightning viewed from the safety of our homes. But consider children who are frightened when taunted with a toy spider. They may soon realize that the spider is not dangerous, leading them to conclude that their fear is not justified. At the same time they know that they have been frightened. Lacking an external reason for their fear, they may attribute it to an internal characteristic of themselves. In this way, they come to label themselves as afraid of spiders.

Older children and adults are much less likely to make these misattributions. When frightened by a sudden loud noise, for example, adults are typically aware that they were startled by its suddenness. They do not attribute their fear to other stimuli that happened to be present, nor do they become afraid of noise.

Fears of particular animals are common in very small children, especially in children who do not have pets. Because the child is small, medium-sized animals may seem large and threatening. Some children seem especially wary of animals' mouths, perhaps fearing that they might be bitten. Through a combination of modeling (seeing others interact with animals without being harmed), parental encouragement, and direct experience, children typically learn that these animals are not really dangerous, and they stop being afraid. Occasionally, however, children continue to perceive themselves as afraid of the animal, even after learning that it is not dangerous. They attribute their fear to themselves, rather than to harm that might befall them. Thus, people with circumscribed phobias have learned to label themselves as fearful, and this self-confirming belief is largely responsible for maintaining their fear.

Implications for Treatment

Because phobias are maintained by the belief that one is phobic—that is, the belief that one will experience fear in particular nondangerous situations—effective treatments of phobic disorders are treatments that change this belief. Thus, expectancy modification is not a nonspecific factor in the treatment of phobic anxiety. Because dysfunctional expectancies are the causes of phobic disorders, expectancy modification is an essential aspect of their alleviation.

If therapeutic improvement is due to expectancy change, then the effectiveness of specific therapeutic procedures will depend on how they are experienced and interpreted by clients. This suggests greater flexibility in adapting treatment techniques to particular clients than would be indicated from many other theoretical perspectives. For example, conditioning explanations of the cause and cure of phobic disorders led to widespread acceptance of what has been called the "golden rule" of *in vivo* exposure (see Rachman, Craske, Tallman, & Solyom, 1986). The golden rule stipulates that during *in vivo* exposure sessions, clients must remain in the feared situation until their fear decreases. According to conditioning theories, allowing them to escape the situation while their fear is maximal should reinforce their avoidance behavior and thereby worsen their condition.

In fact, the opposite occurs. Rachman et al. (1986) tested the golden rule hypothesis by providing eight sessions of *in vivo* exposure to two groups of agoraphobic clients. Clients in one of these groups were told to stay in fear-provoking situations until their fear decreased to half of its original level. Those in the other groups were instructed to leave the situation as soon as their fear reached a particular level. Both groups of clients showed significant and equivalent degrees of improvement. In other words, escape from anxiety does not strengthen avoidance; nor does it impede the therapeutic effects of exposure.

Although any sufficiently credible procedure can produce some reduction in anxiety, all procedures are not equally effective. Some treatment techniques contain elements that help to convince people that they are improving, thereby strengthening the effectiveness of treatment. Built into the most effective behavioral procedures for treating phobic anxiety are features that provide clients with feedback indicating that they are improving. All of these treatments involve repeated or continuous exposure to the feared situation, either in imagination or in real life. Repeated or continuous exposure to any stimulus leads to habituation; in desensitization therapies, habituation is experienced as anxiety reduction.

Anyone who has been to the beach is familiar with the experience of habituation. When we first enter the water, it may feel ice-cold, but it gradually becomes more comfortable. Alternately, we can adapt to the temperature of the water by thrusting part of our body in and out of it. In other words, we can habituate either through continuous exposure or through repeated exposure. That is why repeated exposure to a feared situation can be effective even if the person escapes the situation whenever anxiety is experienced.

In many situations, sensory habituation is only temporary. When one re-enters the water on another day or after sitting in the sun for a while, it feels as cold as it did the first time. In contrast, the effects of habituation in desensitization therapies appear to carry over from one session to the next. This is partly due to the treatment context, which disguises the temporary nature of the habituation that clients experience. Because they are in treatment to overcome their fear, clients interpret their experience of decreased arousal as evidence of treatment effectiveness. This results in their expecting to feel less afraid at the beginning of the next treatment session, an expectancy which, like other response expectancies, is self-confirming.

Evidence for the facilitative role of habituation in treatment was first provided by Lang, Melamed, and Hart (1970), who measured changes in heart rate during desensitization. This allowed them to obtain a measure of the degree of habituation that occurred during repeated imaginings of scenes from the anxiety hierarchy. They reported a correlation of $r = .91$ between the success of treatment and the degree of heart-rate habituation to these scenes. A relationship between within-session habituation and posttreatment improvement has also been reported with other behavioral treatments, and with treatment for obsessive-compulsive disorders as well as for phobias (Borkovec & Sides, 1979; Foa, Grayson, Steketee, Doppelt, Turner, & Latimer, 1983; Watson, Gaind, & Marks, 1972).

Although the data showing a relationship between habituation and fear reduction are compelling, it should be noted that habituation is neither necessary nor sufficient for fear reduction to occur. In the first place, sufficiently credible expectancy modification procedures can produce substantial fear reduction, even though no opportunity for habituation is provided (see Kirsch & Henry, 1977; Kirsch et al., 1983). Secondly, physiological habituation occurs before it is noticed experientially. Therapeutic effects require sufficient time for these changes to be experienced by the patient (Gauthier & Marshall, 1977).

The role of experienced habituation is facilitative. By confirming clients' positive expectations about treatment (or reversing their negative expectations), it enhances the effects of treatment on clients' self-perceptions. Its special importance comes from the fact that it does so experientially rather than vicariously. We are more certain of attitudes and expectations formed on the basis of direct experience than we are of those based on vicariously acquired information, and for that reason, direct experience has a greater impact on our behavior (Fazio & Zanna, 1981; Wickless & Kirsch, 1989).

Foa and Kozak (1986) have argued that the demonstrated superiority of *in vivo* exposure over imaginal exposure may be related to the informational effects of habituation. They note that real-life exposure evokes phobic anxiety more reliably than does imagery, thus providing a greater opportunity for habituation to occur. In contrast, anxiety can be evoked in obsessive-compulsives by imagery exposure as well as by *in vivo* exposure, and correspondingly, both procedures produce similar therapeutic results.

However, the superiority of *in vivo* treatment over imagery therapies may have a simpler explanation. When anxiety to the imagined stimulus has been eliminated, the client cannot be certain of how much this will carry over to real-life encounters. In other words, there is a "transfer gap" between imaginal and *in vivo* exposure (Barlow, Leitenberg, Agras, & Wincze, 1969). Even if the degree of habituation were the same, real-life exposure would produce the most convincing evidence that fear of the actual phobic stimulus has been reduced.

Because of the superiority of *in vivo* treatments, some writers (for example, Emmelkamp, 1982) have recommended that imagery procedures be abandoned except when real-life exposure is impractical, or when the anxiety disorder does not involve an external stimulus. However, imagery can still play an important role in treatment for many clients. Imaginal exposure generally arouses less anxiety than real-life exposure (Foa & Kozak, 1986). Although this may make it less efficient in reducing fear, it also makes it less uncomfortable for clients. Because it leads to a reduction of fear for most clients, imagery can be used to make *in vivo* exposure easier to tolerate. Coupling *in vivo* and imaginal exposure may not enhance treatment effectiveness, but it may make the treatment process easier for the client. That alone is sufficient reason to continue its use. Similarly the use of a graduated hierarchy in either imaginal or *in vivo* treatment is not always necessary, but it can be very useful for clients who feel themselves unable to tolerate sustained imagery or exposure to the situation that most frightens them.

When anxiety is experienced, during either imaginal or real-life exposure, it can be handled in a number of ways. Clients can be taught relaxation, which can be presented as a coping skill to be used in anxiety-provoking situations (Goldfried & Trier, 1974). The relaxation response is then used to reduce the feelings of anxiety, either while remaining in the real or imagined situation or, if need be, immediately after the encounter has ended.

Relaxation training is a pleasant experience for most people. However, in some clients, relaxation training induces anxiety rather than alleviating it (Heide & Borkovec, 1983). For these people, relaxation training can be replaced by instruction in self-hypnosis or pleasant imagery. Although the real or imagined encounter can be ended and returned to without the use of *any* auxiliary technique, relaxation or some alternate response provides the client with the sense that he or she can *do* something to control anxiety, thereby enhancing feelings of personal efficacy.

With clients who experience panic attacks, the roles of dysfunctional beliefs and hyperventilation should be investigated. The belief that panic is an indication of psychosis or a life-threatening physical disorder should be challenged and countered. Clients can be helped to develop more realistic and less threatening interpretations of their symptoms. Through role-playing and other techniques, they can be taught to counter spontaneous irrational thoughts with more appropriate cognitions (see Beck & Emery, 1985).

During a therapy session, hyperventilatory hypocapnea (a decreased amount of dioxide in the blood) can be induced intentionally by rapid breathing (about 40 deep breaths through the mouth per minute for one to three minutes), and the similarity of this experience to the panic attacks can be ascertained (Ley, 1985). The nature of hyperventilation and the purpose of the experiment should first be carefully explained. Although the physical sensations of hypocapnea and panic may be the same, the client is not likely to be as frightened by the experience when he or she is aware that it was intentionally induced by hyperventilation.

If the outcome of this therapeutic experiment is positive—that is, the client reports that induced hypocapnea is similar to the sensations experienced during a panic attack—it can be used in two ways. First, it can provide an explanation of the attacks that is not as frightening as the idea that one is having a heart attack or going crazy, an explanation that will be especially convincing because it was confirmed through direct experience. Second, respiration training can be used to prevent or terminate panic attacks. Clients can be taught that although they may feel they are not getting enough oxygen, they must breathe more slowly and take in less air to end the distressing feelings. Hypocapnea can also be reversed by breathing through the nose at a normal rate with one nostril closed, or by breathing into a paper bag.

If the panic attacks are not induced by hyperventilation, and if relaxation or other coping skills are not always effective in alleviating the anxiety symptoms, clients can be taught to use paradoxical intention to facilitate anxiety reduction. They can be informed (accurately) that their anxiety is produced by the fearful anticipation of its occurrence, and that one way of reducing it is to try to make it worse. They should be instructed to try to increase their anxiety as much as possible when feeling anxious. For those with exaggerated fears of the consequences of anxiety, this can be presented in such a way as to place them in a therapeutic double bind. Intellectually, they may understand that their anxiety is not really dangerous, but they do not believe it emotionally. By staying with an anxiety attack, rather than escaping it, and by maximizing its intensity, clients can learn through direct experience that they will not die or go crazy.

The question arises whether knowing that the effectiveness of a particular procedure is due to expectancy modification precludes its effective use. In regard to treating anxiety disorders, this is clearly not the case. Clients can be informed truthfully that their fears are due to their beliefs and expectations. The dynamic of the vicious cycle can be explained to them, and they can be told that the various techniques they will be using will interrupt the cycle and allow them to change their dysfunctional beliefs in a way that can be accepted emotionally as well as intellectually. Explanations of this sort can be every bit as credible as any other treatment rationale.

RESPONSE EXPECTANCY AND DEPRESSION

6

Over the past two decades, cognitive and behavioral therapists have developed a number of treatments for depression, each linked to a different theory of the causes of the disorder. These treatments are often subclassified as behavior therapies, cognitive therapies, and cognitive-behavior therapies. In fact, most are combinations of cognitive *and* behavioral strategies. For example, one of the techniques included in a popular "behavior therapy" for depression is to teach clients to substitute positive thoughts for negative ones in evaluating aversive events (Lewinsohn, Sullivan, & Grosscup, 1982). Conversely, the most popular form of "cognitive therapy" includes the behavioral strategy of scheduling activities (Beck, Rush, Shaw, & Emery, 1979). Properly speaking, all of these new treatments are multi-component, cognitive-behavior therapies, differing only in the degree to which cognitive and behavioral components are emphasized.

These cognitive-behavioral treatments share a number of common components: They are time-limited, relatively brief (15 to 20 sessions), highly structured, provide clients with a theoretical rationale about the cause and cure of depression, and teach clients skills that can be used outside of treatment sessions to combat their dysphoric moods. In other words, they include all of the ingredients of "placebo therapy" described in Chapter 3 (Fish, 1973; Frank, 1973).

Another common characteristic of these treatments is their effectiveness. As a group, they produce a clinically significant degree of improvement in depressed clients, rivaling or even surpassing that produced by antidepressant medication (Nietzel, Russell, Kelly, & Gretter, 1987; McLean & Hakstian, 1979; Rush, Beck, Kovacs, & Hollon, 1977). There is evidence that drug treatment produces more rapid improvement than cognitive-behavioral psychotherapy. However, within a few weeks, patients treated by psychotherapy catch up with those treated pharmacologically (Elkin et al., 1986). Also, clients treated via cognitive-behavior therapy are less likely than pharmacotherapy patients to relapse within a year after the end of treatment (Simons, Murphy, Levine, & Wetzel, 1986). Finally, in direct experimental comparisons, these treatments have been reported to be superior to psychodynamic and nondirective psychotherapies (McLean & Hakstian, 1979; McNamara & Horan, 1986; Shaw, 1977).

Experimental comparisons of the cognitive and behavioral components of these treatments have shown them to be roughly equivalent in effectiveness. Cognitive procedures were reported to be significantly more effective than behavioral treatment in two studies (McNamara & Horan, 1986; Shaw, 1977). However, the reverse was found to be true in a third study (Hodgson, 1981), and four additional studies have reported equivalent results for cognitive and behavioral treatment strategies (Rehm, Kaslow, & Rabin, 1987; Taylor & Marshall, 1977; Wilson, Goldin, & Charbonneau-Powis, 1983; Zeiss, Lewinsohn, & Muñoz, 1979). Also, meta-analyses have failed to reveal significant differences in outcome as a function of whether treatments were primarily behavioral or primarily cognitive (Nietzel et al., 1987).

The Mechanisms of Change

The fact that various cognitive and behavioral treatment strategies are generally equally effective has presented a theoretical dilemma. Each of these procedures is based on a different theory of depression. Scheduling pleasant activities, for example, is based on the premise that depression is caused by a low rate of response-contingent reinforcement (Ferster, 1973); self-control therapy is based on the premise that depression is caused by negative self-evaluations (Rehm, 1977); and cognitive therapy is based on the premise that depression is due to a negative view of oneself, the world, and the future—views maintained by systematic logical errors in the thought processes of depressed individuals (Beck et al., 1979). Because each procedure is specifically designed to modify the particular thoughts or behaviors that are designated by different theories as the critical antecedents of depression, many theorists have wondered how they can all be effective (for example, Lewinsohn & Hoberman, 1982).

The Multiple Mechanism Model

One way of resolving the apparent paradox is by viewing depression as due to multiple causes. Abundant data indicate that people who are depressed engage in fewer pleasant activities, evaluate themselves less positively, and have pessimistic views of themselves, the world, and the future.[1] Perhaps each of these are partial causes of the disorder. The model illustrated in Figure 6–1 suggests that despite the general equivalence in their effectiveness at reducing depression, each therapeutic procedure does so via a different mechanism. Scheduling pleasant activities leads to a higher rate of positive reinforcement; interpersonal skills training enhances interpersonal relations; and so on. Each of these treatments alleviates depression because each remediates one of the deficits that causes depression.

---

[1]On the other hand, some evidence suggests that it may be nondepressed people, as opposed to depressives, whose thinking is faulty. Although depressed people have more negative perceptions of themselves and situations, those perceptions may be more accurate than those of nondepressed subjects (Alloy & Abramson, 1979; Lewinsohn, Mischel, Chaplin, & Barton, 1980).

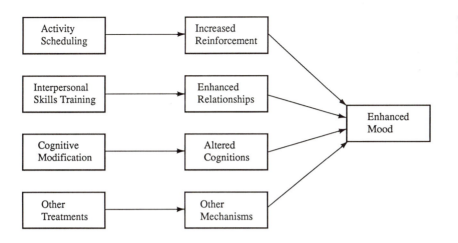

FIGURE 6–1 The multiple mechanism model of treatments for depression.

At least two empirically testable hypotheses can be inferred from the multiple mechanism model. First, even if different treatment procedures are equally effective, a combination of techniques ought to be more effective than any one of them used alone. Second, even if they are equally effective on measures of depression, they ought to have different effects on measures of the hypothesized mediating mechanisms. In other words, scheduling pleasant activities ought to have a greater impact on activity levels; cognitive modification should produce a greater change in cognitions; and so forth.

The first of these hypotheses has been tested in three studies. Consistent with the multiple mechanism model, Taylor and Marshall (1977) reported that a combination of cognitive and behavioral treatment strategies was more effective than either method of treatment used alone. In contrast, Rehm et al. (1987) found that cognitive treatment, behavioral treatment, and a combination of the two were equally effective. Finally, McNamara and Horan (1986) reported that cognitive treatment, with or without behavioral treatment, was more effective than behavioral treatment alone. At best, these studies provide equivocal support for the hypothesis that a combination of cognitive and behavioral strategies is more effective than either type of treatment by itself.

The second hypothesis is more critical to the multiple mechanism model, and studies testing it have produced more consistent results. In the first of these, Zeiss et al. (1979) used three different types of treatment for depressed outpatients: increasing pleasant activities; teaching interpersonal skills; and altering depressive cognitions. These treatments were assessed on a wide variety of instruments, including measures of pleasant events, interpersonal skills, and cognitions. If different treatments produce comparable effects via different mechanisms, one would expect different patterns of results on these measures. However, not only did these treatments result in comparable degrees of improvement in depression, they also produced comparable results on the various process measures. In other words, contrary to the specificity hypothesis, cognitive treatment was no more effective than the other treatments in altering cognitions; scheduling pleasant events was no more effective than the other therapies in increasing the frequency and enjoyability of pleasant events; and training in interpersonal skills was no more effective than the others in enhancing clients' social skills.

A similar outcome was reported by Simmons, Garfield, and Murphy (1984) in a comparison of cognitive therapy (which included both cognitive and behavioral components) and anti-depressive medication in the treatment of depressed outpatients. Both groups showed similar degrees of improvement on measures of depression. However, both groups also showed similar changes on measures of dysfunctional thought processes, despite the fact that no attempt was made to alter these processes among those receiving pharmacological treatment. Furthermore, in both groups the degree of change in depression was linked to the degree of change in cognition. The authors interpreted these results as indicating that cognitive change was a *part* of improvement, but that it was not the *cause* of improvement.

Rehm et al. (1987) tested three versions of Rehm's self-control therapy for depression. One was aimed at increasing pleasant activities, the second at changing subjects' self-evaluations, and the third treatment was a combination of the first two. Not only were all three treatments equally effective in reducing depression, but they also had equivalent effects on specific measures of the frequency of pleasant and unpleasant activities and on measures of cognition. In sum, contrary to the multiple mechanism model, the effects of particular treatments were not specific to the targets at which they are aimed.

Relaxation training and physical exercise are among the procedures used in the past as "nonspecific" controls in psychotherapy outcome studies. More recently, both procedures have been reported to be as effective as cognitive-behavioral therapy in the treatment of depression, and different specific mediating mechanisms have been hypothesized for each (Fremont & Craighead, 1987; Reynolds & Coats, 1986; also see Klein et al., 1985). The antidepressive effects of exercise are hypothesized to be mediated by enhanced physical fitness; those of relaxation by an inhibition of stress-related neurochemical changes.

The hypothesized mechanism by which relaxation training has been linked to changes in depression has not yet been assessed empirically, but mechanisms proposed to account for the effects of aerobic exercise on mood *have* been studied, and the initial data fail to support the specificity hypothesis. Fremont and Craighead (1987) compared the effects of cognitive therapy, aerobic exercise (running), and a combination of the two treatments on the mood states of mildly and moderately depressed subjects. All three groups improved significantly and equally on a variety of measures, and a four-month follow-up evaluation showed that improvement had been maintained. Changes in physical fitness were assessed among subjects who were assigned to the exercise groups, and the correlations between changes in fitness and changes in depression were nonsignificant.

Similar results were reported by Johnston (1987) in a study on the effects of aerobic exercise on the mood states of subjects drawn from a general community population. Johnston found a significant reduction in both depression and anxiety among self-selected participants in a "Fitness for Life" program. However, equivalent improvement was obtained by a control group of subjects enrolled in a variety of adult education courses (for example, basketry, quilting, oil painting, chair-caning, and upholstering). Regression analyses failed to reveal any relation between mood changes and changes in fitness among subjects in the Fitness for Life group. However, subjects' preintervention expectancies about the effects that their respective programs would have on their mood states were significant predictors of their postintervention anxiety and depression scores. Anxiety expectancies accounted for 46% of the variance in the posttreatment anxiety ratings of Fitness for Life subjects, and they accounted for 70% of the variance in the anxiety ratings of adult education subjects. Similarly, expected depression accounted for 47% and 56% of the variance in posttreatment depression scores.

The Common Mechanism Model

Depression is a psychological condition that is marked by sustained dysphoric mood and accompanied by a number of cognitive and behavioral deficits. These deficits include a diminished level of activity; a loss of pleasure in activities previously considered rewarding; social withdrawal; negative self-evaluations (lowered self-esteem); and negative expectations (pessimism). Hypotheses that these deficits are the causes of depression led to the development of treatments designed to modify them directly.

Consistent with each of these hypotheses, treatment outcome data indicate that depression can, in fact, be alleviated to a considerable degree by therapeutic procedures aimed at altering these deficits. On the other hand, depression can also be treated effectively with antidepressant medication, aerobic exercise, or relaxation training, without any specific attention to modifying cognitive or behavioral deficits. Furthermore, the effects of various treatments appear to be nonspecific. Reductions in depression are accompanied by corresponding reductions in its cognitive and behavioral concomitants, regardless of the type of treatment used.

This lack of specificity in the effects of different treatment procedures presents a challenge to theories that associate different causal mechanisms with each treatment. As a result, many theorists have suggested that all of these treatments work by activating a common mechanism (Kornblith, Rehm, O'Hara, & Lamparski, 1983; Lewinsohn & Hoberman, 1982; McLean & Hakstian, 1979; Teasdale, 1985; Zeiss et al., 1979). A model of the common mechanism hypothesis is illustrated in Figure 6–2. According to this model, changes in behavior and cognition are consequences rather than causes of changes in mood. In addition to the data indicating equivalent effects, this model is supported by evidence that depressed mood states, regardless of how they are produced, generate changes in cognitive processes (Blaney, 1986; Bower, 1981; Brewin, 1985; Teasdale, 1983; Zajonc, 1980).

The common mechanism by which various treatments are hypothesized to produce change is typically linked to the features identified by Frank (1973) as

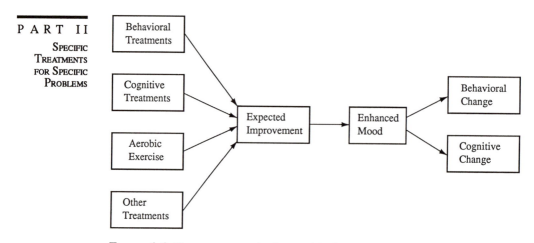

FIGURE 6–2 The common mechanism model of treatments for depression.

common to most therapies: a therapeutic rationale, a healing ritual, and the idea that change is produced by the activity of the client rather than that of the therapist. In addition, the superiority of cognitive and behavior therapies over more traditional psychotherapies is associated with features shared by the newer treatments: a high degree of structure; the teaching of specific skills that can be used outside of the therapy office to combat depression; and a time-limited course of treatment, implying that noticeable improvement should occur in a reasonably short time. These common features should foster two related expectations: that one will in fact get better and that changes in mood can be brought under the client's control.

Still, the effectiveness of pharmacological treatment suggests that the common mechanism model is incomplete, at best. Comparisons of anti-depressive medication with placebo pills indicate that the former has a greater effect (see Elkin et al., 1986). Some of this superiority in outcome may be due to enhanced expectations associated with the side effects of the active drugs used in these comparisons. Side effects provide clues that allow subjects to figure out whether they are in the placebo or active drug condition (Moscucci, Byrne, Weintraub, & Cox, 1987; Ney, Collins, & Spensor, 1986). Subjects who believe they have received the active drug presumably have more positive expectations than those who think they have been given a placebo, and this may produce differences in outcome. Nevertheless, the existing data suggest a pharmacologically specific effect of imipramine on depression.

Reciprocal Causation Models

Although they have similar and in some instances greater and longer lasting effects (Rush et al., 1977; Simons et al., 1986), cognitive-behavior therapies cannot achieve those effects via chemical alteration. Therefore, at least as far as the comparison between drug treatment and psychological treatment is concerned, different causal mechanisms are likely despite the equivalence in outcome

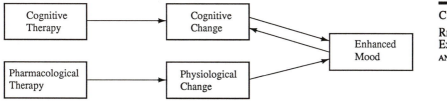

FIGURE 6–3 A reciprocal causation model of treatments for depression.

and the nonspecificity of the effects produced by these different forms of treatment.

Hollon, DeRubeis, and Evans (1987) have proposed a model, illustrated in Figure 6–3, that is based on the idea of reciprocal causation (see also Teasdale, 1983). According to this model, cognitive therapy and pharmacological treatment produce their effects via different specific mechanisms. Cognitive therapy produces changes in depression because of its effects on clients' cognitions. In contrast, the effects of medication on depression are not cognitively mediated. However, changes in depression, regardless of how they are brought about, produce changes in cognition, leading to equivalent cognitive change for all forms of effective treatment. This model is consistent with the lack of specificity in effects reported by Simons et al. (1984) and also with the established superiority of imipramine over placebo treatment.

The cognitive therapy specifically referred to in the model proposed by Hollon et al. (1987) is the one developed by Aaron Beck and his colleagues (Beck et al., 1979), and the cognitive processes that are hypothesized to both affect and be effected by depression are those emphasized in Beck's theory. Specifically, these are negative beliefs and expectations about oneself, the world, and the future; and the errors in logic that are hypothesized to maintain those maladaptive cognitions. However, Beck's cognitive therapy includes many of the treatment components contained in other cognitive-behavior therapies for depression— scheduling pleasant activities, and training in assertiveness, for example. As we have seen, the data thus far provide little evidence to support the efficacy of one cognitive or behavioral technique over another; therefore, there is little empirical justification for singling out these particular psychological mechanisms as the means by which cognitive-behavior therapies alleviate depression.

The reciprocal causation model proposed by Hollon and his colleagues fails to account for the equivalence and lack of specificity of the various component processes of cognitive-behavioral treatments of depression (Rehm et al., 1987; Zeiss et al., 1979), nor can it account for the comparable effectiveness of such interventions as aerobic exercise on relaxation training (Fremont & Craighead, 1987; Reynolds & Coats, 1986). After all, if the effects of pharmacological and psychological treatments are due to different mechanisms, despite the equivalence of their effects on hypothesized intervening mechanisms, then why should the effects of different psychological treatments not be due to different mechanisms as well?

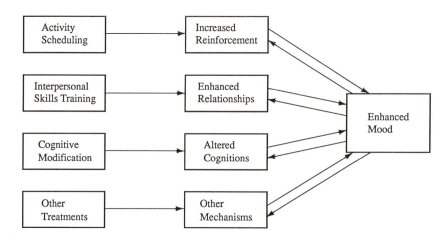

FIGURE 6–4 An expanded reciprocal causation model of treatments for depression.

This problem can be rectified easily by expanding the reciprocal causation model as illustrated in Figure 6–4. According to the expanded model, various cognitive and behavioral procedures operate via different mechanisms. As in Hollon's model, the lack of specificity in the effects of these procedures is due to reciprocal causation. Depression produces a number of cognitive and behavioral deficits. Reducing any one of those deficits reduces depression, which in turn reduces the other deficits.

The problem with the expanded reciprocal causation model is that there is little evidence supporting the contention that the effects of cognitive or behavioral intervention strategies are due to the hypothesized mechanisms on which they are based. Nevertheless, the model is plausible and testable. It would be supported if data could be obtained indicating that changes on variables directly related to intervention techniques preceded those related to other variables, even if the changes were equivalent by the end of treatment. For example, increases in activity levels ought to occur sooner in response to activity scheduling and later in response to other therapeutic interventions.

Multiple mechanism, common mechanism, and reciprocal causation models are not incompatible (Teasdale, 1985). As illustrated in Figure 6–5, the effects of some treatment procedures might be due to more than one causal mechanism. Some treatments may have effects that are specific to the theories from which they were derived (Treatments A and C), as well as effects that are associated with altered response expectancies, whereas the effects of other treatments may be mediated entirely by changes in expectancy (Treatment B). This is not unlike the effects of active medications, which are partly due to the pharmacological characteristics of the drugs and partly due to the expectancies associated with knowing that one is receiving a particular medication (see Chapter 2). Finally, the relation between some hypothesized mechanisms and depression may be reciprocal.

Establishing which mechanisms are operative in various treatments is an important empirical task. Existing data suggest that the actions of imipramine are

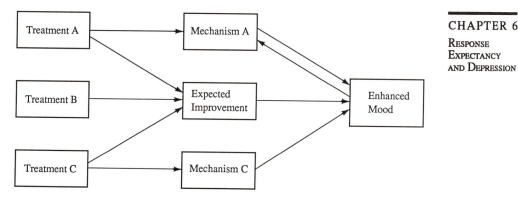

FIGURE 6–5 A combined model of treatments for depression.

best represented by those of Treatment C in Figure 6–5. The actions of placebo treatment are analogous to those of Treatment B. The mechanisms of cognitive-behavioral techniques have not yet been established, but data indicating that negative moods produce negative cognitions suggest that the actions of these treatments are modeled by either Treatment A or Treatment B, but not by Treatment C (Teasdale, 1983).

Expectancy Effects in Treatments for Depression

Regardless of whether specific effects are due to the pharmacological properties of antidepressant medication, increased levels of reinforcement, or changes in thought processes, there are considerable data indicating substantial effects associated with expectancy. Notable is the degree of improvement found among subjects in placebo and other treatment control conditions, but not among waiting-list or no-treatment control subjects. Although cognitive-behavior therapies are significantly more effective than control treatments, these differences are relatively small, especially among moderately depressed subjects (Elkin et al., 1986; McNamara & Horan, 1986). Subjects given control treatments often show substantial reductions in levels of depression, whereas those in waiting-list or no-treatment control conditions typically show little or no change (Elkin et al., 1986; McNamara & Horan, 1986; Shaw, 1977; Taylor & Marshall, 1977; Wilson et al., 1983).[2]

Additional evidence for the role of expectancy in the treatment of depression comes from a study reported by Catanese, Rosenthal, and Kelley (1979). Dysphoric college students were randomly assigned to one of five treatment conditions or a no-treatment control group. In two of the treatment conditions, subjects were instructed to engage in pleasant activities or to imagine pleasant scenes whenever feeling blue. Subjects in two other treatment groups were asked to

[2]In some circumstances, but not in others, waiting-list control subjects do show significant levels of improvement prior to receiving treatment. This is typically found when these subjects have substantial contact with the staff conducting the study, including interviews, phone calls, and extensive assessment procedures (Frank, 1973; Zeiss et al., 1979).

imagine or engage in *unpleasant* events or activities. These subjects were told that the negative images or activities would punish their dysphoric moods. Subjects in a fifth treatment group were instructed to distract themselves by thinking about social issues unrelated to their own problems.

Subjects in all five treatment groups showed substantial gains in their scores on depression inventories, gains that were maintained at a follow-up assessment more than two years after treatment. In contrast, those in the no-treatment condition continued to show relatively high levels of dysphoric mood. Furthermore, there was no difference in improvement among any of the treated groups, except that after treatment and at the two-year follow-up, subjects in the punishment groups reported significantly *fewer* blue moods than those whose treatment involved pleasant images or activities. Because the subjects in this study were suffering from subclinical levels of depression, these data must be interpreted cautiously. Nevertheless, the substantial, long-lasting improvement in the punishment groups is directly contrary to the predictions that would be drawn from behavioral theory, in which depression is seen as a consequence of reduced rates of positive reinforcement and increased rates of punishment.

Finally, preliminary data from a large-scale collaborative research program sponsored by the National Institute of Mental Health also point to the role of expectancy in the treatment of depression (Elkin, Morris, Parloff, Hadley, & Autry, 1985; Elkin et al., 1986). This study investigated the effectiveness of two forms of brief psychotherapy: cognitive-behavior therapy (Beck et al., 1979) and interpersonal psychotherapy (Klerman & Weissman, 1982). The effects of these treatments were compared to those of two control conditions: imipramine, or placebo pill combined with minimal supportive therapy designed to manage the dose levels of the medication. By the end of the treatment program, a significant reduction in depression was found in all four groups, including the placebo pill control group, and the degree of improvement within each of the groups was correlated with patients' expectancies of improvement. Furthermore, among moderately depressed subjects, there were no significant differences among the groups in degree of improvement. For more severely depressed subjects, only imipramine and interpersonal therapy were more effective than placebo treatment, indicating that they may be somewhat more effective than cognitive-behavior therapy for these patients.[3]

Because of the relatively strong showing of interpersonal psychotherapy in this major outcome study, an examination of the nature of this treatment will be useful. Interpersonal psychotherapy is a brief (12-16 weeks) treatment for depression developed by Gerald Klerman and his colleagues. It is based on the premise that depression is caused by four specific types of social and interpersonal problems: (1) inadequate grieving following the death of a loved one; (2) interpersonal role disputes such as sustained marital conflict; (3) role transitions such as divorce, the birth of a child, or a change in social or professional status; and

---

[3]Analyses involving all subjects (both moderately and severely depressed) failed to show any significant differences between cognitive-behavior therapy, interpersonal therapy, or imipramine. This uniformity indicates that the advantage of interpersonal therapy over cognitive-behavior therapy is slight.

(4) social isolation. Treatment involves assessing the particular interpersonal deficit associated with the client's depression and using a variety of techniques to remediate the deficit. Depending on the assessment, the therapist might help the client to complete the mourning process, resolve interpersonal conflicts, alter interpersonal expectations, develop a sense of competence and optimism in relation to a new social role, or establish new and more rewarding interpersonal relationships.

Because interpersonal psychotherapy is a form of brief treatment and many of the targeted changes are difficult to achieve, treatment goals are often limited to starting work on these issues rather than solving them. For this reason, changes in social functioning are not expected until some time after treatment has ended. In fact, experimental tests reveal that although interpersonal psychotherapy produces substantial improvement in depression levels by the end of treatment, changes in social functioning take at least six to eight months to develop (Klerman & Weissman, 1982). How, then, are those short-term changes in depression achieved?

Interpersonal psychotherapy consists of two components. The first is aimed at remediating deficiencies in social relationships, and this is the component that has delayed effects. The second component is aimed at relieving depressive symptoms, and this aspect of treatment is based explicitly on Jerome Frank's (1973) assessment of the common mechanisms of different psychotherapies. To reduce the symptoms of depression, the interpersonal psychotherapist

> attempts to instill in the patient a sense of hope. . . . Depressed patients characteristically feel that their symptoms will never lift. . . . They should be informed that this pessimism, along with other symptoms . . . are all part of this depressive episode . . .
>
> To enlist patients' involvement in therapy, the following information about treatment can be given to them: Depressions do respond to treatment; there are a variety of treatments that are effective; and the treatment that the patient will be undergoing has been shown to be effective in several clinical studies. Most depressives recover promptly with treatment, and the prognosis is quite good [Rounsaville & Chevron, 1982, pp. 108-109].

Therefore, in one of the most effective therapies for depression, depressive symptoms are alleviated by altering clients' depressive response expectancies—their sense of hopelessness about their own feelings of depression.

Depression about Depression

The data reviewed in the previous section indicate that patients' expectations play an extremely important role in the treatment of depression. This raises the question of how the expectancy for improvement alleviates depression. At least part of the answer to this question may be related to John Teasdale's (1985) concept of "depression about depression." A common feature of depression is the belief that one will remain depressed, and because depression is aversive, the expectation that it will persist is an extremely depressing thought. In other words, maladaptive response expectancies can be a cause of depression. Conversely, the belief that one will get better produces a positive emotional state because it replaces the expectancy of an aversive state with the expectancy of a highly desirable one.

The hypothesis that response expectancy can be a cause of depression is consistent both with Aaron Beck's cognitive theory of depression (Beck et al., 1979) and with the theory of learned helplessness (Abramson, Seligman, & Teasdale, 1978). Beck and his colleagues view depression as the result of three cognitive patterns, often referred to as the "cognitive triad": (1) a negative view of the self; (2) a negative view of the world; and (3) a negative view of the future (Beck et al., 1979). The first and third patterns include negative response expectancies. Viewing their feelings of depression as due to irremediable personal defects, depressives expect that they will remain depressed forever.

According to learned helplessness theory, depression is due to the experience of uncontrollable aversive events that people attribute to their own unchanging and unchangeable characteristics (Abramson et al., 1978). These attributions about the cause of the negative events they are experiencing leads them to expect that the aversive outcomes will continue to occur. For example, if you believe that your failure to pass an exam was due to a lack of native ability, you will expect to fail similar tests in the future. Clinically depressed persons often blame themselves for their depression and view this extremely aversive state as being due to a relatively stable and uncontrollable personal deficit. This being the case, they quite naturally expect to remain depressed.

According to Teasdale (1985), the common mechanism shared by different therapies for depression is the capacity to decrease people's depression about their own depression. In addition to effects that may be associated with features specific to these different treatments, they reduce depression by

> helping patients to view it as a problem to be solved, rather than evidence of personal inadequacy, by encouraging expectations that their actions can affect the problem, and by providing them with a structure to test out and repeatedly confirm the effectiveness of their problem-solving actions, thereby facilitating and maintaining a sense of control [p. 161].

This hypothesis is consistent with the evidence that all forms of treatment (including placebo treatment) produce substantial reductions in depression; that highly structured treatments with a credible rationale suggesting relatively rapid improvement are particularly effective; and that the effects of various treatments are not specific to the hypothesized mechanisms on which they are based. But more direct data support the hypothesis that altering depression about depression is an important mechanism of effective treatment.

Fennell and Teasdale (1987) compared cognitive-behavior therapy to "treatment as usual" for depressed clients. Subjects in the treatment-as-usual group received whatever treatments their family doctor would usually have offered, including antidepressant medication and referral elsewhere for psychotherapy. Those in the experimental group were given cognitive-behavior therapy in addition to treatment as usual. Significant differences in improvement between the two groups were observed within two weeks of the onset of treatment and were maintained throughout the duration of therapy. However, the superiority of cognitive-behavior therapy was not found for all patients. Although some subjects responded to treatment rapidly, leading to the statistically significant difference between the groups within two weeks of the beginning of treatment, others improved more slowly. Throughout treatment, the depression scores of these slow responders were not different from those in the treatment-as-usual group. In contrast, rapid responders maintained their gains not only through the end of treatment, but also at three-month and one-year follow-up assessments.

Fennell and Teasdale (1987) then investigated possible causes of the differences between responders and nonresponders to cognitive-behavior therapy.[4] Success in treatment was significantly predicted by two intercorrelated variables: a measure of depression about depression, and a measure of the perceived credibility of the rationale for cognitive-behavior therapy. Depression about depression was measured by assessing subjects' responses to the hypothetical situation of waking early one morning, feeling tired but being unable to get back to sleep, and ruminating about the day ahead. High scores on depression about depression were derived from responses indicating that (1) clients would feel extremely upset in this situation, (2) they would blame themselves for it, (3) they would see it as the beginning of another bout of depression, (4) these negative feelings were not atypical, and (5) nothing they could do would change them. Subjects who responded in this manner were more likely to accept the rationale of cognitive-behavior therapy as credible ($r = .61$), and those who accepted the rationale were less depressed following treatment ($r = -.76$).

Stress, Expectancy, Coping, and Depression

Considerable data indicate that the occurrence of stressful life events, particularly those involving separation and loss, are precipitants of depression (Paykel & Hollyman, 1984). Compared to the general population or to patients with other psychological diagnoses, depressives report a greater number of stressful events up to a year before the onset of their depression, a difference that is especially marked in the weeks immediately preceding the onset of the disorder. On the other hand, the association between life events and depression is moderate, at best. Although losses, separations, and other negative stressors induce dysphoric moods in almost everyone, most people do not become clinically depressed following these events.

Because life events in themselves are not sufficient to bring about the disorder, researchers have sought for psychological variables that might mediate the relation between stress and depression. Two variables in particular have been

---

[4]In reports by Teasdale (1985) and Fennell and Teasdale (1987), these were referred to as "rapid responders" and "slow responders" to cognitive-behavior therapy. However, there is no evidence that cognitive-behavior therapy had any effect at all on these subjects, in view of the facts that (1) subjects in the cognitive-behavior therapy group received the same "treatment as usual" that was given to the control group and (2) the response of "slow responders" was not significantly different from that of control subjects. Hence, "nonresponders to cognitive-behavior therapy" is also an accurate label for this subset of clients.

extensively investigated: social support and coping style (Kessler, Price, & Wortman, 1985). Stress is significantly more likely to cause psychological dysfunction among people who are relatively lacking in social support, and among those who either lack the necessary skills or for some other reason fail to make use of effective coping strategies. It has been suggested that avoidance exacerbates the effects of stress on depression, whereas active coping strategies (for example, reevaluating the meaning of the stressor or doing something to lessen its impact) decrease the negative effects of life events (Billings & Moos, 1984).

Teasdale (1985) has suggested that the likelihood that people will use active coping strategies might depend on their response expectancies. Those who believe that their strategies will successfully alleviate their negative moods will be more likely to use those strategies, whereas those who are relatively pessimistic about the success of their attempts to cope will fail to either initiate or persist in them. They are more likely to see their feelings of depression as uncontrollable, thus initiating a vicious cycle that might result in a full-blown depressive syndrome.

Teasdale's hypothesis was tested in a survey of 472 college students (Kirsch, Mearns, & Catanzaro, 1988). These subjects were asked to complete an inventory of negative life events that they had experienced during the previous year, a measure of family support, a measure of coping styles, a depression scale, and a survey of physical health problems. In addition, they completed the Negative Mood Regulation (NMR) Scale, a measure of coping response expectancies devised by Catanzaro and Mearns (1987). In completing the NMR, subjects rated the degree to which they believed that the use of various coping strategies would enable them to feel better. The NMR includes such items as "I can usually find some way to cheer myself up," and "planning how I'll deal with things will help."[5] People scoring high on the NMR were hypothesized to be more likely to actively cope with stress—by looking for positive aspects of the situation—and less likely to avoid dealing with the stressor—by using drugs as an escape.

It is axiomatic that correlation does not establish causation. However, the statistical procedures of path analysis can be used to test causal relations between correlated variables (Kenny, 1979). We used a path analysis to examine the relations between people's coping response expectancies and the other variables described above. The results of this analysis are shown in Figure 6–6. The numbers in this diagram are path coefficients. Path coefficients are similar to correlations, but they are more conservative because variance associated with other variables has been partialled out. In other words, they represent the *unique* predictive power of hypothesized causal variables, predictive power that is not shared with other variables with which the criterion is correlated. For example,

[5]Coping response expectancies are similar to self-efficacy expectations. However, they can more precisely be interpreted as outcome expectancies. Rather than asking whether people are able to engage in particular coping behaviors, they assess whether people believe that those behaviors would successfully reduce their dysphoric moods.

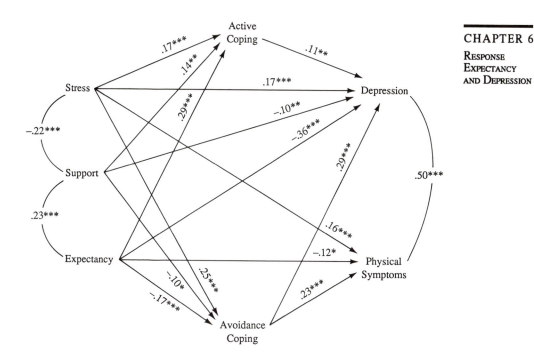

FIGURE 6–6 Structural model of environmental variables (stress and family support), response expectancies, and coping behavior as causes of depression and physical symptoms.

the correlation between stress and depression was considerably higher than the path coefficient between the two variables. The path coefficient shows that the relationship between stress and depression that is independent of people's expectancies, their coping behavior, and the degree of support they received from their families.

The results of our path analysis show that all three of our independent variables are predictors of the ways in which our subjects coped with stress. The greater the amount of stress they experienced, the more likely they were to engage in both active and avoidant coping behaviors. Those with greater family support and more positive response expectancies were more likely to use active coping strategies, whereas those with less family support and more negative response expectancies were more likely to avoid dealing with their problems.

The data on predictors of depression were even more interesting. The zero-order correlation between active coping and depression was nonsignificant. In contrast, the path analysis indicated that with variance associated with all other variables held constant, active coping efforts were indeed associated with depression, *but in a direction opposite to that theoretically predicted.* With expectancy held constant, there was a positive association between depression and active coping.[6] On the other hand, response expectancy had a direct association with depression (and with physical symptoms as well) that was independent of its effects on coping strategies. The more that people expected their coping efforts to succeed, the less depressed they were and the fewer physical problems they reported.

How are these data to be interpreted? As hypothesized by Teasdale (1985), people who believed that their coping efforts would succeed were more likely to attempt to actively cope with their problems. However, their coping efforts were successful only to the extent that they believed they would be successful. People with relatively low coping response expectancies may also initiate coping efforts, but because of their low levels of expectancy, these efforts are not as successful. Because they still feel depressed, these people may persist in coping efforts to some extent, whereas those whose efforts have been successful no longer have as much to cope with. In other words, the active coping strategies that people use to deal with stress may not have an automatic effect on mood. Instead, it is the *belief* that one's mood will change that produces the change.

Alleviating Depression

The data reviewed in this chapter provide clear evidence for a common mechanism in treatments of depression, and identify that common mechanism. Having little else in common, all effective treatments for depression alter clients' expectations about their depressed mood. Consistent with the general response expectancy hypothesis, *believing* that one will feel better is enough to *make* one feel better. In many cases, the change in belief and mood is sufficient to interrupt the vicious cycle produced by the reciprocal relation between cognition and emotion, transforming it into a benign cycle. Feeling better induces a greater sense of confidence, which in turn further enhances one's mood.

Besides this common mechanism, treatments may have effects that are independent of expectancy. However, except for the action of antidepressive medication, the existence of these effects has not been clearly established. Not only do diverse treatments have similar effects on depression, but they also have comparable effects on measures of hypothesized mediating mechanisms. Furthermore, as soon as credible theoretical rationales are developed, procedures that were initially used as "nonspecific" controls (for example, physical exercise and relaxation training) are found to be as effective as better-established therapies and are added to the growing number of effective treatments for depression (Fremont & Craighead, 1987; Reynolds & Coats, 1986).

Therapeutic expectancies remove an important barrier to recovery. Even if there are other causes for a client's depression, rectifying those sources of depression may not be sufficient to relieve the client's dysphoric mood. The

---

[6]With only stress, family support, and avoidance partialled out, the relation between active coping and depression was still nonsignificant. It was only when the effects of expectancy were also controlled that the significant counter-intuitive relation was found.

conviction that one's depression cannot be overcome may be sufficient to maintain a dysphoric mood. For that reason, people who are certain of remaining depressed for a long time may remain depressed even if all other causes of their depression are remedied.

One feature common to effective psychological treatments for depression is that they are relatively brief. Their brevity, in and of itself, conveys a therapeutic message, suggesting to clients that their troubling emotional states will soon be improved. If accepted as true, this message should generate a positive mood change. Just as the anticipation of aversive events produces sadness, the belief that good things will happen generates happy feelings. In contrast, clients who are told that their condition will require years of psychotherapy are hearing a very depressing message, a message that might keep them depressed even if other aspects of the therapy are based on sound principles.

A second feature common to the more effective psychotherapies for depression is that they teach clients strategies that they themselves can implement for control of their dysphoric moods. This aspect of treatment may account for the superiority of cognitive therapy over antidepressant medication as far as relapse rates are concerned. Psychotropic drugs produce temporary states that wear off once the drug is discontinued. In contrast, a skill that is well learned may last a lifetime. It may be that some coping skills have effects that are independent of expectancy, but that has not yet been established. It does seem clear, though, that when a person *believes* that a particular strategy is effective, the belief can make the strategy effective for that person.

Expectancy Modification as a "Specific"

Chapter 3 reviewed data indicating that psychotherapies differ in their effectiveness. Specifically, cognitive-behavior therapies are more effective therapeutic change agents than traditional insight therapies. Further, some evidence suggests that the effects of some of these treatments are greater than those of equally credible treatments that have been devised as "placebo" controls in therapy outcome studies.

On the other hand, data reviewed in Chapter 4 indicated that the effects of systematic desensitization, the most thoroughly studied behavior therapy, can be explained by its effects on clients' expectancies. There is also evidence that the effects of *in vivo* exposure on phobic anxiety are mediated, at least in part, by expectancies. Finally, a good part of the effectiveness of our best psychological treatments for depression appears to be due to expectancy.

Why is it that expectancy plays such a large role in the treatment of anxiety and depression? The answer is that expectancy is one of the causes of these disorders. Phobic disorders are associated with a fear of fear. This is especially clear in the case of agoraphobia, which can be *defined* as a fear of fear, but it is true of other phobias as well. Similarly, many depressed people are depressed about their own feelings of depression. This is not the only cause or maintaining factor of depression, but it does appear to play an important role in many people's depressive disorders. These people have become locked in a destructive feedback loop in which their experiences of anxiety and depression strengthen their expectancies for these negative moods, and their expectancies for negative feelings generate those feelings.

These conclusions about the causes of anxiety and depression have important implications for the way in which these disorders may be treated. The fact that expectancy plays an important part in treatment outcome is no cause for embarrassment; it does not mean that the treatment is ineffective, nor that it is a placebo. In fact, a treatment that reduces anxiety or depression by altering clients' fear-arousing or depressive expectations is as far from being "nonspecific" as any psychological treatment can be. Treatments and treatment components that operate via expectancy modification accomplish their aims by removing one of the specific causes of anxiety and depression.

A CLINICIAN'S GUIDE TO EXPECTANCY MODIFICATION

7

The preceding chapters demonstrate that dysfunctional response expectancies play an important role in maintaining many psychological disorders, and that changing those expectancies is an important part of effective psychotherapy. The next question is "How does one go about modifying a client's dysfunctional expectancies?" Answers to this question are scattered throughout the book. This chapter presents a systematic overview of some strategies for changing a client's expectations.

Expectancy modification has been used, knowingly or unknowingly, by effective therapists since psychotherapy was first practiced. The development of specific therapies for particular disorders (for example, desensitization therapies for phobias, cognitive therapy for depression, sex therapy, and so on) can be seen in part as a refinement of expectancy modification strategies. These therapies permit more efficient and more effective modification of response expectancies, and that is at least one of the reasons for their ability to produce better outcomes. Psychoanalytic treatment is the "Model T" of psychotherapy: It may get you where you are going, but newer models are faster and more reliable.

This chapter reviews the components of effective treatment from the perspective of response expectancy theory. As you read these suggestions for enhancing the effectiveness of treatment, you may notice that they are based to a large degree on experimental data reviewed in previous chapters. This demonstrates the relevance of experimental research to clinical practice.

The Therapeutic Relationship

One of the factors common to all psychotherapies is the establishment of a therapeutic relationship. The essential ingredient of this relationship is trust. The client's trust is important for a number of reasons, one of these being that it fosters acceptance of the therapist's communications. Therapists perceived as trustworthy are likely to be believed; their interpretations are more likely to be accepted as true; and they will therefore be more effective in modifying their client's expectations. That is why it is so important to avoid the use of deception, even when it seems that a "white lie" might speed therapeutic progress.

However, establishing rapport does not mean becoming the client's peer. The role of expert is also useful in promoting trust. Actually, the therapeutic relationship can be thought of as a collaboration between two experts. The client is the world's foremost expert on his or her own subjective experiences, while the therapist is an expert on psychological principles and methods of change. By acknowledging the client's expertise while simultaneously demonstrating confidence in his or her own expertise, the therapist encourages a relationship of mutual respect.

The establishment of rapport is not limited to the initial stages of therapy. For some clients, especially those whose parents were particularly untrustworthy (for example, victims of child abuse), earning trust may be a process that remains uncompleted until the end of therapy, if ever completed at all. These clients test the therapist's trustworthiness again and again, always half expecting the therapist to fail the test and always being a bit surprised when the therapist does not fail.

Being human, even the most skilled and caring therapist will occasionally fail to meet a client's standards, especially if the client has idealized the therapist and has therefore set impossibly high standards. When this happens, the client may express considerable anger at what is viewed as a betrayal. It is altogether natural for the therapist to react to this anger defensively and focus critically on the client's shortcomings (for example, his or her tendency to over-idealize). This may fuel the client's anger, and a pathogenic interpersonal struggle may result. Alternately, the therapist can empathize with the client's disappointment, accept the client's anger, and acknowledge an error, though without engaging in self-denigration. Part of the therapist's message might be: "I'm sorry! I try to do the best I can, but like everyone else, I sometimes make mistakes. I hope that you can accept that, just as I want you to be able to accept yourself as someone who sometimes makes mistakes despite the best of intentions."

Sometimes a more pithy response will do. After patiently listening to a long, angry tirade from a client with a history of developing anger toward therapists (which had frequently been reciprocated), one therapist sat in silence for a moment and then quietly commented, "Wow! You really beat me up today. Is there anything else I've done wrong that you'd like to share with me?" This was delivered without a trace of sarcasm. During the client's angry outburst, the therapist had reminded himself that this was part of the difficulty that had led the client to seek treatment and that in some very important sense, she was doing the best she could. This enabled the therapist to avoid the anger that would otherwise have negated his ability to respond therapeutically. After a minute of stunned silence, the client smiled sheepishly, thanked him, and they said good-bye. The therapist had "passed" that test, and the two resumed a productive relationship the following week.

Role-Playing the Client

Role-playing the client is a particularly effective technique for communicating empathy and enhancing feelings of trust and confidence. Role-playing is used in a variety of therapies, but the technique described here is a novel application developed by Robert Belliveau (personal communication, November, 1981; see also Belliveau, 1988). Properly done, it can be a powerful experience for both therapist and client. In addition to communicating empathy, a role-play by the therapist can actually increase the therapist's empathy with the client and provide fresh insights into the dynamics of the client's feelings. It can give the client the feeling that he or she has been more thoroughly understood than ever before and lower the client's defensiveness and resistance to new ways of thinking.

Before engaging in role-play, the therapist listens carefully to the issues that concern the client, asking questions when needed to fill in necessary details. When the therapist feels that he or she has acquired an accurate understanding of the client's experience, the role-play can be explained as follows: "I'd like to give you some feedback about what I've been hearing, and one method that I've found useful for doing that involves me role-playing you. I'm not going to imitate the way you talk or anything like that. I'm just going to pretend that I'm you, as a way of sharing with you what I've heard. I know this might seem a little strange, but is it OK with you?"

Assuming that the client consents, the therapist might ask whether there is anything about which the client wishes him or her to be particularly sensitive, and the two then change seats. At this point, it is useful to take a few moments to prepare oneself for the role-play. The therapist thinks about what has been seen and heard, not only about particular issues that have been presented and the feelings that have been displayed, but also about the client's background, social history, and values. Next, the therapist imagines being the client; that is, imagines having been brought up in the client's household by the client's parents and having gone through the experiences that the client has described. In other words, the therapist tries to feel what it would be like to have lived the client's life.

Notice that in this preparation for the role-play, the therapist does not imagine that she *is* the client. Instead, she imagines that she has lived through the client's experiences, including those early experiences that shaped the client's attitudes and values. This difference, though subtle, is critical. If the therapist pretended to be the client, he would probably imitate the client's mannerisms, and the client would feel belittled or ridiculed. Instead, the therapist talks and acts like himself as he might have been had he lived through the experiences of the client.

The role-play also needs an imaginary listener. Sometimes this can be oneself, so that the therapist is role-playing the client talking to the therapist. More frequently it is someone in the client's life. One way of selecting an imaginary listener is by asking the client: "If you could choose anyone in the world to share this with, who might that person be?"

Spontaneity plays an important part in the role-play. Rather than plan all her words in advance, the therapist lets them flow freely from the imaginary life into which she has cast herself. In so doing, she may become aware of feelings that the client has not explicitly articulated. In expressing anger, for example, the therapist may become aware of feelings of being hurt that have given rise to the anger. When this happens, the therapist can incorporate those spontaneous thoughts and feelings into the role-play. Sometimes these additions turn out to be off the mark, but more often they are recognized by the client as genuine. When this happens, the client benefits immediately from a deeper understanding of his or her own experience. The role-play experience also reinforces the client's confidence in being understood by the therapist.

At the conclusion of the role-play, therapist and client return to their original seats, and the therapist asks the following questions: "How accurate was that? Was there anything that did not fit or that you would like to correct?" When the role-play has gone well, the client finds little to correct and may express some amazement. When therapists clearly articulate feelings and thoughts that their clients were only vaguely aware of before, clients sometimes ask whether the therapist is a mind reader.

Therapists often present their hunches about clients' experiences in the form of interpretations. For example, a therapist might say, "Besides feeling angry toward your father, I wonder whether you might also feel hurt by him." Clients may either accept or reject these interpretations. They are more likely to accept them when the interpretations have been embedded within a role-play because (1) the role-play increases the accuracy of the therapist's empathy, thereby increasing the accuracy of the interpretation, and (2) the feeling of being profoundly understood, which is a consequence of a successful role-play, lowers the client's resistance to otherwise threatening interpretations.

In couples therapy, role-playing a client can be doubly effective. When the underlying hurt is expressed, instead of the anger produced by the hurt, the spouse is able to listen less defensively and to respond empathically rather than with a counterattack. This can break the vicious cycle that is a trap for many couples, paving the way for deeper understanding and increased intimacy.

Assessment

While establishing rapport, the therapist begins a careful assessment of the problems for which the client is seeking treatment. Among other things, the therapist wants to know whether the client's problems involve nonvolitional responses. Anxiety, depression, sexual disorders, sleep disorders, conversion symptoms, dissociative disorders, obsessions, compulsions, substance abuse, hallucinations—all of these problems involve nonvolitional responses. In contrast, many marital, occupational, and parent-child problems do not. (Typically, clients with these presenting problems are more troubled by the voluntary behavior of others than they are by their own nonvolitional reactions.)

Although therapeutic expectancies are an important factor in the treatment of all psychological difficulties, they are particularly important in treating problems that involve nonvolitional responses. In assessing these problems, the therapist wants to know the degree to which response expectancy maintains the dysfunctional nonvolitional responses. In many instances, dysfunctional response expectancies may be maintained solely by expectancies, particularly in the case of simple phobias and in some sexual and sleep disorders. In these instances, expectancy modification may be all that is needed for successful treatment.

However, response expectancy is not the only factor that can affect a nonvolitional response, and when other causal factors are present, changing expectations may not be sufficient to produce a successful outcome. For example, test anxiety may be due to the perception that one is not bright enough to succeed in academic course work. In this case, effective therapy would involve helping the client to form more accurate self-efficacy judgements or to set more realistic academic and occupational goals. Similarly, a social phobia could be related to a lack of social skills, which results in punishment of the client's attempts at social interactions and a consequent increase in his or her anxiety. In this case, successful treatment would have to include teaching the client the social skills that are needed if social encounters are to have positive outcomes.

If the client in either of these instances has come to label himself or herself as phobic, expectancy modification would also be needed. In other cases, dysfunctional nonvolitional responses may be due entirely to factors other than expectancy. For example, feelings of depression can be produced by a significant interpersonal loss. Some clients are aware that this is the cause of their dysphoric mood and do not regard themselves as particularly prone to depression. These clients need emotional support and may require help in working through the process of grieving. However, even in these cases, dissipation of the negative affect may require the client's belief that it will come to an end. Coping behaviors tend to be effective only to the degree that they are believed to be effective (Kirsch et al., 1988), and the belief that one will remain depressed is sufficient to keep one depressed (Teasdale, 1985).

Although dysfunctional responses are typically ego dystonic, these "symptoms" often serve a positive function for the client as well. A phobic disorder, for example, may provide a means of avoiding certain unpleasant activities without having to confront a domineering spouse. The current functions of apparently dysfunctional response need to be carefully assessed because they are indications of genuine needs of the client. If these needs are not met in other ways—that is, if the positive function of the problem behavior is not neutralized—considerable resistance to treatment may be encountered. The person whose phobia is motivated by avoidance of marital confrontation may require assertiveness training and/or marital therapy before the phobia can be overcome.

However, this does not mean that direct treatment for specific dysfunctions should be withheld until hypothesized "secondary gains" have been handled. On the contrary, problem-focused treatment can be thought of as one of the best means of assessing the degree to which the problem is motivated by these reinforcements. Returning to our example of a phobia that may be motivated by avoidance of marital distress, desensitization treatment could lead to one of three possible outcomes. First, one or another form of resistance to treatment could be encountered, thereby rendering the treatment ineffective. This would be interpreted as evidence in support of the therapist's hypothesis about the need to work on the marital relationship. A second possibility is that the phobia will be eliminated, leading to an increase in marital distress (not only for the client, but for the spouse as well). This would provide motivation for marital treatment that might otherwise have been resisted. Finally, there may be significant improvement in the phobic reaction, with no corresponding deterioration of the marital relationship. When this happens, both the therapist and the client can be grateful that the therapist's hypothesis was wrong and that the therapist had the wisdom to test it before embarking on a lengthy program of treatment for something other than the presenting problem.

In the theories upon which traditional psychotherapies are based, the primary function of all problem behaviors, thoughts, and feelings (which are regarded as symptoms of underlying conflict) is to ward off anxiety that can be traced to unconscious wishes. In addition, they may provide some secondary gains, such as allowing the person to avoid an unpleasant activity. In traditional behaviorist theory, these secondary gains are termed *reinforcement* and are seen as the primary maintaining causes of the problem. However, some dysfunctional responses may have no positive functions. A simple phobia, for example, may have been acquired when a frightening childhood experience led the child to misattribute the fear to stable internal factors (for example, "I was afraid because I have a fear of snakes"). Furthermore, responses that once had a function can persist even when the function is removed. For these reasons, direct treatment of a problem response may be required even if underlying conflicts have been resolved. As Freud (1959b) noted, at some point the phobic individual must confront his or her fears directly.

It is clear that expectancy modification is essential in treating dysfunctional nonvolitional responses. However, even when a client's problems do not involve nonvolitional responses, positive therapeutic expectancies are likely to enhance the effectiveness of treatment. A client who believes that treatment will be effective will be motivated to actively comply with the treatment program, and a client who actively cooperates will experience greater benefits from an effective treatment. Conversely, overly optimistic expectations are likely to be disconfirmed, leading the client to become disillusioned with psychotherapy. For these reasons, promoting realistically positive expectations about the outcome of treatment is an important task with *all* clients. Accomplishing this task requires an assessment of the client's beliefs and expectations about psychotherapy, and correction of misconceptions.

It is also essential to get detailed information on how clients have tried to cope with their problems in the past, how well each of their coping strategies has worked for them, what approaches previous therapists have attempted with them (even if these were for different problems), and how well each of these approaches worked. The answers to these questions allow the therapist to choose more wisely between alternate treatment strategies, and to describe these strategies in ways that are likely to be accepted.

Obtaining detailed answers to these questions is very important. It is not enough to know that hypnosis was effective in treating a particular problem in the past, for example. The therapist should find out how hypnosis was induced, which induction procedures worked particularly well for the client and which seemed to get in the way, what was done after the induction, which suggestions were effective and which were not, and so on. What has worked well in the past for a particular client is a clue to what will work well in the future; what has not worked well is an indication of pitfalls to be avoided.

Learning the Client's "Personal Paradigm"

One important part of the assessment process is to gain an understanding of the client's *weltanschauung*. A *weltanschauung* is a view of oneself and the world, sometimes referred to as a "personal paradigm." It is the network of interlocking beliefs and assumptions (schemas), conscious and unconscious, through which new information is processed. An important part of the *weltanschauung* is the client's perception of the causes of the problems that have led him or her to seek treatment. If the treatment rationale is at odds with the client's firmly held beliefs about the problem, it will be dismissed as incredible, and the client will have negative expectations about therapeutic outcome.

Some beliefs about the causes of problems are not inconsistent with therapeutic interventions and do not need to be challenged. These can be capitalized on even if the therapist has a different view of the causes of the problem and the underlying mechanisms by which a treatment will achieve its aims. The therapist need not feign agreement in order to utilize these potentially helpful beliefs. "If you are right about that," the therapist might say, "then doing *x, y,* and *z* ought to bring about the following changes." It is not important here that the therapist has a different idea about how *x, y,* and *z* might bring about those changes. What is important is that both therapist and client agree that the treatment will lead to improvement.

Some of our beliefs are held without much conviction. We may think that something is true yet be willing to accept another opinion, especially if that opinion comes from someone perceived to have special expertise. Lukewarm beliefs are easily changeable and do not play an important role in one's *weltanschauung*. A credible rationale that is at odds with such beliefs is likely to be readily accepted.

The more difficult situation involves a firmly held belief that inhibits therapeutic progress. For example, one client was convinced that her distressing hallucinatory experiences were produced by the devil as a punishment for past sins. As long as she held this belief, almost any intervention was doomed to failure. Further, the explanation that these experiences were internally generated (and therefore changeable) was sure to be rejected.

The key to changing firmly held dysfunctional beliefs is to treat them as hypotheses that might be true. Similarly, the therapist's contrary beliefs can be presented as hypotheses that might be false. After all, no one has a monopoly on truth. Treating the therapist's and the client's beliefs about the problem as tentative hypotheses eliminates fruitless argument. Instead, it sets the stage for empirical hypothesis testing. For example, the hallucinating client described above happened to be Catholic, and she was able to obtain a blanket absolution from a priest for all of her sins. This was a "no-lose" situation. The priest was able to intervene in a way that a psychotherapist, not having the appropriate credentials for granting absolution, could not. If her hallucinations ceased, her belief about their cause would remain intact, but that particular problem would have been resolved. On the other hand, if she continued to hallucinate, the explanation of her experiences as a punishment for her sins would become untenable, thereby making other interventions more acceptable.

As it turned out, absolution did not rid this client of her hallucinations. However, it was now possible to decrease her fear of them, and with that accomplished, she could stare directly at them when they occurred, rather than turn away from them in terror as she had in the past. She discovered that as soon as she looked directly at the vague apparition that she had glimpsed out of the corner of her eye, it disappeared. Having first been a demonic being and then a full-fledged hallucination, it was now a visual aberration over which the client had considerable control.

Formulating Therapeutic Interventions

Advocates of "placebo therapy" may be relatively unconcerned about the specifics of a treatment, concentrating instead on its credibility to the client (for example, Fish, 1973). The logic of placebo administration is based on the client's belief that treatment X will produce some particular change; that it will result in a reduced fear of heights, for example. If the client believes this premise and then experiences treatment X, the logical conclusion is "I am no longer afraid of heights" (Kirsch, 1978). In this scenario, all that is necessary is that the placebo procedure match the description that convinced the client it would work.

The point of view taken in this book is quite different. Effective therapy is more than just an empty ritual that matches the major premise of a syllogism. This is true even in treating disorders that are generated in large part by dysfunctional response expectancies. Independently of the credibility of their rationales, some procedures are more effective than others in changing expectations. Furthermore, regardless of the degree to which they alter expectancies, some procedures are more effective than others in producing therapeutic change. For the most part, these treatments are termed "cognitive," "behavioral," and "cognitive-behavioral."

Because of the widespread view that psychological problems are rooted in the past, traditional psychodynamic therapy is accepted by the general public as more credible than these newer alternative treatments (Winter, 1980). However, as shown in Chapter 3, treatments that are aimed directly at altering problematic behavior, thoughts, and emotional reactions produce greater therapeutic benefit. These treatments include specific procedures that promote the alteration of dysfunctional response expectancies, and their effectiveness is closely linked with the degree to which they alter those expectancies (Kirsch et al., 1983).

Cognitive-behavior therapies share such components as the use of relaxation procedures, imagery, behavioral rehearsal, and rational persuasion. However, the content of the imagery, the behaviors that are practiced, and the arguments that are presented vary with the problem being treated. Whatever other effects these procedures may have, all of them can be regarded as strategies for modifying response expectancies. The fact that these procedures are tailored to the problem being treated is part of what makes them effective. It makes sense to lay persons and clinicians alike that relaxation should lower anxiety, new behaviors should get easier with practice, and pleasant imagery should reduce feelings of sadness.

A treatment may be perceived as credible only if it fits the characteristics of a particular client. For example, some depressed clients have poor social skills and impoverished social relationships; others harbor a variety of depressing beliefs and expectations; and some suffer from both deficits. These deficits may be consequences of depression, rather than its causes. Nevertheless, as long as a connection between the deficit and the depression is perceived by the client, treating the deficit can produce lasting improvement. However, social skills training will not make much sense to a depressed client with good social skills, and cognitive restructuring will not make much sense to a client who does not have many irrational beliefs. Because treatments that are ill-matched to client's deficits are not very credible, they tend to be less effective for those clients (Heiby, 1986; McKnight, Nelson, Hayes, & Jarrett, 1984).

Their common sense appeal is only one of the reasons for the effectiveness of cognitive-behavioral treatments in modifying expectancies. Another is that they are structured to provide the client with repeated evidence of therapeutic effectiveness. Effective treatment of phobic and obsessive-compulsive disorders, for example, involves repeated exposure to anxiety-provoking stimuli, thereby providing an opportunity for clients to observe that their condition is improving. Conversely, experiences suggesting that the treatment may not be working are actively prevented. For example, in treating erectile dysfunction, coitus may be prohibited until the client's confidence in his ability to attain an erection is well established.

The use of graduated hierarchies, proceeding from more simple to more difficult tasks is a generally effective strategy for two reasons: (1) it is less upsetting to clients than requiring them to attempt a more difficult task at the outset, and (2) it ensures initial success, thereby strengthening positive expectations. Some data appear to contradict this idea (see Barlow & Waddell, 1985). For example, prolonged exposure to a feared stimulus produces, in the short run, a greater initial reduction of fear than does gradual exposure. However, this type of treatment produces a relatively high dropout rate, and those given gradual exposure eventually catch up to those treated by prolonged exposure in the degree to which their fears have been reduced. Further, graduated exposure is more effective than prolonged exposure when hierarchy steps are modified ad hoc in response to the needs of individual clients (Williams et al., 1984). Therefore, in most instances, graduated exposure is the best strategy. The use of practice in imagination and of modeling by the therapist can be recommended for the same reason. Whether or not they add to the ultimate effectiveness of behavioral practice, they can make a behavioral task seem less arduous to the client (Barlow & Waddell, 1985).

For any particular problem, there are a variety of potentially effective cognitive and behavioral treatment procedures. It is a good strategy to use a combination of these, following the old saw of not putting all of one's eggs in one basket. Even so, many choices can be made among equally effective procedures.

For example, should greater weight be placed on imagery procedures, behavioral practice, or cognitive restructuring? Which procedure should be tried first? Should some not be used at all? If relaxation practice is to be included, what form should it take? Should the client be instructed in progressive relaxation, meditation, or self-hypnosis?

Knowledge of what has and has not worked for the client in the past will aid the clinician in making these decisions, as will an understanding of the client's *weltanschauung*. In addition, some of these questions can be left for the client to answer. Clients can sometimes judge what kind of treatment will work best for them, and their judgement about which treatment will work best may be better than the therapist's. The wisdom of clients in choosing appropriate treatments should never be underestimated. Lest we forget, it was Bertha Pappenheim (Anna O.), not her physician, who invented the "talking cure" (Breuer & Freud, 1895).

Experimental data also indicate that allowing clients to choose a treatment can enhance its effectiveness. In one of these studies (Kanfer & Grimm, 1978), all clients were given the same treatment after being presented with three descriptions of it, which they were misled to believe represented different treatment methods. In another study (Devine & Fernald, 1973), four different treatments were described and subsequently administered. In both studies, greater improvement was shown by those who believed they were receiving their preferred method of treatment. Therefore, when deciding between two or more therapeutic approaches, the therapist might do best to allow the client to choose which course to follow. When a client participates in choosing a treatment, he or she is likely to have faith in its efficacy.

One can enlist the client's participation in choosing therapeutic components as follows: "There are a number of strategies that we might try," the client can be told. "Although all of them appear to be effective, some work better with some people and others work better with others. We need to figure out which might be best for you, and although I know quite a bit about these treatment procedures, you are the best expert about yourself. I think that you might be the best judge of which is best suited to you." However, this technique may not be best for all clients. People with a low tolerance for ambiguity or an external locus of control, for example, may feel uncomfortable with the responsibility of choosing between alternative treatments. These clients may have greater faith in a treatment that has been chosen and presented with confidence by the therapist.

The Therapeutic Rationale

When I was first a client, all that I knew about psychotherapy was what I had learned from novels and films. From these sources, I had formed the impression that psychological problems were due to forgotten childhood events, particularly events of a sexual nature. The client's task, I thought, was to relate his or her life history to the therapist in as much detail as possible, with special attention to those incidents that are embarrassing to relate. Through some mysterious process, the therapist would enable the client to remember the missing pieces, at which point all of the client's problems would vanish.

My therapist was analytically oriented, and he patiently listened to my life history, nodded from time to time, took an occasional note, and interjected appropriate "hmm's." His first directive comment to me was delivered after two months of therapy, by which time I had reached the age of 12 in my narrative. "You have a good memory," he said, "but I'm not getting any of the feelings that are associated with the material you are bringing up."

How was I to know that he wanted me to emote in his office? I assumed that he was criticizing me for neglecting to tell him how I had felt during the various incidents that I had described. "Oh! I'm sorry," I said, feeling only slightly embarrassed by this oversight on my part. Then, returning to the incident I had just been describing, I calmly added, "Well, I can remember feeling very hurt...."

It is easy for professionals to forget just how little some of their clients may know about the process of psychotherapy. Even clients who have been in treatment before may have debilitating beliefs about therapy. Some prospective clients are under the impression that a successful outcome requires years of treatment; this belief is often associated with a sense of hopelessness about one's condition and can be one of the causes of depression. Other clients may be looking for a quick fix; unless disabused of this unrealistic attitude, such clients are likely to be disappointed by the typical rate of progress in therapy. With their positive expectations disconfirmed, they may come to regard their trial of psychotherapy as a failure.

Many clients who are new to psychotherapy do not know what to expect, nor what is expected of them. The therapist who inculcates realistically positive expectations will thereby foster therapeutic success. By letting the client know that progress is likely to be gradual at first, the therapist paves the way for taking advantage of random fluctuations in the client's condition. Even the smallest changes in a positive direction can then be noted as an indication of improvement. At the same time, the client can be prepared for the likelihood of substantial improvement in the reasonably near future, thereby countering feelings of hopelessness. Finally, clients need to be prepared for inevitable setbacks, both in therapy and in life. Negative fluctuations that occur during treatment can be welcomed as opportunities for further practice of skills that have been learned. If well prepared for, setbacks that occur after treatment has ended can be accurately interpreted as part of the ups and downs of normal life, rather than as a sign of impending relapse.

One of the most important misconceptions about therapy that needs to be corrected is the idea that the effects of treatment depend primarily on the work of the therapist. This attitude encourages a passive approach to treatment and an overly dependent therapeutic relationship. Successes that are attributed to the therapist's skill rather than to the client's efforts are not likely to produce a sense of mastery or self-efficacy. In contrast, when clients experience their progress as due to their own efforts, they are more likely to continue to improve at the end of formal treatment and less likely to experience a relapse later on. Learning a strategy for coping with anxiety, depression, or other dysfunctional nonvolitional responses is like learning any other skill. A skill is something that can be put into use on one's own and does not require the constant presence of the teacher from whom it was learned (see Vickery et al., 1985). This may be one reason for the lower rate of relapse among depressed clients who have been treated with cognitive-behavior therapy, as compared to patients treated with anti-depressive medication (Simons et al., 1986).

Rationales for Specific Treatment Procedures

Clients need to have a general understanding about the nature of psychotherapy, their role as a client, and the expected course of treatment. They also need to have some degree of understanding about the specific procedures to be used. They need to know what their role is in each intervention, what kind of changes can be expected, and enough about the causal mechanisms involved so they can believe that the procedure is likely to be helpful.

The amount of information needed to satisfy this last requirement varies from client to client. Some clients are very concerned with the details of how and why a particular intervention will achieve its effects, and they will have no faith in a procedure unless it makes sense to them. Others are content to know that the treatment is effective and are unconcerned about causal mechanisms. For these clients, it may be enough to simply tell them that the intervention is known to be effective. Explaining more than is needed may not hinder treatment progress, but it is not likely to enhance it either.[1]

When confronted with the possibility that the outcome of some very effective interventions may be due to expectancy modification, many therapists become concerned with how to explain these procedures to clients who want to know exactly how the treatment will help them. They fear that they will be faced with an uncomfortable choice between lying to their clients or abandoning effective treatments.

Fortunately, there are other alternatives. For example, a therapist can honestly inform a client that "while we have very good evidence that a particular intervention is effective, we are not yet certain of how it achieves those effects." The therapist can then choose a rationale compatible with the client's *weltanschauung* and present it as a possible reason for the effectiveness of the treatment. Because we have not, in fact, reached a consensus about the mechanisms by which therapeutic effects are obtained, no deception is involved when a rationale is presented in this manner, even if the rationale is not the one that the therapist believes.

Yet another alternative involves presenting an expectancy model of a particular dysfunctional response and the treatment procedures that are to be used. For example, in treating some cases of public speaking anxiety, the following rationale can be used:

> Part of what seems to be going on is that you are caught in a vicious cycle that involves your beliefs about yourself. Before you even enter a speaking situation,

---

[1] I am reminded of the young boy who asked his mother, "Where did I come from?" After marshalling her courage and explaining to her son the basic facts of human reproduction, the boy commented, "That's funny! Michael's mommy said he came from Cleveland."

you are convinced that you will become terrified. You expect to shake and tremble, perspire, stutter, stammer, and forget what you were going to say. In fact, just thinking about speaking makes you feel tense and nervous. In other words, a big part of what you are afraid of is your own fear.

We need to interrupt that cycle. To the extent that you can learn to think of yourself as a person who can handle public speaking situations, you will become a person who can handle those situations. And to the extent that you are able to experience yourself being relatively unafraid in a public speaking situation, you will come to see yourself as a person who is not afraid of speaking in public.

We can use a number of procedures to help you change the way in which you think about yourself. One of these is to use imagery combined with relaxation. First we'll work on some relaxation exercises. We can use procedures that are very similar to the ones you used in the yoga classes you told me about. Our aim will be to for you to become confident of your ability to reduce tension and increase relaxation at will.

Next, we'll combine your relaxation skills with some imagery. I'm going to ask you to imagine that you are speaking to a small group of people about a comfortably familiar topic. As soon as you feel yourself getting overly tense, I'd like you to call upon the relaxation response that you have practiced. In that way you can experience yourself reducing your speaking anxiety right here in the safety of my office. Once you've done that successfully, we can move from imagery to behavioral practice. You might begin by delivering a short talk to me, being prepared to do just what you did in your imagery practice. In other words, I want you to become somewhat nervous while speaking to me, so that you have an opportunity to experience your ability to relax away your fear. Direct experiences of this sort are the best way to change your beliefs about yourself.

There are a number of points to notice about this rationale. First, it is consistent with experimental data and is therefore entirely honest. Second, it is based on the idea of response expectancy as a cause and as a treatment mechanism. In that way, it bears some resemblance to the Park and Covi (1965) "sugar pill" rationale described in Chapter 2. Third, it is credible to many clients. Fourth, it illustrates some of the other suggestions that have been made in this chapter. For example, it capitalizes on the client's prior experience with meditation, and it presents a treatment approach that utilizes a graduated series of tasks. It also includes a paradoxical instruction—that of becoming nervous while role-playing a speech in the therapist's office. If the client is indeed afraid of his or her own fear, this instruction will lessen the likelihood that he or she will become nervous. The "failure" to become nervous during the role-play can be used as a sign of improvement and as an indication that the client is ready for a more difficult task. On the other hand, if the client "succeeds" in becoming nervous, the prescribed opportunity for fear reduction has been obtained.

Another important point to notice about this rationale is that it is based on a careful assessment of the client's problem. Neither the rationale nor the treatment it describes is appropriate for all clients requesting treatment for public speaking anxiety. The preceding rationale assumes a client who finds the experience of the fear to be highly aversive. Other clients may be more concerned with their ability to appear knowledgeable and entertaining to an audience. In these latter cases, the treatments and their rationales would have to include procedures directed toward reducing evaluation apprehension and/or increasing public speaking skills.

Implementing Treatments

Many therapeutic guides provide considerable detail about the structure of treatment and the specific order in which treatment components are administered (for example, Barlow, 1985; Beck et al., 1979; Lazarus, 1971; Leiblum & Pervin, 1980). They are replete with case studies, sample dialogues, and specific wordings of therapeutic messages (for instance, relaxation instructions or hypnotic inductions). Detailed instructions of this sort can be very useful as exemplars, and some have been included in this chapter. However, the data on the role of response expectancy in psychotherapy suggests that they be used with caution. From a response expectancy perspective, they should be treated as examples to be freely adapted for use with individual clients, not models to be copied slavishly. The keys to enhancing the effects of treatment are careful observation, flexibility, and experimentation. Psychotherapy has few inviolable rules, and the rules presented in this book, as well as those found in other books, should be taken only as rules of thumb.

An effective therapist should be prepared to modify a treatment procedure to fit the particular needs of a client, even when the contemplated modification seems to violate the very principles on which the treatment was based. The fact that a treatment works does not mean that the theory from which it was derived is true. For example, the navigation of ships based on Ptolemaic astronomy worked quite well for centuries despite the fact that the earth was not really the center of the universe. Similarly, systematic desensitization is an effective treatment for phobias, despite the fact that the reciprocal inhibition theory on which it was based has been shown to be incorrect. Previous chapters have shown that expectancy modification is one of the active mechanisms of effective psychotherapy. This provides a theoretical rationale for altering even those treatment components that would otherwise be regarded as essential.

Even the most effective therapeutic interventions fail with some clients, and it is not always possible to predict in advance whether a particular procedure will work with a particular client. For that reason, interventions should be thought of and presented as experiments that may or may not work. When they fail, other treatment approaches can be tried. If treatment is ultimately to be successful, both clients and therapists must have permission to fail.

One way of dealing with failure at a therapeutic task is to interpret it as a sign that the client was not quite ready to undertake it, implying that he or she is likely to be more successful once adequate grounding has been prepared. There are a number of ways to construct intermediate steps. For example, a less difficult task can be chosen as a sub-goal. Alternately, the therapist can make the task easier by providing some assistance. Agoraphobic clients, for example, might be accompanied on outings before attempting the same excursions on their own. The therapist can also model tasks for the client, prior to having the client attempt them. Practice in imagination can proceed behavioral practice. A task can be accomplished first through hypnosis and then without hypnosis. Behaviors can be engaged in initially for very brief periods of time, and the length of time can then gradually be increased. Clients who "cannot" say something as part of an interpersonal role-play can be asked first to whisper the individual words one at a time, then to begin stringing them together, and finally to gradually increase the volume until they are shouting them.

These examples follow the rule of thumb that it is more effective and more humane in the long run to structure a graded series of tasks than it is to require a difficult task without such careful, step-by-step preparation. However, even this rule of thumb can be broken in particular instances. Chapter 10 describes a gradual step-by-step process of merging the personalities displayed in multiple personality disorders. A therapist was prepared to use this procedure with a particular multiple personality client whom he was seeing. First, however, the different personalities had to be convinced that they were really the same person.[2] Once this was accomplished, the client (in the guise of the most resistant personality) expressed eagerness to stop being separate and asked how long this would take. Taking this as a cue, the therapist immediately altered his strategy and informed her that they might be able to bring about the merger at that very moment, if she was really ready, but suggested that she consider the possibility of waiting until the following week. She chose to go ahead, and the fusion was brought about quickly and easily via hypnosis. A graduated hierarchy of successive approximations probably would have worked just as well with this client. But it would have been a waste of time, and it would have prolonged the client's discomfort unnecessarily.

Sometimes a therapist is faced with the opposite problem, and even the most minutely graduated series of tasks and sub-tasks fails to produce the intended result. This can be an indication of a misassessment. For example, it may be a sign that other issues must be addressed before a particular problem can be tackled. In this case, the key is to examine the various functions of the problem behavior and the particular problems that might ensue if it were changed. Does marital stability, for example, depend on the maintenance of the problem? In other cases, treatment failures may be related to a misunderstanding of the nature of the problem. A skill deficit, for example, can mistakenly be treated as an anxiety problem or vice versa.

When failures of this sort occur, the therapist should be prepared to change directions in midstream. For example, early in the therapist's work with the multiple personality client described in Chapter 10, he attempted to help her

---

[2]Clients are often resistant to accepting the multiple personality diagnosis, thinking it bizarre that personalities whom they think of as entirely separate people are really parts of themselves. Inevitably, however, there are many logical inconsistencies that can be brought to the client's attention. For example, how is it that these different people always live in the same house and that when one moves, the others move? Why is it that the driver's license in the possession of one personality has another personality's name on it? Why is a person present in the session (after having switched personalities) not able to remember arriving? A gentle but persistent focus on these inconsistencies can gradually wear down the delusion that each personality is a physically separate being.

become more assertive using typical cognitive-behavioral procedures. This attempt was notably unsuccessful, and no amount of breaking down tasks into easier steps seemed to help. It eventually became clear to the therapist that they were failing because his client already possessed the skills that he was trying to teach her. The problem was that she had segregated those skills to different personalities. As "Elly" she was unassertive, but as "Betty" she had all the assertive skills she needed. Allowing Elly to behave assertively would have violated the role boundaries she had created, and efforts to produce changes of this sort were therefore doomed to fail. What needed to be changed was her belief in Elly and Betty as separate personalities.

Ending Therapy

When terminating the therapeutic relationship, one wants to promote continued progress outside of treatment and to guard against relapse. This can be done by (1) structuring various components of treatment as skills that the clients are learning, (2) gradually transferring control of treatment to clients, (3) warning them to expect the fluctuations of success and failure that are typical of life, and (4) demonstrating to clients their ability to confront many issues on their own.

The goal is to teach clients to be their own therapists (Kirsch, 1978b). As particular strategies are repeated in therapy sessions, the client will become familiar with them and can gradually learn to anticipate the therapist's next response. When ready to intervene in a way that he or she has intervened in the past, the therapist can ask the client to predict what will happen next. "This is somewhat similar to other situations we have dealt with, isn't it? For example, you may recall how I responded when you brought up the question of X. Do you recall what I said (or did, or asked, or suggested) then?...That's right, and I also said Y and suggested Z. What do you think I might say (or ask, or suggest) in this situation?"

This involves a somewhat subtle but important role-shift toward the end of therapy. The client is now taking on the dual roles of client and therapist. The therapist is shifting into the role of supervisor and only dealing with the client's problems indirectly. As the client learns to instigate coping strategies on his or her own, dependence on the therapist lessens. This prepares the client for life without therapy, which is, after all, the ultimate goal of effective treatment.

At the same time, the door must be left open for the client to return to the therapist if necessary. Although a sense of confidence in being able to handle particular problems alone can aid in preventing relapse, so too does the knowledge that additional help is available. Knowing that the therapist is still available lowers the client's anxiety about failure and thereby makes failure less likely.

A Final Word

This chapter has reviewed a number of techniques, strategies, and procedures that can be used in changing dysfunctional response expectancies. Many of the

122

techniques are based on cognitive-behavioral therapies, which have been shown experimentally to be more effective than traditional insight-oriented treatment. Others are derived from clinical research and practice. However, one expectancy modification technique that has not been explored in this chapter is hypnosis.

Hypnosis is viewed by many clinicians as an arcane procedure to be feared and avoided. Part III reviews the experimental literature on hypnosis and shows that fear of hypnosis is unwarranted. In terms of its causes and effects, hypnotic phenomena are no different than nonhypnotic phenomena. Once the fear of hypnosis is overcome and its principles are laid bare, it can be used as a technique to enhance the effects of psychotherapy.

HYPNOSIS AND HYPNOTHERAPY

PART

III

DEMYSTIFYING HYPNOSIS

8

Although the power of placebos is not fully understood, we do know that expectancy effects can be substantial. Placebos can alter feelings, behavior, and physiological function. They can also enhance the effectiveness of psychological treatments (Mavissakalian, 1987).

The therapeutic effectiveness of placebos presents the clinician with a dilemma. On one hand, we want to maximize the therapeutic impact of our treatments. On the other, we want to avoid deceiving our clients. The client's trust is one of the most potent weapons in our therapeutic arsenal. A violation of that trust could render therapy injurious rather than helpful.

Hypnosis can provide a solution to this dilemma. The effects of hypnosis are similar to those of placebos. It can be used to alter mood states, reduce pain, and modify skin conditions (Wadden & Anderton, 1982). It can also be used to enhance the effectiveness of psychotherapy. For example, when meta-analysis was used to compare the average effects of psychodynamic therapy to those of cognitive and behavior therapies, the latter were found to be more effective. However, when hypnosis was added to psychodynamic treatment, its effectiveness was enhanced to the point that it surpassed all other forms of treatment (Smith et al., 1980). Similarly, for those clients with positive attitudes and expectations toward it, hypnosis can augment the effectiveness of cognitive and behavior therapies (Spinhoven, 1987).

This chapter and the next demonstrate that the effects of hypnosis are greatly dependent on expectancy. Nevertheless, hypnosis is not a placebo. Placebos are substances or procedures that are presented deceptively as having physical characteristics that they do not in fact possess. In contrast, hypnosis is almost always presented truthfully as a psychological procedure.[1] In fact, when commonly held myths about hypnosis are debunked, its effects are enhanced rather than

---

[1]Unlike modern hypnosis, mesmerism was believed by its proponents to be a physical intervention and therefore could be classified as a placebo. In contrast, I know of only three contemporary instances in which hypnotic inductions were presented as physical procedures (Council et al., 1983; Glass & Barber, 1961; Kroger & Schneider, 1959).

diminished (for example, Diamond, 1972). Therefore, hypnosis can be regarded as a nondeceptive method of duplicating the effects of placebos.

Many clinicians are leery of using hypnosis with their clients. They think of it as an arcane procedure of dubious effectiveness, that they do not understand. It may be associated in their minds with magic, mysticism, and a mysterious altered state of consciousness in which the subject relinquishes control to the hypnotist. Some of these ideas can be traced to the beliefs and practices of mesmerists in the late 18th and early 19th centuries. Others are the products of sensational novels, plays, and films. The behavior of highly hypnotizable subjects seems so different from ordinary experience as to lend credence to these myths. Given appropriate suggestions, hypnotized subjects appear to lose volitional control over simple physical movements, display selective amnesia, report experiencing suggested visual and auditory hallucinations, and in general, mimic all of the symptoms of conversion and dissociative disorders.

Despite these factors, hypnosis is not magical or mysterious. This chapter argues that these behaviors are produced by the same factors that produce nonhypnotic behavior: expectancies, abilities, motives, and the like. Hypnosis is no more mysterious than systematic desensitization or other therapeutic procedures involving imagery or relaxation, and clinicians should be no more afraid of it than they are of progressive relaxation.

Another belief inhibits the use of hypnosis in psychotherapy—the myth that hypnosis requires a great deal of specialized training in order to be used safely and properly. This myth stems from the mistaken notion of hypnosis as a special altered state of consciousness analogous to sleep. As with sleep, people can fall into this special state and have to be wakened from it when the session is over. The idea of hypnosis as a special state of consciousness leads to such worries as "What do I do if I can't get my client out of hypnosis?" In fact, learning to use hypnosis is no more difficult than learning to use any of the clinical techniques that are the stock and trade of cognitive behavior therapists. Once the real nature of hypnosis is understood, it becomes apparent that the idea of a client being "stuck" in hypnosis is about the same as that of a client getting "stuck" in relaxation. The purpose of this chapter is to demystify hypnosis. Just as demystifying hypnosis enhances the responsiveness of hypnotic subjects, so too does it disinhibit the therapist from using it with clients.

What Is Hypnosis?

Hypnosis is frequently defined as an altered state of consciousness (trance) in which people are especially responsive to suggestions. However, because many theorists doubt that hypnosis really is an altered state, this definition begs the question. A more neutral definition proposed by Kihlstrom (1985) leaves little room for improvement: "Hypnosis may be defined as a social interaction in which one person, designated the subject, responds to suggestions offered by another person, designated the hypnotist, for experiences involving alterations in perception, memory, and voluntary action" (pp. 385–386).

As a result of copious research, experimenters agree about most of the general parameters of hypnosis. It is known that people vary widely in their response to hypnosis; that responsiveness is more or less normally distributed in the population; and that it depends far more on attributes of the subject than it does upon the skill of the hypnotist. Experimental studies reveal that some very sophisticated hypnotic inductions are no more effective than simple and easily learned standardized procedures (for example, Mathews, Kirsch, & Mosher, 1985). Although clinicians have spent many thousands of dollars to learn specialized induction and "trance deepening" techniques, it would appear that much of this money has been wasted.

It is also known that most, if not all, hypnotic phenomena can be experienced through suggestion alone, without being preceded by a hypnotic induction. The effect of induction procedures is to enhance suggestibility. On the other hand, most claims that hypnosis can enhance overt behavior beyond normal motivated capacities have been disconfirmed, as has the belief that it can enhance the accuracy of memory or allow access to unconscious mental contents. About the only hypnotic "miracle" that has been substantiated is the effect of hypnosis on skin conditions (Barber, 1978), and as shown in Chapter 2, through the use of placebos, this appears possible without hypnosis as well.

Hypnotic responsiveness is measured on a number of standardized scales, most of which are highly correlated with each other (for example, Barber, 1969; Shor & Orne, 1962; Spanos, Radtke, Hodgins, Stam, & Bertrand, 1983; Weitzenhoffer & Hilgard, 1959, 1962; Wilson & Barber, 1978). Typically, these scales begin with a hypnotic induction procedure in which relaxation is repeatedly stressed. This is followed by a number of "test suggestions" that are used to assess a subject's level of responsivity. These include ideomotor items, in which nonvolitional movements are suggested—for example, the suggestion that an arm is becoming lighter and is rising upward by itself; challenge items, in which an inability to accomplish a normally easy task is suggested and the subject is then challenged to accomplish it—for example, the suggestion that an arm has become stiff and rigid, and that the subject cannot bend it; and suggestions for alterations in thinking or perception—for example, hallucinations. Among the more dramatic effects that are assessed on these scales are age regression, selective amnesia, positive and negative hallucinations,[2] and the inability to smell ammonia.

In addition to producing the behavior suggested in these standardized test items, hypnosis has been demonstrated to be effective in the treatment of pain, asthma, and warts (Wadden & Anderton, 1982). Experiments also suggest that hypnosis might be used to enhance the functioning of the immune system (Hall, 1984) and that suggestion, even without a hypnotic induction, might decrease blood loss during surgery (Bennett, Benson, & Saigo, 1985).

---

[2]A *negative visual hallucination* is a failure to see something that is clearly present in the visual field. Hypnotic hallucinations are not restricted to visual phenomena, however. Rather, they can be suggested for any sensory modality.

Are Hypnotic Responses Genuine?

Although wart removal, immunologic function, and blood loss are not under voluntary control, most of the overt responses of hypnotized subjects are well within the bounds of normal volitional behavior. People can intentionally raise their arms or keep them rigid. They can pretend to see things that are not there, to have failures of memory, or to have a loss of sensation. In other words, most hypnotic responses can easily be fabricated. Although few if any theorists in the field believe that hypnotized subjects are merely faking, the dramatic nature of some of the self-reported effects of hypnosis has prompted some people outside of the field to dismiss it as a sham.

Convinced that hypnotic behavior could not be faked well enough to fool an expert, Martin T. Orne (1959) developed an experimental strategy to demonstrate that hypnosis was genuine. Orne's strategy involves pretesting potential subjects for hypnotizability and selecting two groups of subjects for further study. One group consists of subjects who achieve very high scores on hypnotic susceptibility scales; the other group is composed of subjects with very low scores. The low hypnotizable subjects are told that they will be hypnotized by a second experimenter, but that they are not to go into a trance. Instead, they are to try to fool the second experimenter by pretending to be hypnotized.

In the role of second experimenter, Orne was certain that he would easily be able to recognize which of the subjects were faking and which were not. In study after study, however, no differences were found between the two groups:

> Not only were simulators able to perform the many feats of strength—such as remaining suspended between two chairs—without hypnosis, but they also showed themselves capable of tolerating painful stimuli without flinching . . . and were able to apparently recall material that ought to have been beyond their ken. . . . Simple behavioral tasks did not effectively discriminate between them, nor did a variety of procedures that tried to evaluate the individual's trust in the investigator (whether, for example, when told there was a chair behind him, he would sit down without actually testing its presence) [Orne, 1979, p. 535].

The few differences that have been found were due to a tendency of simulators to outperform highly hypnotizable subjects who had not been instructed to simulate. For example, simulators were more likely to report experiencing suggested visual hallucinations as indistinguishable from genuine perceptions, whereas genuine subjects were more likely to describe their images as vague, fuzzy, and transparent (Spanos, 1986).[3]

---

[3]The description of visual hallucinations as transparent has been interpreted by some as evidence of a special state of consciousness (Orne, 1959). According to this argument, transparency is an example of "trance logic," a tolerance for logical incongruity that is thought to be characteristic of hypnosis. Spanos (1986), however, has argued convincingly that reports of transparency can more easily be interpreted as a failure to be completely successful in generating the suggested image: "Most people who try to imagine with their eyes open report that their visual images tended to be nonlifelike. Such images are described as vague, fuzzy, of short duration, incomplete—and transparent" (Spanos, 1986, p. 463).

The simulator design has a generally recognized deficiency: Although a failure to find differences between reals and simulators makes it impossible to rule out the hypothesis that the reals were faking their responses, it does not establish that they *were* faking. It is still possible that the same overt behavior was due to two different mechanisms. Despite its lack of parsimony, this latter interpretation is accepted by all current theorists. Nevertheless, the data are disquieting, and they lead theorists to cite extra-experimental evidence in support of their belief in the genuineness of most subjects' responses. For example, the fact that hypnotizable subjects respond to some suggestions but not to others has been interpreted as evidence that they are not faking (Orne, 1979), as has the reported reduction of pain in clinical situations (see Wagstaff, 1981, however, for a rebuttal to this argument).

The typical failure of the traditional simulator design to discriminate between "real" subjects and those who are faking led to the development of an alternative referred to as the "surreptitious observation design" (Kirsch, Silva, Carone, Johnston, & Simon, 1989). The simulator design was modeled on the double-blind design used in drug research (although it is only single-blind, in that the simulators obviously know that they are simulating). Our expansion of the simulator design was inspired by the balanced placebo design described in Chapter 2. We reasoned that people who were faking would have less reason to do so if there was no one present to fool. Based on that assumption, we asked simulating and nonsimulating subjects to experience the same tape-recorded hypnotic induction and test suggestions two times, first alone and then with an experimenter present. We told them that they would later be asked to rate the two experiences comparatively, so that we could establish whether people experience hypnosis more intensely when they are alone or when an observer is present. As in the traditional simulator design, simulators were asked to try to fool the observer and were told that part of the purpose of the study was to determine whether this could be done. Unknown to any of the subjects until their participation was over, they were being surreptitiously observed by means of a video camera hidden in the room.

In these surreptitious observation experiments, simulators were substantially less responsive when observed surreptitiously than when openly observed. This verifies the success of this attempt to arrange the situation so that subjects would not suspect they were under observation. In contrast, nonsimulating subjects were as responsive when they thought they were alone as they were when they knew they were being observed. This confirms what hypnosis investigators have long believed, but have not previously been able to demonstrate experimentally: that the effects of hypnosis are real. Little, if any, of the behavior of highly responsive subjects appears to be faked. Instead, it would appear that their behavior is a generally accurate reflection of their subjective experience. In response to test suggestions, hypnotized subjects really do experience selective amnesia, nonvolitional movements, perceptual distortions, and the other effects that they report.

It is important, however, to distinguish between the terms *nonvolitional* and *involuntary*. To say that something is occurring nonvolitionally is to say that it is experienced as happening automatically; that is, without conscious volitional effort. The term *involuntary* carries the additional connotation of being un-preventable and occurring against one's will. Hypnotic responses may occur involuntarily in this stronger sense of the term for some subjects, particularly if they believe that an inability to resist is characteristic of deep hypnosis (Lynn, Nash, Rhue, Frauman, & Sweeney, 1984; Spanos, Cobb, & Gorassini, 1985). However, most successful hypnotic subjects report that although they experience responses as occurring without direct volitional effort, they are also aware that they could cease responding at any time. In fact, many of them ingeniously develop intentional cognitive strategies in order to bring their hypnotic responses about, just as actors may intentionally concentrate on upsetting memories or fantasies in order to produce tears (Barber, Spanos, & Chaves, 1974). As is true of actors producing tears, the strategies are entirely volitional, but the resulting response is experienced as an automatic consequence of their intentional behavior.

When interpreting the data of these surreptitious observation experiments, we must be cautious for another reason. In the traditional simulator design, differences between simulating and nonsimulating subjects are sometimes interpreted as evidence of a trance state. This interpretation is not warranted. Such differences suggest only that the nonsimulating subjects were probably not faking their responses. Similarly, our results indicate that faking accounts for little if any of the behavior of highly responsive subjects, but they are not evidence of an altered state. In fact, the results tell us nothing about the causes of these changes in experience.

Is Hypnosis an Altered State of Consciousness?

Despite general consensus about the effects of hypnosis, there is acute and sometimes bitter controversy about the mechanisms by which those effects are obtained. Lawrence Stone's (1972) statement about the study of 17th century English history can be applied to theories of hypnosis: "This is a battleground which has been heavily fought over, and is beset with mines, boobytraps and ambushes manned by ferocious scholars prepared to fight every inch of the way" (p.xii). At the center of this controversy is the idea of hypnosis as an altered state of consciousness. This view of hypnosis has dominated scientific and lay thought for more than a century. Since the 1950s, however, the "state" view has been increasingly challenged by a group of "nonstate" theorists (Barber, 1969; Barber, Spanos, & Chaves, 1974; Kirsch, 1985a; Sarbin & Coe, 1972; Spanos, 1982, 1986; Wagstaff, 1981), who reject the idea of "trance" as an explanatory concept. In their view, the effects of hypnosis can be fully accounted for in terms of people's beliefs, expectancies, motives, and abilities.[4]

---

[4] In the 1970s everyone appeared to agree that the state-nonstate question was one of the most contentious issues in the field of hypnosis (Sheehan & Perry, 1976). Later, even this came into dispute, as some theorists declared it to be a dead issue. However, nonstate theorists have not recanted, and more traditional theorists continue to define hypnosis as an altered state. This state of affairs led one prominent nonstate theorist to suggest that if the controversy had died, someone should have informed him as to how it had turned out (Coe, 1983).

Hypnosis was once believed to be a unique physiological state that was in some ways similar to sleep. The word *hypnosis* was taken from the Greek word *hypnos,* which means sleep, and the supposed hypnotic state, frequently referred to as "artificial somnambulism," was seen as analogous to sleepwalking. However, it has since become clear that hypnotized people display none of the physiological indices of sleep, nor of any intermediate state between wakefulness and sleep. In fact, considerable research has failed to find any physiological changes unique to hypnosis. Instead the physiological changes that occur in response to typical hypnotic induction procedures appear to be those that are also found in response to meditation, progressive relaxation, autogenic training, and other methods of inducing relaxation (Edmonston, 1981).

Given the content of typical inductions, it is not surprising that the effects of a hypnotic induction should resemble simple relaxation. For example, the hypnotist might say:

> Let yourself relax completely. Relax all the muscles of your body. Let all the tension drain out of you as you become more and more deeply relaxed. Imagine yourself lying on a beach on a warm summer's day, without a care in the world, completely at ease...

It is no wonder that when asked to describe in their own words the subjective state that they experience following a hypnotic induction, the only characteristics upon which even the most responsive subjects can agree is that they feel relaxed, carefree, at peace, calm, and unafraid (Edmonston, 1981). Nor is it any wonder that when first encountering hypnosis, behavior therapists, whose treatment procedures include the use of relaxation training followed by therapeutic imagery, are frequently unable to discern any differences between hypnosis and some of the treatments they already use.

In the absence of any distinguishing physiological or subjective characteristics of the state of consciousness that follows a hypnotic induction, the definition of hypnosis as an altered state has been justified by its effect on suggestibility. As Clark Hull wrote in 1933:

> The only thing which characterizes hypnosis as such and which gives any justification for calling it a "state" is its generalized hypersuggestibility. That is, an increase in suggestibility takes place upon entering the hypnotic trance. The difference between the hypnotic and normal state is therefore quantitative rather than qualitative. No phenomenon whatever can be produced in hypnosis that cannot be produced to lesser degrees by suggestions given in the normal waking condition. The essence of hypnosis lies in the fact of *change* in suggestibility [Hull, 1933, p. 391].

More than a half-century of subsequent research has substantiated Hull's assertion that the various phenomena elicited in people after they have been subjected to hypnotic inductions—including such dramatic effects as selective amnesia, pain reduction, and alterations in skin conditions—can also be produced by suggestion alone, though to a lesser degree (Barber, 1969, 1978). More recently, it has also been established that the increase in suggestibility produced by a trance induction can also be obtained by providing people with information and instructions aimed at enhancing their motivations, attitudes, and expectancies. This groundbreaking work was initiated by Theodore X. Barber (1969) and his colleagues, who have convincingly demonstrated that the idea of a hypnotic trance is not needed to explain increased suggestibility.

Barber's initial experimental strategy was based on providing subjects with "task motivational instructions." Instead of listening to a hypnotic induction, subjects were told that their ability to imagine was being tested. They were strongly urged to cooperate with the experiment by actively imagining the suggested effects, and they were told that others had been successful in doing so. In study after study, Barber and his colleagues observed the effects of these instructions and compared them to the effects of a standard hypnotic induction; in study after study, the effects of task motivational instructions were found to be comparable to those of hypnosis.

Barber measured these effects in two ways: (1) by observing subjects' overt responses to hypnotic suggestions, and (2) by having them describe their subjective experiences (for example, by asking them "When I said that your left arm felt light and was rising, did your arm feel light or did you raise it deliberately in order to follow instructions or to please me?"). This assessment of subjective responses is particularly important because the presence of these subjective experiences has been proposed as the essential criterion of hypnosis (see Bowers, 1966; Orne, 1959).

A frequent criticism of Barber's work has been that task motivational instructions may place greater pressure on subjects for compliance than traditional hypnotic inductions. Such task motivational statements as "Everyone passed these tests when they tried," "I want you to score as high as you can," and "If you don't try to the best of your ability, this experiment will be worthless and I'll tend to feel silly" (Barber, 1969, p. 46) were seen as particularly problematic. Messages of this sort might lead some subjects to pretend to be more responsive than they actually are. Whether task motivational instructions are more likely than trance inductions to result in faked responses is not yet known. However, other methods of duplicating the effects of trance inductions on suggestibility have been devised, methods that do not involve the high-pressure statements contained in task motivational instructions.

Hypothesizing that responding to hypnotic suggestions involved an easily learned imaginative skill, Comins, Fullam, and Barber (1975) replaced the typical hypnotic induction with detailed instructions on how to use goal-directed fantasies to produce the experience of suggested effects. For example, subjects were shown how to experience arm levitation by imagining that large helium-filled balloons were attached to their hands. Subjects who were given these instructions were told that they would not be hypnotized, but were asked to use these goal-directed fantasies to enhance their response to suggestions. This procedure was as effective as a trance induction in enhancing suggestibility.

Katz (1978) used these instructions in goal-directed imagery as the basis of what he referred to as a "skill induction." Instead of telling subjects that they would not be hypnotized, Katz told them that goal-directed imagining *was* hypnosis and that hypnosis was not, as many people mistakenly believe, a profoundly altered state of consciousness in which subjects come under the control of the hypnotist. Subjects were then taught to develop their own imaginative strategies for generating hypnotic experiences. Research on this skill induction has shown it to be as effective, and in some instances even *more* effective, than a traditional trance induction in enhancing both behavioral and subjective responses to standard hypnotic suggestions (Council, Kirsch, Vickery, & Carlson, 1983; Katz, 1978, 1979; Vickery, Kirsch, Council, & Sirkin, 1985).

Unlike induced states of consciousness, learned skills do not disappear at the end of a session. For example, once you have learned to ride a bicycle, you retain that skill; you do not have to be retaught each time you want to ride. For that reason, the effects of the skill induction generalize to later hypnotic sessions, and prior skill training can enhance the effects of a hypnotic induction. In contrast, a trance induction adds nothing to the effects of skill training (Vickery & Kirsch, 1985; Vickery et al., 1985). This is particularly important in clinical practice. It suggests that responses to hypnotic interventions might be enhanced by instructions and practice in responding without a trance induction. It also provides an alternative procedure that might be more effective with clients who are leery of hypnosis.

When confronted with evidence that simple instructional procedures are as effective as trance inductions, some state theorists suggested that these instructions might also induce a hypnotic trance. Others suggested that people may spontaneously slip in and out of trance, which is also hypothesized to account for normal waking suggestibility (Sheehan & Perry, 1976). The common assumption of these two arguments is that the presence of an altered state of consciousness can be inferred from people's subjective responses to hypnotic suggestions.

Using response-to-suggestion as the criterion of a trance state entails two problems. First, it uses circular reasoning, thereby rendering the altered state hypothesis untestable (Barber, 1969). If the presence of a hypnotic state is inferred from subjects' responses to test suggestions, there is no way of demonstrating or refuting the hypothesis that those responses are dependent on that state. Second, as John Chaves has noted, if subjects spontaneously slip in and out of hypnosis, then

> it would seem that much research in psychology has been negated since very few if any investigators control for this variable. Carried to its logical conclusion, it would be necessary for all experimenters in psychology—irrespective of whether they are studying learning, reaction time, psychophysics, psychophysiology, or whatever—to periodically insure that their subjects had not slipped into hypnosis [quoted in Barber, 1969, pp. 223-224].

It is possible, of course, that different procedures (trance inductions, task motivational instructions, skill inductions, and so on) produce the same effects via different mechanisms. If this is the case, however, it remains to be empirically demonstrated, and until it is, parsimony demands that we assume a common mechanism. As argued above, there is no reason to believe that task motivational instructions or skill inductions create an altered state of consciousness. Nevertheless, they are as effective as trance inductions in enhancing suggestibility. Therefore, the existing data indicate that the notion of a special state of consciousness is not needed in order to account for hypnotic phenomena.

On the other hand, the fact that alterations in conscious state are not causes of increased suggestibility does not mean that these changes in conscious state do not exist. Following a hypnotic induction, many people report that they feel themselves to be in an altered state. Although most highly responsive subjects reject this idea and instead describe hypnosis as a "normal state of consciousness that simply involves the focusing of attention" (McConkey, 1986, p. 314), there is no reason to doubt the truthfulness of the substantial minority who do report experiencing an altered state. However, rather than being a cause of other hypnotic phenomena, alterations in conscious state appear to be just one more effect of hypnosis, as much in need of explanation as hand levitation, catalepsy, amnesia, and other directly and indirectly suggested effects.

The Neodissociation Theory of Hypnosis

A century ago, the mind was believed to be a collection of associated ideas. Based on this theory of associationism and noting the similarity of hypnotic responses to hysteria and multiple personality, a number of 19th century scholars—including Binet, Charcot, Janet, and Freud—hypothesized that all of these phenomena were due to "dissociation," the splitting off of a group of associated ideas from the rest of consciousness. This idea has recently been resurrected, with modifications, by Ernest R. Hilgard (1979).

Hilgard's neodissociation theory is based on a series of studies involving the suggested occurrence of a "hidden observer." In a typical hidden observer experiment, subjects who have been selected for their ability to experience suggested pain relief in hypnosis are given the following instructions *after being hypnotized*: "When I place my hand on your shoulder, I shall be able to talk to a hidden part of you that knows things that are going on in your body, things that are unknown to the part of you to which I am now talking" (E. Hilgard, 1979, p. 59). They are then given suggestions for analgesia and subjected to a painful stimulus. Reports of their levels of experienced pain are obtained with and without the hidden observer signal (the hand on the shoulder). Typically, about half of the subjects who are tested in this manner show evidence of a hidden observer. That is, when touched on the shoulder, they report higher levels of pain, though not as high as the pain levels reported without any suggestion of analgesia at all. Hidden observer phenomena have also been observed through "automatic writing" and for hypnotic deafness as well as hypnotic analgesia.[5] On the basis of this evidence, Hilgard proposed that hypnotic responses are partial dissociations in which consciousness is temporarily divided into two parts separated by an "amnesic barrier."

[5]Following a suggestion for hypnotic deafness, some subjects respond to the question "Can you hear me?" by answering "No!" Even those who fail to respond to this ploy recover their hearing when the hypnotist *tells them* that they are once again able to hear (Barber et al, 1974). This could be interpreted as a spontaneous display of dissociation or as an indication of faking combined with naivete.

Unlike earlier state theorists who looked for phenomena unique to hypnosis, Hilgard views dissociation as a common occurrence in nonhypnotic contexts as well as in hypnosis. It is not unusual for people to engage in two activities simultaneously—driving a car and holding a conversation at the same time, for example—while being more aware of one than the other. From this perspective, hypnotizability can be thought of as a capacity for dissociative experiences. Using a wide variety of tasks, Stava and Jaffa (1988) tested this hypothesis by measuring people's dissociative capacities in nonhypnotic contexts. Subjects were assessed for their ability to simultaneously attend to two different tasks (divided attention), to attend to a single task while ignoring other stimuli (selective attention), and to recall information that they had been told to ignore (incidental learning). None of these abilities were related to their hypnotizability.

One of the pitfalls in theorizing about hypnosis is mistaking effects for causes. Hilgard (1979), for example, has come to regard altered states of consciousness as an effect of hypnosis, rather than the cause of hypnotic responses as earlier theorists had proposed. A similar case can be made for dissociation. Recall that the hidden observer is explicitly suggested by the hypnotist. In this respect, it is not different from any other hypnotic suggestion (hand levitation or selective amnesia, for example). This is not to say that dissociations are unreal. "Dissociation" is a descriptive label for a kind of hypnotic response that some subjects experience. However, it is not an explanation of hypnotic behavior; rather, it is one of the many responses to suggestion that needs to be explained.

The issue here is whether hidden observer instructions uncover an existing dissociation that can account for hypnotic analgesia and other effects, or whether they create a dissociation in addition to those effects. Nicholas P. Spanos and his colleagues at Carlton University in Canada have reported two studies that address this issue directly. In the first of these studies (Spanos & Hewitt, 1980), one group of subjects was given the usual hidden observer instruction, coupled with suggestions for analgesia. For a second group, the hidden observer suggestion was administered with one important modification. Instead of being told that the hidden observer was *more* aware of what was going on in their bodies, these subjects were told that the hidden part of them was so deeply hidden that it was *less* aware. Instead of reporting more pain when the hidden observer signal was given, these subjects indicated that less pain was experienced by their "hidden observers" than by their "normal" hypnotized selves.

In a second study (Spanos, Radtke, & Bertrand, 1984), hidden observer instructions were coupled with a suggestion to forget a list of words that subjects had learned. The results of this procedure were analogous to those found with hypnotic analgesia: Subjects recalled the words when touched on the shoulder, but not when the hypnotist's hand was removed from their shoulders. However, subjects in a second group were told that there were two hidden parts of themselves, each associated with a different cerebral hemisphere. They were further informed that one hemisphere stored concrete information and that the other stored abstract information. The experimenter then contacted each of the two "hidden observers" sequentially, one by touching the subject's right shoulder, the other by touching the left shoulder. Depending on which shoulder had been touched, subjects recalled either the concrete or the abstract words from the list they had learned.

Taken together, these two studies convincingly demonstrate that the hidden observer effect is due to specific information that is conveyed to the subject. Depending on the wording of the suggestion, the hidden part can be either more or less aware of painful stimulation, and numerous hidden parts can be created, each with its own specialized memories. This is similar to clinical cases of multiple personality, in which varying numbers of personas can be evoked, each of which may or may not be amnesic for particular other personas. In multiple personality disorders, "dissociation" is a description of the phenomenon that needs to be explained; it is not an explanation of that phenomenon. Similarly, in hypnosis experiments the hidden observer is one of many suggested effects; it is not an explanation of those effects.

Hypnosis and Imaginative Involvement

One of the best documented facts of hypnosis is its apparent stability. Scales measuring hypnotizability show a reliability that would be envied in most other areas of psychological assessment. Different hypnotizability scales are highly correlated with each other, and test-retest correlations are also remarkably high, even when test sessions are separated by as much as ten years (E. Hilgard, 1979; Morgan, Johnson, & Hilgard, 1974). This has led many researchers to conceive of hypnotizability as a stable trait.

The idea of hypnotizability as a trait has generated hundreds of attempts to find other personality characteristics with which it might be correlated. Most of these attempts have failed. Hypnosis does not appear to be reliably associated with the personality traits measured by a wide variety of assessment instruments (Barber, 1964). In fact, only two kinds of variables have frequently been found to be correlated with hypnotic responsiveness. The first is people's attitudes and expectancies about their own hypnotizability; the second is the tendency to become involved in such commonplace imaginative activities as looking at clouds, daydreaming, and reading novels, a trait known as *imaginative involvement* or *absorption*. Moderate correlations with hypnotizability have frequently been reported for both of these variables (see references in Council, Kirsch, & Hafner, 1986). Also, when interviewed in depth, highly responsive subjects, sometimes referred to as hypnotic virtuosos, typically report that ever since childhood they have had a very rich fantasy life and very vivid imagery (J. Hilgard, 1970; Wilson & Barber, 1983).

These studies led Jim Council and me to assume that absorption and expectancy were independent factors producing hypnotic responses, and we therefore included measures of both variables in one of our studies (Council et al., 1983). However, the results of that study led us to suspect that the relationship between absorption and hypnotizability might be an artifact. We found that although absorption was correlated with hypnotizability, it was more highly correlated with hypnotic response expectancies, which were, in turn, even more highly correlated

138

with hypnotizability. Furthermore, when we partialled out variance associated with expectancy, the relationship between absorption and hypnotizability was nonsignificant.

These findings led to closer examination of earlier studies, and in almost all of them it was found that the absorption scale was administered in a context that was clearly associated with the subsequent test of hypnotizability. We began to suspect that the absorption scale might be reactive. Because the items on absorption scales are so obviously related to our culturally transmitted view of hypnosis (for example, "If I wish, I can imagine that my body is so heavy that I could not move it if I wanted to"), people scoring high on these scales might be led to expect that they are better hypnotic subjects than they otherwise would have thought. In other words, the relation between hypnotizability and absorption, as measured in these studies, might actually be an expectancy effect. We hypothesized that people scoring high on absorption scales were more responsive because filling out the scale led them to *believe* that they would be more responsive.

The absorption scale was administered to two large groups of subjects (Council et al., 1986) in order to test this hypothesis. As in prior studies, one group was tested for hypnotizability in the same context in which the absorption scale had been administered. For the other group, the absorption scale was administered as part of a study with no obvious connection to the subjects' later experience of hypnosis. As predicted, it was found that absorption was correlated with hypnotizability only when the scale was administered in a hypnotic context.

The preceding study has now been independently replicated with different measures of imaginative involvement, different subject populations, and a number of procedural variations (de Groot, Gwynn, & Spanos, 1988; Drake, Nash, Spinier, & Welsberg, 1986; Lynn, Seevaratnam, Rhue, Neufield, & Dudley, 1985; Rhue, Lynn, Vinocour, Clark, & Weiss, 1986). These studies confirm the fact that in order to find an association between hypnotizability and absorption, subjects must recognize that the items on the scale are related to hypnotizability. In addition, de Groot et al. (1988) were able to demonstrate that measuring absorption and hypnotizability in the same context affects hypnotizability, rather than merely changing the way in which people respond to the absorption questionnaire.

Hypnotic Responsiveness and Goal-Directed Imagery

Imaginative involvement need not be interpreted as a stable trait. Instead, one might view it as a strategy used by good hypnotic subjects in order to generate suggested experiences. There are two sources of evidence for this hypothesis. First, most subjects who are successful in responding to various suggestions report that they have engaged in various imaginative strategies in order to bring those responses about. Specifically, they report using *goal-directed fantasies* to generate suggested effects (Barber et al., 1974). Goal-directed fantasies involve imagining situations that would cause the suggested response to occur. The second source of evidence in support of this form of the imaginative involvement hypothesis is the finding that brief training in goal-directed imagining enhances responsiveness to hypnotic suggestions (Diamond, 1972; Vickery & Kirsch, 1985; Vickery et al., 1985).

On the other hand, the degree of response enhancement produced by giving instruction in goal-directed fantasies is not very great, and many people appear unable to generate hypnotic responses despite using goal-directed images. Why? Perhaps these people do not experience hypnotic phenomena because they are unable to become sufficiently involved in their fantasies. However, Steven Jay Lynn and his colleagues have suggested another explanation (Lynn, Snodgrass, Rhue, & Hardaway, 1987): The effects of goal-directed fantasies may depend on people's beliefs and expectations about their effects. Maybe the unresponsive subjects do not perceive a link between their use of imagination and the experience of hypnotic effects.

In order to test this hypothesis, Lynn et al. (1987) presented a series of typical hypnotic suggestions to two groups of subjects. Subjects in one group had been selected on the basis of their high suggestibility scores on a previous test. The others were selected because they were relatively unresponsive to suggestions. Both groups were told that the suggestions were part of a "test of imagination." They were asked to imagine each of the test suggestions, but not to make any movements in response to them. Half of the subjects in each group were also asked to generate goal-directed fantasies as a means of facilitating their involvement in the suggested imaginings.

The suggestions were then presented, behavioral responses of the subjects were scored, and they were asked to write essays describing their thoughts, feelings, and actions during each of the suggestions. These essays were rated for (1) degree of absorption in goal-directed fantasies, (2) the extent to which subjects perceived a link between imagination and experiencing the involuntary movements contained in suggestions, and (3) the experience of nonvolitional movement.

Regardless of instructions, highly hypnotizable subjects became absorbed in goal-directed fantasies, believed that imagination could produce involuntary movements, moved in response to the suggestions (despite the instructions to resist), and reported that they experienced the movements as involuntary. In contrast, low hypnotizable subjects did not generate goal-directed fantasies unless instructed to do so. However, those who *were* so instructed reported as many fantasies as the high hypnotizables, and the content analysis of their essays indicated that they were as able as the highly hypnotizable subjects to become engrossed and absorbed in these fantasies. However, they did not hold the belief that absorbed imagining could produce involuntary movements, and they did not respond behaviorally as much as the high hypnotizables. Further, across all subjects, the degree to which suggested movements occurred was best predicted by their beliefs that imagination would produce movement ($r = .64$). The correlation between fantasy and behavioral response was nonsignificant.

The results of this study suggest that the degree to which people are able to become involved in goal-directed fantasies does not differentiate suggestible from nonsuggestible people. Both groups are able to become equally involved in

140

these fantasies. However, highly suggestible subjects *believe* that their involve-ment in these fantasies will lead to the nonvolitional production of the suggested response. Therefore, they spontaneously generate goal-directed fantasies that enable them to experience the suggested response. Low and suggestible subjects do not believe that suggested responses can be produced by intentionally imagin-ing events that, if they actually occurred, would produce the response. For that reason, they do not generate goal-directed fantasies unless specifically asked to do so, and even when they do engage in goal-directed imagery, it fails to produce the suggested response.

Imagery, Counter-Imagery, Expectancy, and Response

According to the goal-directed imagery hypothesis, successful responding to hypnotic suggestions should require concentration on suggestion-related imagery and rejection of conflicting ideas and thoughts. However, a number of studies have shown that given appropriate expectations, highly hypnotizable subjects are able to display hypnotic responses while imagining conflicting events, and they are able to resist suggestions despite intense subjective involvement in goal-directed imagery (Lynn, Nash, Rhue, Frauman, & Sweeney, 1984; Spanos, Cobb, & Gorassini, 1985; Spanos, Weekes, & de Groh, 1984; Zamansky, 1977).

Because these findings were limited to the small proportion of people who achieved very high scores on hypnotic susceptibility scales, Kirsch, Council, and Mobayed (1987) decided to examine the relationship between imagery and expectancy in a more representative sample of the general population. We had subjects experience the same set of hypnotic suggestions twice in a single hypnotic session. On the first trial, they were asked not to engage in any intentional imagery at all. On the second trial, instructions for intentional imagery were embedded in the suggestions. For half of the subjects, the imagery instruc-tions were congruent with the suggestions—for example, they were asked to imagine holding a heavy dictionary while arm heaviness was suggested. The remaining subjects were given counter-imagery instructions—for example, during the arm heaviness suggestion they were told to imagine a strong stream of water pushing their arms upward.

In addition to varying the nature of the imagery, we also varied information about the effects that these imagery strategies would have. Half of the subjects were told that hypnotic effects were due to imagination, that goal-directed imagery should enhance those effects, and that counter-imagery should inhibit them. The others were told that hypnotic effects depended on distracting the conscious mind so that suggestions could be acted on unconsciously. According to this rationale, goal-directed imagery should inhibit hypnotic responding by keeping the conscious mind focused on the suggestion, whereas counter-imagery might facilitate responding by distracting and confusing the conscious mind.

Figure 8–1 shows the effects of imagery and expectancy on subjects' be-havioral responses to six hypnotic suggestions. Baseline scores were obtained without imagery. Imagery scores indicate subjects' responses to the same sugges-tions when instructions for goal-directed imagery or counter-imagery were added.

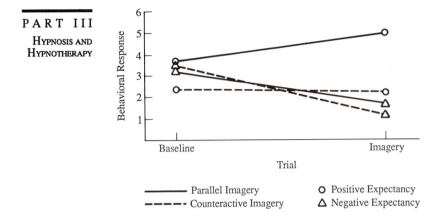

FIGURE 8–1 The effects of goal-directed imagery and counter imagery as a function of expectancy instructions. SOURCE: Reprinted from Kirsch et al., 1987.

The effects of goal-directed imagery are shown by the solid lines; those of counter-imagery by dotted lines. As you can see, goal-directed imagery enhanced responsiveness substantially when coupled with positive expectancy information, but it decreased hypnotizability to an equal degree when coupled with negative expectancy instructions. Counter-imagery inhibited responsiveness only when coupled with negative expectancy instructions; in the positive expectancy condition, it had no effect whatsoever on subjects' responsiveness.[6]

This study suggests that imagery strategies do not have an automatic effect on responsiveness to hypnotic suggestions. Instead, their effects depend on people's expectations. Imagery enhances responsiveness when people expect that to be its effect, but decreases responsiveness to an equal degree when negative expectations are held about its effects.

Another aspect of these data is worth noting. The idea that hypnotizability is a fixed trait is based on the finding that test-retest correlations of responsiveness are typically quite high. However, in this study the test-retest correlation was only .32, a level of association that accounts for only 10% of the variance. This low level of association was due to the intervening expectancy manipulation, which accounted for 46% of the variance (equivalent to a correlation of .68). It suggests that hypnotizability may not be a stable trait after all. Instead, the high test-retest correlations that are more typically found may be due to the fact that subjects' hypnotic response expectancies have not changed appreciably between testing sessions.

In sum, the relation between absorbed imagining and hypnotic responsiveness depends on people's beliefs and expectations. Subjects who are engrossed in suggestion-related imagery fail to experience hypnotic effects unless they

---

[6]The failure of counter-imagery to enhance responsiveness, despite instructions suggesting that it would, may have been due to the unbelievability of those instructions. We found that subjects in the counter-imagery conditions *expected* to be less responsive than those in the goal-directed imagery conditions.

believe that imagery can generate those effects. Conversely, people can respond to suggestions even when engaging in conflicting fantasies.

Hypnosis and Expectancy

If the dramatic effects of hypnosis are not due to an altered state of consciousness, dissociation, or goal-directed imagery, what does cause them? What appears to be undeniable is that people's beliefs and expectations are extremely important factors. The malleability of hidden observer phenomena has led some theorists to interpret it as an expectancy effect (Spanos, 1982, 1986). Correlations between expectancy and hypnotizability are higher than those between imaginative involvement and hypnotizability, and the latter correlations have been shown to be a measurement artifact due to the effects on expectancy of administering measures of imaginative involvement in a hypnotic context.

Similarly, the effects of goal-directed imagery appear to be mediated by expectancy. Although teaching subjects to use goal-directed imagery increases their responsiveness to test suggestions, the same degree of response enhancement can be achieved by merely telling subjects that they can expect to become more responsive on subsequent trials (Vickery & Kirsch, 1985). Also, goal-directed imagery can either enhance or impair responsiveness, depending on subjects' beliefs about its effects.

From the days of Mesmer until modern times, expectancy has been viewed as an unwanted artifact, and considerable experimental effort has been devoted to controlling its effects in order to uncover the presumed underlying essence of hypnosis (Orne, 1959). One result of this research has been to push back the boundaries of hypnosis as more and more effects are revealed to be "artifactual." Richard St. Jean (1986) has compared this process to peeling back the leaves of an artichoke in order to find its heart. However, as we continue to peel back the leaves, it is becoming apparent that there may be no heart to uncover. Chapter 9 presents and evaluates an expectancy theory of hypnosis. According to this theory, expectancy is an *essential* aspect of hypnosis, perhaps its most essential aspect.

AN EXPECTANCY
MODEL OF HYPNOSIS

Both hypnosis and placebos can be used in alleviating pain, tension, and skin conditions. The perceptual distortions often cited as the hallmark of hypnosis can also be reproduced by placebos. For example, by falsely informing subjects that they were ingesting a drug that produced psychedelic flashbacks, Heaton (1975) obtained subjective reports of hallucinations, numbness, tingling sensations, dream-like feelings, and altered time perception. Placebos have also been used to produce the same degree of enhancement to hypnotic test suggestions as that produced by trance inductions (Glass & Barber, 1961). Given this degree of similarity in their effects, it is reasonable to suspect that hypnosis and placebos involve similar mechanisms. From this point of view, hypnotic responses are hypothesized to be a function of subjects' hypnotic response expectancies.

A considerable amount has been written about the role of expectancy in hypnosis (see Orne, 1959; Sarbin, 1950). The expectancies that these theorists have written about are role expectancies; that is, people's beliefs about the effects of hypnosis. Many people with appropriate role expectations are poor hypnotic subjects. This fact has led to the proposal that hypnotic responding requires particular talents or abilities (Sarbin, 1950) or that it involves an altered state of consciousness (Orne, 1959).

Response expectancy theory suggests another possibility. Genuine hypnotic responses are characterized by changes in experience, especially experiences of involuntariness or automaticity. These are exactly the kind of experiences that can be produced by response expectancies, as amply documented in our review of placebo effects (Chapter 2). From this perspective it is not enough for a person to believe that a particular response is consistent with the role of hypnotized subject. Instead, the person must believe strongly enough that he or she will *personally* experience the response.

Hypnotic role perception is only one type of belief that influences hypnotic response expectancies. Other important cognitions include people's perceptions of the situation as "hypnotic" and their beliefs about their own susceptibility to hypnosis (Barber et al., 1974). These three cognitions—situational perceptions, role expectancies, and self-perceptions—interact to produce hypnotic response

145

expectancies. People will believe that a particular hypnotic response (for example, selective amnesia) will occur only if they interpret the situation as hypnotic, perceive the response as characteristic of hypnosis, and judge themselves to be good hypnotic subjects.

This chapter examines data concerning the effects of situational perceptions, role expectancies, and self-perceptions on hypnotic behavior. These data show that expectancies play a major role in the production of hypnotic responses. Self-perceptions determine *whether or not* hypnotic responses will occur; situational perceptions determine *when* they will occur; and role perceptions determine *what* those responses will be.

Situational Perceptions

The modern history of hypnosis began with the work of Franz Anton Mesmer, a Viennese physician who lived from 1734 to 1815. Mesmer believed that an invisible magnetic fluid permeated the universe. According to Mesmer, this fluid was the cause of gravitation, magnetism, and electricity, and also had profound effects on the human body. Imbalances in magnetic fluid caused nervous illnesses, and the restoration of balance through mesmerism was the method by which these illnesses could be cured. At first, Mesmer used actual magnets in his practice, placing them on his patients' bodies in order to redirect the ebb and flow of the hypothesized magnetic fluid. Later, he decided that the human body was itself a kind of magnet, capable of magnetizing inanimate objects and curing disease.

A "traditional" hypnotic induction involves intoning suggestions for relaxation, drowsiness, and sleep to comfortably seated subjects. Induction procedures were considerably more varied 200 years ago. Inductions of the 18th century included touching patients with magnets, massaging their bodies, staring fixedly into their eyes, having them stand by a "magnetized" tree, or giving them "magnetized" water to drink. Group inductions were facilitated by using a large vat of "magnetized" water with protruding iron rods that the patients touched.

The most controversial of the 18th century induction procedures involved having a woman sit with her knees pressed firmly between the thighs of the mesmerist, who applied pressure to her "ovarium," meanwhile stroking her body until she began to convulse. This was referred to as "making passes." According to Binet and Fere (cited in Sheehan & Perry, 1976), many women were so pleased by the convulsive crisis produced by this induction that they followed Mesmer down the hall and begged him to repeat the treatment.

The first experimental demonstration that hypnotic effects are due to people's beliefs and expectations was reported in 1785 by a French Royal Commission established to investigate mesmerism. Among the illustrious members of this commission were Benjamin Franklin, then the American ambassador to France; Antoine Lavoisier, the founder of modern chemistry; and the infamous Dr. Guillotin, best known for his mechanical solution to the mind-body problem. The commissioners devised a series of experiments that included some surprisingly sophisticated expectancy control procedures. For example, a tree in Benjamin Franklin's garden was "magnetized" by one of Mesmer's disciples, but the experimental subject was intentionally brought to the wrong tree. Another subject was told that a container of water had been "magnetized;" in fact it had not. Yet another subject was misinformed that the mesmerist was "magnetizing" her from behind a closed door.

The success of these expectancy manipulations led the commissioners to conclude that the effects of mesmerism were due to imagination and belief. These 18th century experiments are remarkable for their methodological sophistication, and are the first demonstrations of the role of expectancy in the phenomenon from which modern hypnosis evolved. They effectively demonstrate that hypnotic phenomena depend on people's beliefs about the procedures being used, rather than on the procedures themselves.

Modern Replications of the Royal Commission's Experiments

Although most contemporary hypnotic inductions involve suggestions for relaxation, those instructions do not appear to be necessary for enhancing suggestibility. Mesmeric inductions in the 18th century, as mentioned, typically did not include relaxation instructions. More recently, Banyai and Hilgard (1976) tested the effects of an "active-alert" induction, in which references to sleep or relaxation were eliminated, and spontaneous relaxation was prevented by having subjects pedal a stationary bicycle while being hypnotized. Banyai and Hilgard reported that this induction was as effective as a standard relaxation induction in facilitating responses to standard hypnotic suggestions.

Except for the inhibition of relaxation, the induction used by Banyai and Hilgard was similar to standard trance induction procedures. Although their study shows that relaxation is not essential to hypnosis, it leaves open the possibility that some other features of standard hypnotic inductions may be indispensable. More convincing evidence that the effects of hypnotic inductions do not depend on their procedural components can be found in studies comparing the effects of traditional inductions to placebos. Three studies have replicated the experiments of the French Royal Commission by applying procedures that subjects were led to believe would physically cause them to experience a trance state, but that shared little in common with typical hypnotic inductions.

The first modern replication of the Royal Commission experiments was inadvertent. Kroger and Schneider (1959) believed that their "brain wave synchronizer" was a bona fide scientific tool for inducing hypnotic trance. The synchronizer was a variable-speed stroboscopic light that was said to induce trance by altering people's alpha brainwave rhythms. However, it was subsequently shown that its effectiveness depended on subjects being told that hypnosis was being induced (Hammer & Arkins, 1964).

The second contemporary study on the use of a placebo as a hypnotic induction was reported by Glass and Barber (1961), who gave subjects an inert pill, described as a "powerful hypnotic drug" that would induce hypnosis. The placebo was as effective as a standard hypnotic induction in raising levels of response to suggestion. In a conceptually similar study (Council et al., 1983), a psychophysiological laboratory was used as a setting to lend credence to a false biofeedback procedure. Subjects were told that hypnotic trance was associated with high amplitude "theta" brainwaves, and that having their own theta waves fed back to them over earphones would increase the amplitude of those waves and automatically put them into a deep trance. They were wired to a polygraph and then viewed their "brainwaves" on an oscilloscope and heard a false feedback tone through headphones. As was true of Glass and Barber's placebo pill, this procedure was equivalent to a standard trance induction on most measures of hypnotic response.

In sum, the experimental data are consistent with the evidence of history, and taken together, these two sources of data point to one inescapable conclusion: No specific procedures are necessary for eliciting hypnotic phenomena. In this respect, hypnotic inductions are similar to placebos (and in some cases have been placebos). Placebos can be composed of water, cornstarch, sugar, or almost any other substance. They can be administered as pills, capsules, injections, or surgical procedures. The only factor common to all placebos is the implication to subjects that they are receiving active treatment. Similarly, the only factor common to all successful hypnotic inductions is the subject's belief in their effectiveness.

If there is such a thing as a hypnotic state, then expectancy is all that is needed to produce it in susceptible subjects. However, the evidence reviewed in Chapter 8 indicates that the concept of an altered state is not needed in order to explain the increase in suggestibility associated with hypnosis. From a "nonstate" perspective, the data indicate that the experiences and behaviors labeled "hypnotic" occur in any situation that the subject perceives as "hypnotic."

Role Perceptions

The responses of people mesmerized in the 18th century were almost as varied as the procedures used to mesmerize them. According to the report of the French Royal Commission (Franklin et al., 1785/1970), some patients became calm and relaxed and appeared to be insensitive to stimulation, whereas others reported painful sensations and exhibited a variety of other physical symptoms. The most dramatic response to mesmerism was a convulsive "crisis" that lasted up to three hours. With wild looks in their eyes, mesmerized subjects laughed, cried, shrieked, and thrashed about, eventually falling into a stupor. In the 18th century, it was this convulsive crisis, rather than the trance behavior with which we are familiar today, that was seen as the definitive characteristic of mesmerism.

Why did 18th century subjects respond to mesmeric inductions with violent convulsions? From where did the "crisis" come? One part of the answer to this question involves Mesmer's first hypnotic subject. Another is related to the similarities between mesmerism and rites of exorcism.

Mesmer's first subject was Francisca Oesterline, a young Viennese woman who first visited Mesmer in 1773 because of an hysterical disorder that included convulsions among its many symptoms (Mesmer, 1779/1980). Finding orthodox medical treatment of no avail, Mesmer decided to apply magnets to his patient's body, a new and highly controversial form of treatment. Mesmer may have been particularly inclined to try a magnetic cure because of his longstanding interest in the related phenomenon of gravitation, and for that same reason, he may have shown particular excitement in the new experimental treatment. In any case, Fräulein Oesterline suffered an attack on July 28, 1774, and Mesmer responded to it by placing magnets on her body. According to Mesmer, the effect of this procedure was to produce some painful sensations, followed by a remission of his patient's symptoms. Subsequent treatments reliably produced the convulsions from which she suffered, and Mesmer discovered that he could control the location of his patient's convulsions by touching or pointing to various parts of her body, a phenomenon that he proudly demonstrated to others.

Mesmer's magnetic treatment of Fräulein Oesterline gradually led to her recovery, and the story of her cure brought him new patients. Knowing the story of Fräulein Oesterline's treatment, these new patients must also have known of her convulsive response to it, and that knowledge may have led them to expect a similar response. But how did Fräulein Oesterline get the idea of responding with convulsions?

Symptoms of conversion disorders have generally corresponded to people's beliefs, and convulsions had been a well-known symptom of hysteria for thousands of years. It is therefore possible that Fräulein Oesterline's cultural knowledge of convulsive disorders was an important cause of her seizures. More recently, convulsions had also been interpreted as a symptom of demonic possession, and the ability to control them was used by exorcists to make a differential diagnosis between hysteria and possession. It happened that at the time of Fräulein Oesterline's treatment, the exorcisms of Father Johann Joseph Gassner were being widely discussed in Viennese society (Mesmer, 1779/1980), and it is almost certain that she knew of his work. The resemblence of Gassner's exorcisms to mesmerism—as revealed in the following eyewitness account—is too extraordinary to be merely coincidental:

> Gassner told the first [patient] to kneel before him, asked her briefly about her name, her illness, and whether she agreed that anything he would order should happen. She agreed. Gassner then pronounced solemnly in Latin: "If there be anything preternatural about this disease, I order in the name of Jesus that it manifest itself immediately." The patient started at once to have convulsions. According to Gassner, this was proof that the convulsions were caused by an evil spirit and not by a natural illness, and he now proceeded to demonstrate that he had power over the demon, whom he ordered in Latin to produce convulsions in various parts of the patient's body; he called forth in turn the exterior manifestations of grief, silliness, scrupulosity, anger, and so on, and even the appearance of death [quoted in Ellenberger, 1970, p. 54].

The similarities between his own "magnetic" cures and Gassner's exorcisms did not escape the attention of Mesmer (1779/1980), who concluded that the well-known priest was unknowingly curing his petitioners by means of animal magnetism. In both situations, localized convulsions were first induced and then shifted from place to place on command. It therefore seems quite likely that Fräulein Oesterline's knowledge of this phenomena led to her own localized convulsions in response to Mesmer's cues.

As mesmerism developed and spread, the behavior of mesmerists came to resemble that of exorcists even more closely. At the same time, the behavior of mesmerized subjects became more and more similar to that of alleged demoniacs (Spanos & Gottlieb, 1979). Besides convulsions, mesmerized subjects and demoniacs displayed the "appearance of death" (now called a "trance" state), spontaneous amnesia, insensitivity to pain, and perceptual alterations. Thus, the roles of hypnotist and subject were modeled on the analogous roles of exorcist and the possessed.

Experimental Data on Hypnotic Role Expectancies

The importance of people's beliefs about the effects of hypnosis has been emphasized in the theoretical work of Theodore R. Sarbin and his colleague William C. Coe (Sarbin, 1950; Sarbin & Coe, 1972). Drawing on social psychological role theory, Sarbin conceived of hypnotic behavior as a social role that people enact. Sarbin's position has frequently been misunderstood as suggesting that people who appear to be hypnotized are faking, an easy misinterpretation given his description of hypnotic subjects as akin to actors playing a dramatic role. Nevertheless, it is a mistake to confuse role theory with faking. The role of hypnotized subject is actually no different from other social roles. To say that a person has taken on the role of parent, spouse, teacher, student, therapist, or client does not mean that he or she is faking. Although it is not a pretense, the behavior of a parent, student, therapist, or client is determined in good measure by the person's conception of that role.

One of the earliest experimental demonstrations of the effects of role perceptions on hypnotic experience and behavior was reported in a classic article by Orne (1959). In one class where hypnosis was demonstrated at Boston University, the students observed hypnotized subjects displaying "dominant arm catalepsy." The hypnotist lifted the subject's dominant hand to shoulder level and then gently let it go. Catalepsy consisted of the arm staying up rather than dropping after the hypnotist let it go. Of nine subjects who had seen the catalepsy demonstration, all but two showed "spontaneous" (that is, not explicitly suggested) catalepsy when subsequently tested in hypnosis. In contrast, only three of the control subjects from the class not shown the catalepsy demonstration kept their arms up when tested for unsuggested catalepsy.

Popular fiction has portrayed the deeply hypnotized subject as unable to resist the hypnotist's suggestions, and highly suggestible subjects generally behave as if this were so. In fact, the apparent inability of subjects to resist a suggestion has been described as part of the "essence" of hypnosis (Orne, 1959). However, two studies have shown convincingly that the inability to resist suggestions depends on subjects' role expectancies (Lynn et al., 1984; Spanos et al., 1985). In these studies, highly responsive subjects were instructed to resist responding overtly to suggestions, while at the same time imagining the suggestions as vividly as possible. Prior to being hypnotized, some subjects were told that the ability to resist suggestions while vividly imagining them was a hallmark of deep hypnosis; the others were told the opposite. In both studies, subjects who had been told that successful resistance was an indication of deep hypnosis successfully resisted test suggestions, whereas those who were not so informed did not.

One of the most dramatic effects of hypnosis is selective amnesia. Amnesia occurs most frequently when explicitly suggested during the hypnotic session, but sometimes it appears "spontaneously." However, the spontaneity of unsuggested amnesia may be more apparent than real; it may be due to people's beliefs about hypnosis. Young and Cooper (1972) tested this hypothesis by misinforming one group of subjects that truly hypnotized people, after being awakened, do not remember what has happened during hypnosis. Another group was told that this was not true. Following these lectures, 48% of the subjects in the first group, as compared to only 15% of the second, agreed with the statement "If I were to be hypnotized I would not remember what had happened after I woke up" (Young & Cooper, 1972, p. 858). More importantly, 37% of the first group passed a test of hypnotic amnesia (forgetting at least seven of the 11 hypnotic suggestions), whereas only 10% of the second group displayed amnesia. Thus, most of those who expected to be amnesic were amnesic, whereas those who expected to remember the session were able to do so.

Highly responsive subjects given a suggestion to forget certain information act as if their memories are blocked by a powerful amnesic barrier. All sorts of maneuvers have been tried to induce subjects to breach suggested amnesia. Subjects have been (1) told that people typically remember more on a second trial; (2) asked to list forgotten items in chronological order; (3) challenged to try harder to remember; (4) urged to be honest; (5) attached to a polygraph; and (6) shown videotapes containing the information that they had been asked to forget. Although these procedures enhance recall to some degree, none results in substantial breaching of amnesia (Dubreuil, Spanos, & Bertrand, 1983; Ham, Radtke, & Spanos, 1981; Howard & Coe, 1980; Kihlstrom, Evans, Orne, & Orne, 1980; McConkey & Sheehan, 1981; Schuyler & Coe, 1981).

With these studies in mind, Christopher Silva and I decided to test whether we could induce highly responsive subjects to breach amnesia completely by altering their expectancies (Silva & Kirsch, 1987). Half of the subjects were told that deep hypnosis enhances people's memories, allowing them to penetrate amnesic barriers. The others were told that amnesia suggestions are so powerful that deeply hypnotized subjects cannot recall the forgotten material no matter how hard they try. All of the subjects were then presented with the same audiotaped procedure. After a hypnotic induction, the voice on the tape asked them to recite six words that they had memorized. Amnesia for the words was then suggested and subjects were challenged to remember. Hypnosis was then "deepened" by a counting procedure, and the subjects were challenged once again. Finally the amnesia suggestion was canceled and subjects were asked to recite the list of words.

Figure 9–1 shows the mean number of words that subjects recalled on each of the four trials. The first set of bars indicates that prior to the amnesia suggestion, subjects were able to recall all six words. The second set of bars indicates that the amnesia suggestion was highly effective; both groups of subjects recalled an average of about one word. However, after "deepening" hypnosis, the same

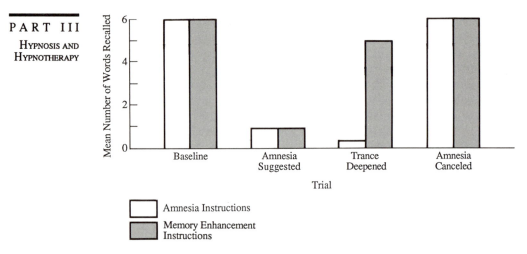

FIGURE 9–1 Mean number of words recalled on each trial as a function of expectancy instructions. SOURCE: Reprinted from Silva & Kirsch, 1987.

challenge produced a substantial between-group difference in behavior. Subjects who had been told that memory was enhanced in deep hypnosis now remembered an average of five of the six words. In contrast, those who had been given information stressing the power of amnesia suggestions tended to recall even fewer words than before.

Figure 9–1 tells only part of the story. Figure 9–2 shows a frequency distribution of the number of words recalled on the critical trial (trial 3). This was after hypnosis had been "deepened," but before the amnesia suggestion was canceled. In "deep hypnosis," all but two of the subjects given memory enhancement expectancies completely breached the suggested amnesia by remembering all six words. In contrast, none of the subjects not given these instructions breached amnesia. This indicates rather clearly that hypnotically induced amnesia is largely under the control of subjects' expectations.

Role Perceptions and Altered States of Consciousness

Other than feelings of relaxation and well-being, most people who have been hypnotized, including those who are very responsive to hypnotic suggestions, report little alteration in their general state of consciousness (Edmonston, 1981; McConkey, 1986). Nevertheless, many subjects do report various unsuggested changes in experience, bolstering the belief that hypnosis is an altered state of consciousness. Because there is little reason to doubt the veracity of these reports, we can conclude that hypnotic inductions do produce altered states in some subjects, although those alterations should be regarded as hypnotic effects rather than as causes of other hypnotic effects.

Viewing altered states of consciousness as one of the many effects that can be produced by hypnotic procedures leads to the question of how they are

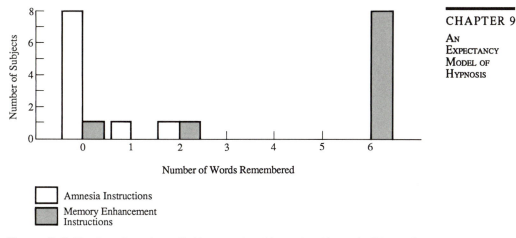

Amnesia Instructions
Memory Enhancement
Instructions

FIGURE 9–2 Number of words recalled by amnesic subjects after "deepening" hypnosis as a function of expectancy instructions. SOURCE: Reprinted from Silva & Kirsch, 1987.

produced. As a hypnotic effect, rather than a causal mechanism, one would suspect that altered states are produced by the same mechanisms that produce other hypnotic effects. In particular, people can be expected to experience alterations in consciousness that correspond to their beliefs about hypnosis.

In a nonhypnotic context, the ability of expectancy to influence states of consciousness has been convincingly demonstrated in a series of studies designed by William B. Plotkin and his colleagues (Plotkin, 1979). In the most compelling of these studies, subjects receiving genuine alpha wave biofeedback were given intermittent verbal feedback indicating either success or failure. Prior to being connected to the biofeedback equipment, they had been given varying information about the characteristics of the state of consciousness that would be produced by the changes in brain waves. For half of the subjects, these characteristics were those that are typically reported as the "alpha experience." They were told that their thoughts would slow down, eventually stopping entirely as they entered an "egoless" state characterized by little or no awareness of themselves as separate individuals. The others received descriptions that in most respects were the opposite of the usual alpha experience. These subjects were told that their thought processes would speed up and that they would become very keenly aware of their personal identities.

Although subjects in all four groups were equally able to enhance their production of alpha brainwaves, the reports of their subjective experiences contained dramatic differences. Whereas most subjects in the "failure" conditions reported "nothing unusual," almost all persons in the "success" groups reported experiencing changes in their conscious state. However, the nature of those changes varied as a function of the information they had received. Depending on the experimental condition they were in, subjects reported that their thought processes either slowed down or became more rapid, and that they became either more or less aware of themselves as distinct individuals. These data suggest that both the occurrence and the nature of changes in consciousness during alpha biofeedback training are dependent upon subjects' expectations.

Henry (1985) demonstrated a similar correspondence between expected and experienced alterations in conscious state within a hypnotic context. Instead of manipulating role expectancies, Henry assessed people's beliefs about the experiential characteristics of a hypnotic "trance" state. In order to test the hypothesis that role perceptions influence the subjective experience of trance, it was necessary to find a set of subjective experiences about which people have divergent preconceptions. A large pool of potential bipolar items were assembled, and subjects were asked to indicate the direction of change that they thought would be experienced by a hypnotized subject. In other words, they were asked to indicate whether hypnosis would produce more or less relaxation, more or less control of movement, and so forth. The criterion for retaining an item in the final version of the scale was an endorsement rate of not more than 60% in either direction. Subjects were then asked to predict whether they would personally experience each of those changes in consciousness when they were subsequently hypnotized.

The degree of change in state of consciousness that subjects expected to experience significantly predicted the number of unsuggested alterations in experience that they subsequently reported. In turn, changes in experience predicted responsiveness to test suggestions. However, the nature of those changes in experience was largely determined by subjects' preconceptions. Depending on their expectancies, hypnotized subjects described "trance" as a state in which time either passed more slowly or more quickly than usual; logical thought was either more or less difficult than normal; the hypnotist's voice sounded closer or farther away than before; sounds were more muffled or more clear than usual; and so on.

Henry's data suggest that there is no particular state of consciousness that can be labeled a "hypnotic trance." Rather, there are a variety of changes in experience that are interpreted as evidence of "trance" when they are experienced within a hypnotic context. Some of these are directly suggested in typical inductions (for example, relaxation); others occur as a function of subjects' preconceptions. To the degree that changes in conscious state are experienced and interpreted as evidence that a hypnotic trance has been achieved, subjects come to believe that they will be able to experience suggested effects. This expectation is capable of generating those effects.

Self-Perceptions of Hypnotizability

Research on situational perceptions and role perceptions demonstrate a strong link between hypnosis and expectancy. Susceptible subjects act out their preconceptions of hypnosis whenever they judge the situation to be "hypnotic." But what is a susceptible subject? Accounting for individual differences in hypnotic responsiveness has been one of the most important and most difficult problems in the literature on hypnosis. As a supposedly stable trait, hypnotizability has the unusual characteristic of not being reliably correlated with any other personality trait. Apparent associations with absorption or imaginative involvement have turned out to be artifacts mediated by subjects' expectancies. Similarly, evidence seeming to point to hypnosis as an imaginative or dissociative skill can better be accounted for in terms of expectancy. It therefore seems reasonable to hypothesize that individual differences in hypnotizability may be associated with differences in people's beliefs and expectations.

When subjects are asked to predict their responsiveness, these predictions are reliably correlated with subsequent tests of hypnotizability (see Shor, 1971). However, the degree of association is only moderate, typically accounting for about 10% of the variance. If hypnotizability is largely due to expectancy, then the two variables ought to be more highly correlated.

This problem is not unlike that encountered by Ajzen and Fishbein (1980) in evaluating the relationship between intention and behavior. According to their "theory of reasoned action," intentions are the immediate determinants of volitional behavior. However, people's intentions change over time, and so they are not always good predictors of behavior. This is particularly true when some unanticipated event occurs that leads people to change their minds about an intended course of action. For example, you might be intending to embark on a European vacation next year, but unforeseen financial reverses could cause you to change your mind. Voluntary behavior is controlled by a person's *current* intentions, not by those that were held in the past.

Chapter 1 noted the formal similarity between intentions and response expectancies. Both are subjective probabilities that particular responses will occur, and both are hypothesized to be the immediate determinants of those responses. But whereas intentions are subjectively held probabilities of the occurrence of volitional responses, response expectancies are anticipations of nonvolitional responses. Just as intentions can change over time, so too can response expectancies, especially those that have not been stabilized by means of a confirming experience. People who have never experienced hypnosis and who think of it as something quite different from anything they have experienced before, are likely to have very tentative hypnotic response expectancies. One person may expect to experience a relatively high level of response; another may expect to be totally unhypnotizable. Neither, however, is likely to be very confident of his or her prediction.

In most experiments that evaluate the relationship between hypnotic response expectancies and hypnotizability, an important event intervenes between the assessment of expectancy and the assessment of responsiveness to suggestion. That event is the hypnotic induction, a ritual that often contains various procedures deliberately aimed at modifying subjects' expectations. For example, one of the most common components of hypnotic inductions is the "eye closure" technique. Subjects are told to stare fixedly at a target high in their visual field and are then told that their eyes are getting tired, that it is becoming more and more difficult to keep their eyes open, and that they are beginning to close of their own accord. Of course, staring at a fixed target would cause eye strain even without the suggestion, but it is hoped that subjects will ignore that fact and attribute the heaviness of their eyelids to the hypnotist's suggestions. Because

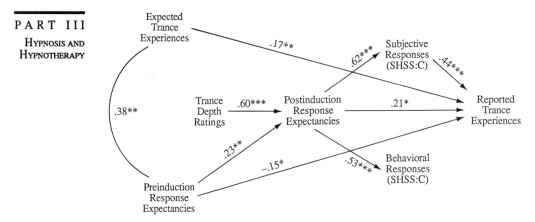

FIGURE 9–3 Causal model of preinduction and postinduction expectancies as determinants of hypnotic responding. SOURCE: Adapted from Council et al., 1986.

hypnotic inductions contain procedures of this sort, they may change people's expectancies about how responsive they will be to suggestions. According to the response expectancy hypothesis, it is these latter expectancies that determine their responsiveness.

One form of evidence for this hypothesis lies in comparisons of correlations between expectancy and suggestibility as a function of whether a trance induction is used. When it is, these correlations are moderate at best. However, when baseline suggestibility is tested, or when trance inductions are replaced by brief instructions in how to use imaginative strategies to produce hypnotic responses, the correlations are substantial (Council et al., 1983; Kirsch, Council, & Vickery, 1984).

A more direct test of the hypothesis that hypnotic inductions change people's expectations is provided by a study in which response expectancies were assessed both before and after a standard hypnotic induction procedure (Council, Kirsch, & Hafner, 1986). Ten hypnotic suggestions were to be administered. Prior to the induction, subjects were asked to predict how many of these suggestions they would be able to experience. After the induction, *but before the administration of the test suggestions,* they were asked to provide a rating, on a scale of 1 to 5, of their depth of trance and to once again predict the number of suggestions to which they would respond. As in many other studies, preinduction expectancies were only moderately correlated with subsequent responsiveness. In contrast, postinduction expectancies were very highly correlated with the number of suggestions to which subjects responded.

Because correlation does not establish causation, a path analysis was used to further examine the data from the preceding study. The results of this analysis are shown in Figure 9–3. The first thing to notice in this diagram is that although subjects' ratings of trance depth were significantly correlated with responses to test suggestions, the causal paths between these variables were not significant (and are therefore not shown). The causal paths between trance depth and responsiveness to suggestions were not significant because subjects' postinduction response expectancies, with which the trance depth ratings were strongly associated, were much better predictors of hypnotic responsiveness. In other words, expectancies predicted subjects' responses to test suggestions even with effects associated with trance depth partialled out. The reverse, however, was not true. With variance associated with expectancy statistically controlled, trance depth ratings did not predict hypnotic responsiveness at all. These data can be interpreted as follows: *After experiencing hypnotic inductions, people's conclusions about how deeply entranced they are alter their response expectancies, which, in turn, determine their levels of responsiveness to suggestion.*

Two other aspects of these data are worth noting: (1) though statistically significant, the association between preinduction and postinduction response expectancies was quite low; and (2) the means of these two measures of expectancy were not significantly different from each other. These data tell us that response expectancies change substantially during a hypnotic induction, but that the direction of the change is not consistent. Hypnotic inductions enhance the expectancies of many subjects and lower the expectancies of others.[1]

How is it that the same induction procedure has different effects on the expectancies of different people? Notice that two variables in Figure 9–3 have not yet been described: "reported trance experiences" and "expected trance experiences." Trance experiences were measured at the very end of the experimental session on the Inventory of Hypnotic Depth (Field, 1965), a standardized scale that includes such items as "I felt dazed," "I did not know where I was," "Things seemed unreal," "It was a very strange experience," and "It seemed completely different from ordinary experience." Expected trance experiences were assessed at the very beginning of the study on a scale composed of similar items.

Also notice that although these trance experiences and the expectancy of their occurrence are related, neither are directly associated with ratings of trance depth. But how could this be? People's judgements of their depth of trance are presumably based on their experience of the kind of changes in consciousness that are assessed on the Inventory of Hypnotic Depth. In fact, if they have not yet been tested with hypnotic suggestions, on what else could their depth ratings be based?[2]

In fact, people must take two factors into account in judging the degree to which they are hypnotized. One of these factors is the extent to which they have experienced changes in experience. It is this factor that is measured by scales like the Inventory of Hypnotic Depth. The second factor involves people's preconceptions about the nature of hypnosis, a factor that was examined in a study reported by Kevin McConkey (1986). Prior to their first experience of hypnosis, some people believe that hypnosis is "an altered state of consciousness, quite different from normal waking consciousness," whereas others believe that it is "a

---

[1]It is important to recall that the preinduction expectancy measure asked subjects to predict how responsive they thought they would be *after* experiencing a hypnotic induction. Expectancies for hypnotic responding without an induction are significantly lower than those predicated on an induction (Council et al., 1983).

[2]Trance depth was rated by subjects on a scale of one ("not hypnotized at all") to five ("very deep") in response to the question, "How deeply hypnotized are you?"

normal state of consciousness that simply involves the focusing of attention" (p.314). These preconceptions lead to different criteria for judging the degree to which one has been hypnotized. Two people may experience the same degree of alterations in experience, but if they have different criteria for judging trance depth, they will reach different judgements about their depth of trance. Those who believe that hypnosis involves a very profound change in conscious state are likely to be disappointed with the effects of a typical induction procedure. They would probably conclude that they had not been very deeply hypnotized; as a result, they would not expect to be very responsive to suggestions. In contrast, people who experience the same changes in conscious state but think of hypnosis as a normal state of focused attention would judge themselves to have been successfully hypnotized and would therefore be likely to retain their positive response expectancies.

Evidence in support of this hypothesis can be found in McConkey's study. Prior to experiencing hypnosis for the first time, more than 80% of low hypnotizable subjects believed that hypnosis was a dramatically altered state of consciousness. In contrast, medium and highly hypnotizable subjects were more likely to approach their first hypnotic experience with the preconception that hypnosis was a normal state of focused attention.[3] A second source of evidence for this hypothesis comes from studies aimed at modifying hypnotizability. These studies suggest that reponsiveness to suggestions are enhanced when people are told that hypnosis is not a drastically altered state of consciousness (Council et al., 1983; Diamond, 1972; Katz, 1978, 1979; Vickery et al., 1985).

To summarize, people who believe that hypnosis is a drastically altered state of awareness may initially believe that they are hypnotizable, but their overly stringent criterion for judging themselves to be hypnotized leads to disconfirmation of that expectancy. Failing to achieve the degree of alteration in consciousness that they believe to be the hallmark of hypnosis, they decide that they are not hypnotized and therefore no longer expect to experience suggested effects. In contrast, people who believe that hypnosis is a normal state of focused attention— as did most of McConkey's medium and highly hypnotizable subjects—may experience the same, modest alteration in conscious state following an induction. But unlike those with more extreme preconceptions, they interpret those changes as evidence that they *are* hypnotized, and they therefore expect to be successful in experiencing subsequent suggestions.

The preconceptions of susceptible and unsusceptible subjects are analogous to the expectancies induced in the placebo (decaffeinated) coffee study described in Chapter 2. The expectancies of subjects given the apparent equivalent of eight cups of caffeinated coffee were similar to the preconceptions of McConkey's low hypnotizable subjects in that they were anticipating very dramatic changes in experience. These subjects had their expectations disconfirmed and showed little change in either experience or physiology. In contrast, subjects who thought they

---

[3]McConkey reassessed his subjects' beliefs about hypnosis after they had been hypnotized. Interestingly, the experience of hypnosis further convinced them that hypnosis was not an altered state.

were getting moderate doses of caffeine expected moderate changes in experience, reported experiencing those changes, and showed corresponding changes in blood pressure. Similarly, those subjects in McConkey's study who did not expect too much of a change in conscious state were most likely to be responsive to suggestions.

Enhancing Hypnotizability by Modifying Expectancies

The close connection between expectancy and hypnotizability has been most clearly revealed in a study conducted by Cynthia Wickless and myself (Kirsch & Wickless, in press). Two procedures were used to convince people that they were good hypnotic subjects: a verbal expectancy manipulation, consisting of feedback from bogus personality tests; and an experiential expectancy manipulation devised by David Wilson (1967) to enhance waking suggestibility.

In the verbal expectancy manipulation, subjects were misinformed that the tests they had taken indicated they had special talent for hypnotic responding. In the experiential expectancy manipulation, a variety of perceptual effects were suggested and then surreptitiously produced via hidden lights and audiotape recordings. For example, following the suggestion that subjects would see the color red, a faint red tinge was surreptitiously imparted to the room by means of a hidden light bulb. Similarly, tape recorded music was played to insure that subjects would experience a successful response to the suggestion that they would hear music.[4] Following these experiences, standard tests of hypnotizability were administered.

Four groups of subjects were tested. The first was a control group, in which neither expectancy manipulation was used; the second group was given the verbal expectancy manipulation; the third group was provided with experiential feedback; and the fourth group was given a combination of both verbal and experiential feedback. The effects of these procedures are shown in Figure 9–4. As you can see, the verbal manipulation produced a small increment in responsiveness to hypnotic suggestion. However, the experiential manipulation produced a very large effect. Most impressively, in the group that experienced both expectancy manipulations, 73% of the subjects were found to be highly hypnotizable and 27% were moderately hypnotizable. There were no unhypnotizable subjects! These data suggest quite convincingly that with sufficiently strong expectations, everyone is hypnotizable.

After the main part of the study was over, subjects were called back and debriefed. They were told that everyone had been given the same feedback from the supposed personality tests, and they were shown the hidden panel of lights and the tape recorder that had played the music. It was explained that the purpose of the deception was to raise their expectations so they would be enabled to more successfully experience subsequent suggestions on their own. They were also offered an opportunity (which none refused) to reexperience hypnosis, using the

---

[4]We used Philip Glass's "Music With Changing Parts," which has been described as "trance music" by some critics and has been used by stage hypnotists in their performances.

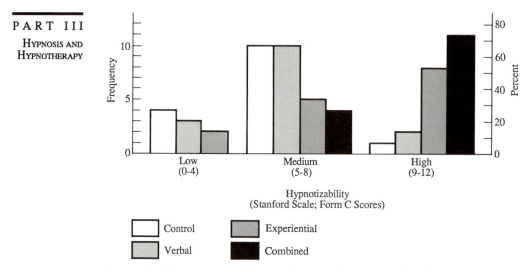

FIGURE 9–4 Frequencies of high-, medium-, and low-susceptible subjects as a function of verbal and experiential expectancy manipulations. SOURCE: Wickless & Kirsch, in press.

same hypnotizability scale that had been used in the first session (minus the suggestions for light and music, of course).

Even after being debriefed, these subjects maintained their high levels of hypnotizability. This is not as surprising as it may at first seem. Although they now knew that the lights they had seen and the music they had heard were not the effects of hypnotic suggestions, they were also aware of having successfully experienced suggested effects that were not aided by artificial means. Therefore, their positive beliefs about their own hypnotizability remained intact.

This study confirms the wisdom of many of the techniques commonly used in hypnotic inductions. Experienced hypnotherapists suggest responses that would occur even without the suggestion; they interpret any behavior observed as evidence that the client is becoming hypnotized; and they use a variety of strategies to prevent clients from experiencing failures (for example, suggesting that the person's arm might or might not feel so light that it will rise into the air). All of these methods are ways of enhancing people's expectancies about their hypnotizability (Barber et al., 1974). However, convincing people that they are highly hypnotizable is not an easy task. The surreptitious confirmation of suggested effects used in the Wilson (1967) and Wickless and Kirsch (in press) studies is unique in its ability to enhance hypnotic response expectancies to such a dramatic degree. Surreptitious confirmations can be thought of as particularly effective hypnotic inductions, but they may not be practical in clinical settings.

Hypnosis as Expectancy Modification

The data reviewed in this chapter reveal a very close association between hypnosis and response expectancy. A good hypnotic induction is whatever the subject believes an induction to be. Similarly, hypnotic experiences, including the experience of "trance," are whatever subjects believe them to be. In other words, good hypnotic subjects experience what they believe to be "hypnotic phenomena" in situations that they judge to be "hypnotic." Further, expectancies are a major determinant of hypnotizability. People who are convinced that they will experience hypnotic responses are likely to experience those responses, whereas those who are certain that they will not experience hypnosis find those expectations confirmed as well.

Expectancy appears to be all that is needed for a procedure to be efficacious as a hypnotic induction, and it also appears to be the sole determinant of the experiences and behavior of good hypnotic subjects. However, it may not be the only factor determining how responsive a person is to hypnosis. It is possible that hypnosis also requires abilities that are not possessed by all people. Also, people who believe that hypnotic responding is completely automatic and requires no activity on their part will require stronger expectancies in order to successfully experience hypnotic suggestions. This may explain the fact that the expectancy manipulations in the Wickless and Kirsch (in press) study were not equally effective for all subjects. Nevertheless, the data demonstrate that expectations play a major role in determining who will experience hypnotic phenomena, when they will experience them, and what those experiences will be.

From this point of view, hypnosis can be regarded as a nondeceptive means of eliciting placebo effects.[5] The use of placebos in treatment is problematic because of the deception that is typically involved. In order for the placebo to be maximally effective, patients must be convinced that they are receiving a physically active treatment. But the use of hypnosis does not require misinformation. In fact, when the myths of hypnosis are debunked and subjects are told that they will not experience a profoundly altered state of consciousness, the effects of hypnosis are enhanced rather than diminished. This view of hypnosis has numerous implications for clinical practice, implications that Chapter 10 explores in detail.

---

[5]A classic study by McGlashan, Evans, and Orne (1969) is often interpreted as indicating that expectancy only accounts for part of the analgesic effects of hypnosis. In that study, subjects who had been preselected for high hypnotizability demonstrated greater apparent tolerance of a pain-inducing task following hypnosis than they did following ingestion of a placebo pain reliever. However, a number of design problems make these data difficult to interpret. First, Stam (1987) demonstrated that the task used to induce pain allows subjects to display greater tolerance by reducing their rate of work (and thereby reducing the intensity of the pain stimulus). Second, the placebo was delivered in a Darvon capsule, from which only limited pain relief would be expected. Third, because the subjects had experienced high levels of response to hypnotic suggestion (that was the basis for their inclusion in the study), they would presumably expect greater pain relief from a hypnotic suggestion than they would from Darvon. As shown in Chapter 1, the degree of pain relief that is produced by a placebo is proportional to its believed effectiveness. These design defects have been rectified in more recent studies, the results of which are entirely consistent with the hypothesis that placebo and hypnotic analgesia are due to similar mechanisms (Baker & Kirsch, 1987; Stam, 1987).

HYPNOTHERAPY

Clinical Applications of the Expectancy Model

Placebos used alone can bring about substantial improvement in such conditions as agoraphobia and depression and can enhance treatment outcome when combined with psychotherapy (Elkin et al., 1985, 1986; Mavissakalian, 1987, 1988). It would be helpful to clients if we could augment the effectiveness of treatment in this way. However, the administration of placebos entails a deception that might ultimately undermine clients' trust in their therapists. The addition of hypnosis to psychotherapy is a way of circumventing this obstacle to the utilization of the placebo effect in clinical practice. Hypnosis can enhance the effectiveness of therapy for some clients and may be a virtually indispensable technique in the treatment of multiple personality and other dissociative and conversion disorders.

This chapter explores the use of hypnosis as an expectancy modification procedure in psychotherapy. The use of hypnosis in therapy can be divided into three phases: preparation, induction, and clinical application. In the first phase, clients' beliefs about hypnosis are explored and corrective information is provided. The purpose of this preparatory phase is to foster the kinds of attitudes and expectations that are most conducive to the experience of hypnosis. This is typically followed by a formal induction ritual, which ratifies the idea that hypnosis is being used and thereby enhances the expectation that suggested effects will be experienced. Because hypnotic inductions typically involve instructions for deep relaxation, the induction procedure may itself have clinical utility for some clients. More frequently, it will be followed by suggestions that focus on the issues for which treatment has been sought.

Clinical suggestions for each of these phases are presented in the first part of this chapter. This is followed by an explanation of how hypnosis may be used in the treatment of hysterical disorders, particularly multiple personality disorder, which appears to be increasing in epidemic proportions. Finally, the idea of hypnosis as the prototype of psychotherapy is presented. The use of hypnosis as a model for nonhypnotic treatment can enhance a therapist's ability to modify pathogenic expectations.

Preparing Clients for Hypnosis

Many commonly held misconceptions about the nature of hypnosis can interfere with its use in treatment. Most of these misconceptions are related to the idea of hypnosis as an altered state of consciousness, typically referred to as a "trance." Some people who have never experienced hypnosis interpret the meaning of a trance as no longer knowing where they are; losing control of their behavior; and feeling profoundly different than they do in the "normal waking state." They may believe that the hypnotist will have power over them, and that when awakened they will have no memory of what has transpired.

These misconceptions can inhibit the experience of hypnotic phenomena in three ways. First, some clients fear the loss of control that they mistakenly think hypnosis entails. As a result, they intentionally resist the hypnotist's suggestions. Second, lay conceptions of the hypnotic trance imply that subjects should take a passive role and merely wait for changes to occur. This discourages people from generating goal-directed fantasies or developing other strategies to facilitate their response to suggestions. Finally, the trance view of hypnosis generates unrealistic internal criteria for concluding that one has been hypnotized. Two people may experience the same state of relaxation, but one may interpret her relaxed feelings as an indication that she has succeeded in becoming hypnotized, while the other interprets the same feelings as a failure. Believing that she is hypnotized, the first person is more likely to be able to experience hypnotic suggestions.

Prior to the first attempt at hypnosis, clients' preconceptions about hypnosis should be elicited and their misconceptions corrected. They can be told that there is nothing mysterious about hypnosis; that it is a normal state of focused attention rather than a profoundly altered state of consciousness; and that it will not feel much different from meditating or relaxing. Most importantly, they can be informed that they will remain in complete control of themselves; that they will only experience those things that they wish to experience; and that they will be able to remember everything that occurred within the hypnotic session.

In addition to providing clients with disinhibitory information, it can be helpful to supply them with facilitative information that may make it easier for them to experience suggested effects. This kind of information is designed to elicit clients' active cooperation rather than merely removing their fears. Clients are told that hypnosis is something that they do, rather than something that is done to them; and that hypnotic suggestions are experienced more vividly when people actively imagine their occurrence. Suggested arm heaviness, for example, can be experienced more easily if subjects intentionally imagine that their arms are becoming heavier. For some, this is facilitated by imagining situations that would make one's arm feel heavy, such as holding a heavy dictionary in the palm of one's hand.

Clients can also be told that the experience of hypnosis depends on their beliefs and expectations. Having never experienced hypnosis before, they are likely to wonder whether they are "really" hypnotized or whether they are merely fooling themselves. They may feel divided about the answer to this question, feeling the suggested experiences and at the same time doubting these experiences. The therapist can facilitate the experience of hypnosis by instructing clients to lay aside their doubts and decide temporarily to go along with the suggested experiences. Clients need not forget their skepticism, but the doubts can remain in the background until after the hypnotic experience, at which point they can reconsider them if they wish.

Telling people that hypnosis is a normal state of focused attention, rather than a drastically altered state of consciousness in which the subject's behavior is controlled by the hypnotist, amounts to providing information that is inconsistent with the views of hypnosis that are often presented in the media. For that reason, it may not be fully accepted by some clients. A useful strategy for reinforcing a more accurate view of hypnosis is to provide clients with hypnotic-like experiences prior to inducing hypnosis.

One way of providing clients with direct experience of hypnotic responses is to demonstrate the Chevreul pendulum illusion. This can be done by asking the client to hold a small pendulum between the thumb and forefinger of one hand and to concentrate on the idea that it will swing in a particular direction—that is, back and forth, sideways, clockwise, or counterclockwise. The therapist suggests that the client focus attention on the pendulum, rather than on the hand that is holding it. The client can be told that the pendulum should not be swung intentionally, but neither should there be a concentrated effort to hold it steady. Instead, the hand holding the pendulum should be ignored. The client's concentration should be focused on the bottom of the pendulum and the desired direction. Typically, the pendulum will begin to move in the suggested direction.

The Chevreul pendulum illusion is very easy, and most people are successful when they attempt to experience it. Nevertheless, it is experienced as uncanny. The pendulum appears to be moving of its own accord, without physical effort on the part of the subject. While this is occurring, the therapist can point out that the client is not in an altered state of consciousness and that the experience is entirely under his or her control. All that the therapist has done is to suggest an experience; it is the client that is making the suggested experience occur. The client can stop the pendulum from swinging any time that he or she wishes. To demonstrate the effect even more convincingly, the therapist can suggest that the client make the pendulum change directions. The change in direction is experienced as unconnected to any intentional physical movements, yet it is entirely under the client's control.

After demonstrating the pendulum illusion, the therapist may wish to demonstrate another relatively easy hypnotic effect. Arm heaviness is one of a number of good choices for this. Subjects are asked to hold out one arm, palm up, and to imagine holding something very heavy. The hypnotist asks them to imagine that the arm is becoming heavier and heavier. "Of course, you could probably resist the feeling of heaviness if you really wanted to," the therapist might say, "and you could keep your arm up. But if you want to experience arm heaviness, you can do that too. Just imagine a heavy dictionary in the palm of your hand, and imagine the feeling of heaviness that it is causing . . . " When outward signs of arm heaviness are noticed, suggestions for arm lowering can be added: "Your arm may feel so heavy that you can feel it moving lower and lower, as it is pulled down by the heavy weight . . . " Although arm heaviness is not as easy to experience as the pendulum illusion, it too can be achieved successfully by most cooperative subjects. When the client experiences arm heaviness prior to trance induction, the idea of actively generating responses in a normal state of consciousness is experientially reinforced.

The provisions of disinhibitory information, instructions in goal-directed fantasy, and pre-induction practice in generating hypnotic experiences have been shown to increase responsiveness to hypnotic suggestions (for example, Council et al., 1983). In fact, when presented as "hypnosis," the further addition of a formal hypnotic induction procedure may not add to responsiveness at all (Vickery et al., 1985). On the other hand, the average degree of response enhancement that these procedures produce is relatively small. They do not change poor subjects into hypnotic virtuosos.

Two methods have been found to produce a more substantial enhancement of suggestibility. One is to instruct subjects to respond voluntarily (for example, by lifting their hand when given a suggestion for arm levitation) while using goal-directed fantasies to help them experience the response as involuntary (see Gorassini & Spanos, 1986). This substantially enhances the subjective experience of hypnotic suggestions, including the experience of involuntariness. It also increases the number of responses to which subjects respond behaviorally.

A second method of substantially increasing hypnotic responsiveness is to surreptitiously provide environmental confirmation of some suggested effects, as was done in the study described in Chapter 9 (Wickless & Kirsch, in press). Once subjects in that study had experienced self-generated responses without environmental enhancement, explaining the deception did not lower their responsiveness. Instead, they maintained their high levels of suggestibility.

Neither of these enhancement strategies may be very useful in clinical settings. Most good hypnotic subjects report experiencing hypnosis without being aware of intentionally generating suggested movements. Telling these subjects that they must physically make suggested responses may detract from their perceptions of the power of hypnosis and might thereby decrease its effectiveness in enhancing treatment expectancies. The use of surreptitious environmental feedback is even more problematic in clinical settings, where even the temporary use of deception is unwise. These experimental demonstrations are important because of their implications about the determinants of suggestibility, rather than their direct applicability to clinical situations.

Fortunately, for most clinical applications, the usefulness of hypnosis is independent of the client's level of hypnotizability (Wadden & Anderton, 1982), and even where associations are found, as in the treatment of pain, asthma, and skin conditions, the correlations tend to be modest (see Baker & Kirsch, 1987). For that reason, the more simple, though less effective, procedures described earlier are probably sufficient for clinical practice.

Hypnotic Inductions

Because hypnotic responsiveness depends more on characteristics of the subject than it does on the skill of the hypnotist, the ability to induce hypnosis is easy to acquire. Anyone who has learned to teach relaxation to clients has learned to induce hypnosis. Progressive relaxation, autogenic training, and similar procedures become hypnotic inductions as soon as they are labeled as such. In fact, any procedure that is believable to the client will suffice as a hypnotic induction. Verbatim inductions are readily available (see Barber, 1969), as are detailed descriptions of various induction techniques (see Udolf, 1987).

Although relaxation instructions can be used unaltered as a hypnotic induction, a number of strategies have been developed specifically for that purpose. For the most part, these induction techniques appear to have been designed expressly to alter people's hypnotic response expectancies. One commonly used strategy is to watch the subjects' responses and comment on their occurrence. The purpose of this is to reinforce the idea that the responses suggested by the hypnotist are beginning to occur, thereby ratifying the idea that hypnosis is being induced. For example, when people are instructed to relax, they begin to breathe more slowly. When this happens, the hypnotist might say, "Your breathing is becoming slower and slower as you begin to enter hypnosis."

The popular "eye closure" induction is another example of this strategy. As described previously, subjects are asked to stare at a target that is somewhat higher than their normal field of vision. The hypnotist then suggests that the subject's eyes are becoming heavy and tired, and that they will soon close. Again, it is hoped that the inevitable feelings of eyestrain will be attributed to hypnosis rather than to the natural effects of staring at a target.

Another expectancy-based induction strategy is to prevent subjects from perceiving that they have failed to experience a suggested response. For example, arm levitation and arm heaviness can be coupled, the subject being told that one outstretched arm is becoming lighter while the other is becoming heavier (Udolf, 1987). If the more difficult arm levitation response is obtained, its experience will strengthen the subject's belief that he or she has been hypnotized. If not, the focus can be shifted to the sensations of heaviness in the other arm.

A variation on this technique involves asking the subject to hold out only one arm and suggesting that it will either become heavier or lighter, the hypnotist not knowing which will occur. The hypnotist might say, for example, "I don't know whether you will feel your arm becoming lighter and lighter, so light that it will rise into the air all by itself, or whether it will become heavier and heavier, so heavy that it will slowly descend to your lap as you become more and more deeply hypnotized. Perhaps your arm is becoming lighter now, lighter and lighter with each breath you take . . . " Depending on whether signs of arm levitation are observed, the hypnotist either continues to focus on levitation, or switches to arm heaviness by saying, " . . . or perhaps you are more aware of the growing feeling of heaviness in your arm . . . "

Although most inductions include suggestions for relaxation, these are not needed for many applications of hypnosis. In some subjects, relaxation instruc-

167

tions can produce intense anxiety (Heide & Borkovec, 1983). For these subjects, relaxation instructions can be replaced by suggestions for euphoria or for alert, focused attention. Subjects are at least as responsive to these "alert" inductions as they are to more traditional relaxation inductions (Banyai & Hilgard, 1976; Gibbons, 1976).

Because hypnosis does not depend on any particular set of procedures, not even relaxation, hypnotic inductions can be tailored to the specific characteristics of the client. For example, one subject who wished to experience hypnosis found herself laughing whenever anyone tried to hypnotize her. Rather than leaving her with the feeling that she was not a good subject, one hypnotist agreed with her that hypnotic inductions could be very funny and asked whether she would mind if he began working with her. As soon as the hypnotist began a typical induction patter, she began laughing. Continuing the induction, he began to laugh with her. "How funny hypnosis is," he said, laughing between each phrase. "Hypnosis can be one of the funniest things in the world. Even the word is funny. *Hypnooooosis!* And wouldn't it be funny if your arm began to rise into the air all by itself? That might be the funniest thing ever . . . " Her arm slowly began to rise and her laughter soon tapered off.

These induction strategies are not new. Eye-closure, for example, was used in the 19th century by James Braid, who believed that a trance state was produced physiologically by fatigue of the eye muscles. A psychological interpretation of these strategies was offered by Milton Erickson (1980), who termed them "utilization techniques." The essential feature of utilization techniques is the use of the subject's attitudes, beliefs, and naturally occurring behaviors as components of the induction procedure.

A study by Smith (1985) indicates that under some conditions, incorporating subjects' naturally occurring behavior in the hypnotic induction enhances their responsiveness to hypnosis. However, these effects are quite small, especially when compared to the wide range of individual differences in susceptibility. For example, despite his exceptional talent as a hypnotist, Erickson (1980) reported that one of his subjects required 300 hours of systematic training before displaying "valid" hypnotic behavior. Hopefully, this subject was not a clinical patient, since the effectiveness of most clinical applications of hypnosis is unrelated to hypnotic "depth."

Clinical Applications of Hypnosis: The Power of a Word

The ease with which effective inductions can be learned has resulted in the proliferation of "hypnotherapists" with little or no clinical training. Many of these people learn a few basic induction techniques and set up shop. To enhance their credibility, some of these lay hypnotherapists obtain certificates from organizations set up merely for that purpose. Although these people may be able to induce hypnosis well enough, they do not know what to do after the induction.

To most lay people, and to some professionals as well, hypnotherapy is viewed as a particular form of treatment that can be compared to other types of therapy. The conventional image of hypnotherapy involves a therapist who induces a hypnotic state in the client and then suggests that a particular symptom will disappear. An overweight client might be told that high-calorie foods will no longer taste good; a smoker, that the craving for nicotine will vanish; a phobic client, that his or her fear will be reduced; and so forth.

In the 19th century, the direct removal of symptoms through suggestion was the most common form of hypnotic treatment. Today, it is the exception rather than the rule. More typically, hypnosis is combined with various nonhypnotic treatment strategies. *Any nonhypnotic therapy can be augmented with hypnosis. Conversely, any hypnotic procedure can be used without being labeled "hypnosis."* Thus, rather than being a specific form of therapy, hypnosis is a procedure that can be used as an adjunct to other therapies. Viewed from this perspective, hypnotherapy is merely the addition of a hypnotic induction to a treatment that could also be administered without hypnosis (Spinhoven, 1987). For example, when hypnotherapy was singled out as a type of treatment in meta-analytic studies, the treatments referred to were instances of psychodynamic therapy facilitated by hypnosis (Smith et al., 1980). The meta-analytic data presented by Smith et al. suggest that the simple addition of hypnosis to psychodynamic therapy substantially increased its effectiveness.

The clinical use of hypnosis requires extensive training; however, this need not consist of specialized training in hypnosis. Because hypnotherapy is the combination of hypnosis with nonhypnotic psychotherapy, experienced clinicians need not have extensive training in hypnosis in order to begin incorporating hypnotic procedures in their work. The principles of effective hypnotherapy are the same as the principles of effective psychotherapy.

Some therapies differ from hypnotherapy in name only. Systematic desensitization, for example, involves teaching progressive relaxation to clients and then having them imagine nonfearful encounters with a feared stimulus. Progressive relaxation is a common method of inducing hypnosis, and instruction to imagine a desired response is a common form of hypnotic suggestion. For that reason, the use of desensitization or of relaxation training as forms of hypnotherapy merely requires labeling them as such. In fact, "hypnosis" was used instead of progressive relaxation in many of the earliest reported cases of systematic desensitization (see Spinhoven, 1987).

Unlike a rose, treatments by another name may not be the same to many clients. For that reason, resistance to some clinical interventions can be overcome by carrying them out in a hypnotic context. For example, while one client was being instructed in progressive relaxation, she suddenly opened her eyes and exclaimed: "This is stupid. I can't do it. It just makes me feel more uptight and nervous." She was asked whether she had ever experienced hypnosis, and her reply was that she hadn't, but that she found the idea intriguing. After talking with her about the nature of hypnosis, the therapist began a standard hypnotic induction stressing muscular relaxation. This time she was able to comply with the relaxation instructions without distress. The client was then taught *self-hypnosis,* which in content was essentially the same as instructing her to practice a relaxation exercise.

One of the values of using hypnosis as an adjunct to therapy is that it may enhance clients' expectations of a positive outcome, and in so doing, it can enhance the effectiveness of treatment. On the other hand, some clients have negative attitudes toward hypnosis. For these clients, labeling the procedure "hypnosis" can decrease treatment effectiveness (Hendler & Redd, 1986). In other words, the effects of adding "hypnosis" to treatment depend on the beliefs and expectations of the client.

Fortunately, little can be done with a hypnotic induction that cannot be done without it. For that reason, one of the best responses to clients who resist the idea of hypnosis is simply not to use it. Instead, consider what you would do after the induction, and apply those procedures without labeling them hypnosis. For example, people who are unresponsive to hypnosis report little reduction in pain following a hypnotic treatment. However, when the same treatment is not defined as hypnosis, they indicate as much pain reduction as highly hypnotizable people (Spanos, Kennedy, & Gwynn, 1984).

The use of hypnosis can also backfire when clients' attitudes toward it are positive, but their expectations are unrealistic. This is similar to the experimental finding that people who think of hypnosis as an altered state are less likely to be successful in experiencing suggested effects. In clinical contexts, this problem occurs when people expect hypnosis to do the work for them, and it is most likely to occur when people seek hypnotic treatment for problems of habit control (for example, smoking or overeating). Their hope is that hypnosis will magically transform them into nonsmokers or more reasonable eaters. Alternately, they may be looking for an excuse for failure: "I tried hypnosis, and even *that* didn't work!"

This does not mean that hypnosis cannot be used in treating these problems. It does mean that *how* hypnosis is used must be carefully explored with the client. Hypnosis is not a panacea. It can be used to augment cognitive-behavioral strategies, particularly when clients are taught self-hypnosis to practice at home in lieu of relaxation and in conjunction with cognitive (imaginal) rehearsal of new patterns of thought and behavior (see Spinhoven, 1987). However, before hypnosis is used, the nature of hypnosis and its role in treatment should be carefully explained. Hypnosis can augment the effects of behavior therapy, but only for clients whose attitudes and expectations are appropriate to its use.

Hypnosis and Hysteria

A relationship between hypnosis and hysteria has been recognized explicitly ever since Charcot's demonstrations that conversion and dissociative symptoms can be elicited and removed by hypnotic suggestions. As a result of these demonstrations, Binet, Janet, and Freud, all of whom studied with Charcot, developed theories of dissociation as explanations of conversion disorders, dissociative disorders, and hypnosis (see Breuer & Freud, 1895/1955). In the 19th century, the mind was most commonly described as a collection of associated ideas, a doctrine known as "associationism." According to dissociation theories, conversion symptoms were expressions of groups of associated ideas that had been cut off from their associative connections with the rest of consciousness, thus forming an organized second consciousness. Multiple personality was viewed as a particularly pervasive dissociation, and hypnosis was commonly viewed as an "artificial hysteria."

Current theorists also recognize a relation between hypnosis and hysterical disorders.[1] Some see self-hypnosis as the mechanism by which dissociative symptoms are acquired and maintained (see Bliss, 1986), a view that is similar to that proposed by Breuer and Freud (1895/1955). Others breathe new life into the early theories of Breuer, Freud, Charcot, Janet, and Binet by viewing dissociation as the basic mechanism of hypnosis (Hilgard, 1979). Using a framework that has much in common with response expectancy theory, Sarbin and Coe (1979) suggested that hypnotic responses and hysterical symptoms may be products of self-deception and self-persuasion. People with hysterical or hypnotically induced amnesia, for example, have come to believe that they cannot remember and they behave accordingly.

Despite their differences in theoretical orientation, these writers agree that hypnosis and hysteria are closely related. The reason for this convergence is the degree of similarity between hypnotic responses and the symptoms of conversion and dissociative disorders. Hypnotized subjects are asked to experience paralysis, amnesia, anesthesia, involuntary movements, and hallucinations. In fact, hypnotizability is measured as the number of conversion and dissociative symptoms that the person is able to display.

Despite the similarities between hysteria and hypnosis, there are two important differences between the phenomena (see Hilgard, 1984). Hypnotic subjects actively cooperate in producing hypnotic responses, whereas hysterics report them as being ego-dystonic (though they may also accept their dysfunction with *la belle indifférence*). Also, hypnotic responses are short-lived, whereas hysterical symptoms may persist for years.

These differences between hypnosis and hysteria may partly be due to differences in motivation between hypnotic subjects and hysterics. There is general agreement that the symptoms of hysteria are motivated behaviors (Sackeim, Nordlie, & Gur, 1979), although the hypothesized nature of this motivation varies predictably between theories. Psychodynamic theorists propose that hysteria is motivated by unconscious conflict, for example, whereas behavioral theorists look for current external reinforcement (recognized as "secondary gain" by psychodynamic theorists). But whatever the motivational sources of hysteria, they are likely to be quite different from the motivation that most people have for experiencing hypnosis. Nevertheless, despite differences in motivation, the similarities between hypnotic responses and hysteric symptoms suggest that both may be brought about by the same underlying mechanism. Although unconscious

---

[1]In 1980, the classification of dissociative and conversion disorders as forms of hysteria was abandoned (American Psychiatric Association, 1980). In this discussion, I have used the term *hysteria* as it has been used historically, to refer to both dissociative and conversion disorders. Conversion disorders involve a psychologically caused loss of physical functioning—paralysis, blindness, or loss of sensation, for example. Dissociative disorders involve disturbances of memory or identity, as in amnesia or multiple personality disorder.

conflict or social reinforcement may be initiating causes of hysteria, response expectancies may be the mechanism by which the symptoms are maintained.

Evidence of the role of expectancy in the maintenance of hysteric symptoms is provided by Schreiber (1961) in the following description of the treatment of hysteria by an elaborate placebo ritual in the Soviet Union:

> We use a form of indirect suggestion psychotherapy to remove the fixated symptoms of hysteria, otherwise unyielding to ordinary methods.
>
> A week before treatment starts, the patient is informed at considerable length that his illness is functional in character, distinguished by conversion phenomena. The patient is assured, however, that he is to be treated in a manner that will be of considerable help. After spending several days in expectation of the "medication" intended to remove the symptoms of his ailment, the patient is conducted to the treatment room and invited to lie down on a couch. He is then informed that the "medicine" will be poured slowly on a special mask and assimilated by his organism by means of breathing in the evaporated drug. He is furthermore assured that the substance brings no unpleasant reactions whatsoever, such as nausea or headache. These remarks help considerably to avoid any possible complications arising in auto-suggestion. The patient is then told, in a manner well adjusted to the level of his education, that he will feel much better, that the symptoms of his disease are a product of cortical inhibition and that the drug, being a powerful stimulating substance, is intended to remove the inhibition. It is explained, for instance, that the patient's hyperkinesia is determined by excitation of brain cells, and that the drug, by calming the nervous system, puts them back into a normal state.
>
> Immediately after this, a registered nurse begins to pour, drop by drop, some aromatic liquid, such as menthol dissolved in alcohol, on the mask already on the patient's face. The whole procedure of treatment takes no more than ten minutes. In the meantime, a discussion is conducted with some other physician concerning the effectiveness of the treatment, with which the latter concurs. They point out that the drug has an excellent effect upon the nervous system and is capable of removing many pathological manifestations. No remarks are addressed directly to the patient; from the very beginning of the treatment he remains a passive listener to the conversation conducted only between the two physicians; the conversation is actually a question of indirect suggestion.
>
> This method of treatment has been used by us for a great variety of symptoms, including hysterical contracture, hyperkinesis, partial paralysis, astasia-abasia [inability to stand or walk without legs wobbling or collapsing, although the patient has normal control while sitting or lying down], mutism, and persistent vomiting [pp. 85–86].

Conventional wisdom suggests that psychological symptoms ought not to be removed until their causes are uncovered and corrected. Attempts to do so are predicted to fail, to be temporary, or to result in symptom substitution. In fact, when hysteria was treated via direct suggestions for symptom removal in the late 19th century, relapse was reportedly common. However, the success of behavior therapy in treating phobic disorders calls this assumption into question. Direct treatment of phobic anxiety is effective and does not result in symptom substitution (Paul, 1967b). One cannot automatically generalize Paul's data to hysterical disorders, but neither can one automatically rule out the possibility that these conditions might also be directly modifiable. Further, a dysfunctional response may continue even after removal of the reason for its initial occurrence. For these reasons, attempts to directly alter hysteric responses may frequently be warranted.

Because of the similarities between hypnosis and hysteria, hypnotic treatment may be the treatment of choice for these disorders. Although conversion disorders are far less common then they were in the past, a number of case reports indicate that conversion symptoms can be treated successfully via hypnosis (see Udolf, 1987), and in some of these cases, the essence of treatment was direct suggestion for symptom removal.

Hypnotic Treatment of Multiple Personality: A Case Study

In contrast to conversion disorder, the diagnosis of multiple personality has increased dramatically (Bliss, 1986). People with multiple personality diagnoses are almost invariably good hypnotic subjects, and hypnosis allows easy access to each of the personalities. For this reason, it may be virtually indispensable for the treatment of this disorder.

The case reported here demonstrates the hypnotic treatment of multiple personality from a response expectancy perspective (Kirsch & Barton, 1988). Two interventions are described. The first involved the creation of a "hidden observer" to obtain a coherent life history. The second technique used successive approximations to diminish the degree of experienced separation between personalities, ultimately leading to complete role-integration. Each of the steps in this series of successive approximations also lessened the disruption to daily life that the role-separation engendered.

These interventions were generated on the basis of a number of assumptions. The first assumption is that each of the personalities was conceived of as an integrated set of self-schemas. Self-schemas are beliefs about oneself, including beliefs about how one responds to various types of events. If we think of ourselves as honest, for example, what we mean is that we expect to be truthful in a wide variety of situations. If we see ourselves as nervous, we expect to feel tense quite a bit of the time. In other words, self-schemas are largely composed of perceived capabilities, propensities, and response expectancies.

Multiple personality disorders are conditions in which a person has multiple self-concepts. Each personality has its own set of self-confirming response expectancies, including the belief that it has no knowledge of the internal experiences of other personalities—that is, selective amnesia. Thus, a second assumption was that the barriers between personalities were maintained by the client's belief in their existence. In other words, "Alice" could not remember "Betty's" behavior because she did not *believe* that she could remember her behavior. As far as Alice and Betty were concerned, they were two different people.

A third premise upon which these interventions were based was that anything that can be experienced following a trance induction can be experienced just as strongly without a trance induction. Hypnotic inductions were used as expectancy modification procedures that provided a means of temporarily altering the client's beliefs about herself. Post-hypnotic suggestions were used to stabilize these altered beliefs outside of a hypnotic context.

Creating a Hidden Observer

Since believed-in personalities are frequently amnesic for other internal personas, obtaining a coherent case history can be difficult. A "hidden observer" (referred to by the client as her "central switchboard") was created as a means of circumventing this problem. The idea of creating a hidden observer was inspired by three sources: (1) Allison's (1974) report of his discovery of an "inner self" in a multiple personality client; (2) Hilgard's (1979) description of the "hidden observer" in experimental hypnosis; and (3) Spanos and Hewitt's (1980) demonstration of the hidden observer as an experimental creation. No assumption was made of a pre-existing "inner self" or "hidden observer." The "central switchboard" was created, rather than uncovered, as an aid to therapy.

The following procedure was used to create the hidden observer. Prior to induction, the client was told that because the "personalities" shared a common nervous system, at some level she had access to all of the memories of all of them. It was stressed, both prior to and following induction, that this "central switchboard" was not a personality. Hypnosis was induced with instructions to "go even deeper than ever before." The suggestion of a hidden part of herself that was not a person, but that had access to the memories of all her personas, was then repeated, and a request was made to speak to that hidden observer. A chronological history was then obtained, including the circumstances surrounding the creation of each persona.

An unintended result of this procedure was a spontaneous fusion of the personalities, lasting for about two weeks. The client described her experience of the fusion as tenuous, reporting that it required considerable effort to hold the parts of her personality together. She was told that this was an indication that she was not yet quite ready for complete fusion, and that following formal fusion, she would experience her unity as effortless. Thus, in addition to providing a more complete case history, this procedure provided the client with a temporary experience of role-integration.

Alice: A Case of Multiple Personality

Alice was the middle child of a professional couple. She reported a pattern of physical abuse (severe beatings) and sexual abuse (examining her genitals) by her father beginning when she was about 4 years old. It was at this age that she created Betty, whom she would pretend to be during abusive episodes. Betty was a strong, tough person who was capable of withstanding mistreatment. In grade school, Alice created a third personality, whom she later named Cathy after a girl she had met in junior high school. Cathy's function was to develop the social skills necessary to relate to the other children at school. In later years, both Betty and Cathy reported engaging in homosexual relationships.

Alice reported that her father raped her for the first time when she was in sixth grade. The following year, in the guise of a new personality, Donald, she began playing with a group of children who drank, smoked, and were frequently truant. Donald retained an awareness of Alice and later of Elly, but not of the other personalities. His function was to prevent them from acting out sexually, which he did by causing them to experience psychogenic pain as a punishment for thinking about subjects that were taboo.

Experiencing difficulty with her schoolwork, Alice created Elly while attending a private prep school. Elly became the "primary" personality, the most frequently present persona in and out of therapy sessions. The name Alice became attached to a childlike persona that lived in the past, recalling earlier events with hallucinatory intensity. The final personality to develop was Francis, who was heterosexually active, but who used sex as a substitute for emotional attachment and therefore felt sexually exploited.

Although she began forming alternate personalities at the age of four, the separation between them became rigid only later in her life. Initially, there appears to have been a recognition that she was one person pretending to be another as a means of handling particular stressors. Around puberty, the personalities began to more fully believe in themselves as separate individuals, each claiming amnesia for behavior occurring in the guise of at least some of the other personalities.

This history, which is consistent with many others that have been reported, suggests the following etiology of multiple personality. Multiple personality frequently occurs in response to severe and prolonged child abuse, especially incest (Wilber, 1984).[2] Initially, the child pretends to be someone else during abusive episodes, as a way of coping with the abuse. Later this strategy may be used to cope with less extreme stressors. Finally, the child comes to regard the personalities he or (more typically) she has created as different people. This is especially likely to occur if the person has been exposed to stories in the media about the phenomenon of multiple personality. Because people typically do not have direct access to the experiences of others, amnesia for the experiences of other personas is consistent with the multiple personality role. It is also a prominent feature of popular presentations of the disorder.

Fusion Through Successive Approximation

The idea of structuring successive approximations of single personality functioning was derived from the behavior therapy literature, where it has been shown to be effective in treating a variety of disorders (for examples see Emmelkamp, 1982; Hewett, 1965). Strictly defined, successive approximation or shaping is an operant procedure in which a graded series of responses is systematically reinforced by a therapist or experimenter. However, Emmelkamp and Ultee (1974) have demonstrated that when progress toward a goal is naturally reinforcing, additional therapist reinforcement may be unnecessary. The use of a series of

---

[2]Most children who are sexually abused do not develop multiple personality. However, most people who are diagnosed as multiple personality report severe abuse.

graded steps toward a goal is a feature of many behavioral techniques (see Jones, 1924; Wolpe, 1958). In the present case, the use of hypnosis to elicit the new response can be seen as analogous to prompting. Instructions to repeat the response without hypnosis were the means used to remove the prompt.

As a first step toward eventual integration, a dialogue was structured between Elly and Cathy by means of the following suggestions. Prior to hypnotic induction, it was agreed that hypnosis would be used to allow Elly to "listen in" while Cathy spoke and vice versa. Hypnosis was then rapidly induced by means of a cue previously established via a post-hypnotic suggestion. Next, Elly was reminded that she would be able to "stick around" while the therapist spoke to Cathy. Cathy was then called forth and informed that Elly was "present." Cathy and Elly then held their first conversation, punctuated by the therapist calling their names as the means of bringing about a switch from one to the other. This conversation ended Elly's doubts about her multiple personality diagnosis.

The next step, at a subsequent session, was to have Elly accomplish the switch to Cathy without the therapist's intervention. Before and after induction of hypnosis, it was suggested that she would be able to do so merely by calling Cathy's name. After Cathy had been called forth by Elly, the therapist told her that she could call Elly back in a similar manner. Following their conversation, hypnosis was terminated.

The third step was to teach Elly and Cathy to hold conversations outside of hypnosis. This was done by first inducing hypnosis, allowing them to converse briefly, and then telling them in a confident tone that they would be able to continue in the same manner outside of hypnosis. Hypnosis was then terminated, and Elly was encouraged to resume her conversation with Cathy.

When Elly returned for her therapy session the following week, she reported that she and Cathy had continued having conversations during the week. This provided an immediate benefit in handling some of the inconveniences of role-separation. For example, if she suddenly found herself on the street not knowing where her car was parked, she could now talk to Cathy and ask if she knew where the car was.

The inconvenience of this method of "intracommunication" was that it required privacy in order for the client to avoid embarrassment. Therefore, the next step was to convert the conversations to the subvocal level. The therapist explained that since they shared one body, Elly and Cathy did not need to speak aloud in order to communicate. Instead, they could think to each other. Hypnosis was then induced, and a suggestion for subvocal communication was given. Prior to terminating hypnosis, the therapist explained that subvocal communication could be continued outside of hypnosis. Hypnosis was then terminated, and Elly was asked to resume her subvocal dialogue.

The next step in breaking down the barriers between the personalities was to have them share memories, first in hypnosis and then outside it. This was explained as being different from the earlier subvocal conversations. Cathy was asked to select a nonthreatening—that is, nonsexual—memory to share with Elly, then to allow herself to be open to Elly while recalling the event she had chosen to share. In this way, some of Cathy's memories were experienced by Elly as memories, though without the conviction that they were her own memories. No attempt was made to have all memories shared via this method. Rather, this procedure was used as a means of providing the client with experiences of herself as an undivided person. For similar reasons, the successive approximation procedure was not repeated for all possible pairs of personalities.

The final step of the successive approximation procedure was to formally fuse the various personalities into one. Resistance to fusion was expressed as two basic fears. The first was that each of the personalities had characteristics that others did not want to share. For example, Elly had expressed confusion for some time as to what her sexuality would be if she were to fuse with the others. She experienced herself as a virgin who feared and avoided sex. In contrast, Betty and Cathy had been homosexually active, and Francis had been heterosexually active. A second concern centered around the perceived positive characteristics of particular personalities. These were recognized as useful in some situations, and the client expressed fear that they would be less available after role-integration.

In previous reports of treatments of multiple personality, concerns of these sorts were handled by working through underlying conflicts that presumably made particular memories unacceptable, and by negotiations between the personalities as to which behaviors would be retained or relinquished (Confer & Ables, 1983; Gruenewald, 1984; Thigpen & Cleckley, 1957). In contrast, the approach used in this case was to begin with two personalities that were relatively compatible with each other, stressing that none of the attributes or strengths of either would be lost in the integration, and assuring the client that as a unitary person she would be capable of deciding how to behave in particular situations. In other words, she would be able to respond to a situation as she would have as Elly or Cathy, but with an awareness of choice and without the need for dissociation. Similarly, sexuality was framed as an issue that did not need to be decided in advance.

The element that was most important in reducing resistance to fusion was the prior implementation of the successive approximation steps described above. Cognitive barriers between the initially fused personalities had already been considerably weakened. They had not only carried on daily conversations outside of therapy, but had done so subvocally, in much the same way that people think to themselves. Also, in sharing some of Cathy's memories, Elly had an experience of what it might be like to be her. In a sense, the fusion was partially accomplished before it was formally begun.

The formal fusion was a four-stage process. First, Elly and Cathy were fused via direct hypnotic suggestion: "Elly and Cathy, you can begin to draw closer and closer together now . . . becoming closer and closer . . . beginning to merge into one person . . . a person with all of the memories of Elly and all of the memories of Cathy . . . with all of the strengths of Cathy and all of the strengths of Elly . . . merging . . . merging . . . becoming one . . . you can remember being Cathy . . . and you can remember being Elly . . . completely together now . . . one person. . . ."

Alice was incorporated in the same hypnotic session, Betty was added during the next session, and Donald two months later. The client adopted a lesbian lifestyle, reported that Francis had "left," and resisted the idea of recovering the memory of being Francis, feeling that she would be more comfortable without those memories. However, three months later, Francis re-emerged twice, for a period of a few hours each time. Following these incidents, the client agreed to a completion of the fusion process.

Once the personalities were fused, there was no need for negotiation over which characteristics should be retained. As had been suggested, Elly acquired the ability to feel and behave as each of them had individually, but with the same degree of choice experienced by all of us as we fulfill our multiple roles in life. Thus, the results of fusion confirmed that a lengthy negotiation process had not been necessary.

Two- and Three-Year Follow-ups

Treatment was terminated after the client obtained employment out of state. However, a follow-up visit was arranged two years after the initial fusion (three years after initiating the successive approximation strategy). During this interview, the client reported that gains she had made via these procedures had remained stable, and that no further episodes of role-separation had occurred. An unsolicited letter was received from the client a year and three months later, in which she reported continued improvement in social and occupational functioning, including a heterosexual relationship of seven months duration. No instances of role separation were reported.

Gruenewald (1971) has cautioned therapists against showing too much interest in secondary personalities or using hypnosis as a therapeutic tool with these clients, suggesting that these therapist behaviors might reinforce the maladaptive dissociative processes. These cautions were heeded in the initial stage of therapy for this client, during which the diagnosis of multiple personality was confirmed. However, a different strategy was employed once the diagnosis was confirmed. The client's phenomenological experience was accepted as genuine, and an empathic therapeutic relationship was established with each of the personalities. It was felt that the client's experience could be more easily changed if it was accepted first than if it was fought against directly. At least in this case, the use of hypnosis combined with empathic interest in all of the personalities led to rapid changes in experience and behavior, changes that had not been brought about during years of prior non-hypnotic treatment.

Hypnosis as an Analogue of Psychotherapy

This chapter has explored some of the implications of response expectancy theory for the use of hypnosis in psychotherapy. In a broader sense, however, hypnotic inductions can be viewed as analogues of the modification of response expectancies in psychotherapy. Hypnotic treatment was the progenitor of modern psychotherapy and contains many similarities to the most effective contemporary treatments.

Hypnotic inductions and psychotherapy both begin with the provision of information designed to acquaint the client or subject with their respective roles. As with hypnosis, psychotherapy clients are informed that effective treatment requires their active cooperation and participation. They are told that psychotherapy is not something that is administered to passive patients, as is often the case in physical medicine. Rather than something that is done to them, therapeutic change is something that they accomplish.

As in hypnosis, treatment effectiveness may be enhanced if a credible rationale is presented. The rationale may vary as a function of the therapist's beliefs and the client's attitudes. Dysfunctional conceptions about the nature of therapy (for example, the idea that the therapist is the one who does the work) are corrected, but other beliefs that the client holds might be accepted by the therapist and incorporated into the treatment and its rationale.

As in hypnosis, an overestimation of the effectiveness of therapy can be counterproductive. A client who has positive, but unrealistic, expectations about treatment and who therefore expects very quick substantial change is likely to be frustrated. When the rate of change does not live up to the client's expectations, those expectancies are likely to change, resulting in the belief that therapy will not be helpful. More functional beliefs include the ideas that change will begin gradually, that therapeutic progress will be uneven, and that setbacks are to be anticipated. This allows clients to interpret small changes as evidence of therapeutic improvement and inhibits them from interpreting setbacks as evidence of failure.

Effective therapists are also likely to make use of the hypnotic technique of utilization. Changes in the client's behavior are interpreted as indications of the effectiveness of the client's work in therapy. When improvement is attributed to treatment, and especially when it is attributed to the client's efforts rather than those of the therapist, a benign cycle is established. Enhanced positive expectations encourage more therapeutic change, which further enhances the client's expectations in a positive feedback loop.

Some theorists, viewing hypnotic inductions as methods of producing a particular state of consciousness, have proposed specific procedures for producing that state. In the 18th century, for example, the use of magnetism was considered indispensable; in the 19th century, the production of eyestrain was seen as necessary by James Braid and his followers; and in our century, hypnosis has been closely linked to relaxation (Edmonston, 1981). However, none of these procedures appear to be necessary for the production of hypnotic effects. Instead, the essential features of an effective hypnotic induction depend on the subject's beliefs and expectations, and skilled hypnotists vary their procedures to fit the characteristics of their subjects.

Most clinicians believe that the specific components of their treatments produce effects that are independent of their clients' beliefs and expectations. They assume that those treatment components are essential to treatment outcome, and that they must therefore be careful not to alter the treatments in ways that might disrupt the action of hypothesized theoretical mechanisms. For example, in treating phobic disorders through systematic desensitization, behavior

179

therapists have been cautioned that the anxiety hierarchy must consist of carefully graduated steps. Similarly, proponents of *in vivo* flooding caution that the client must remain in the anxiety-arousing situation until some reduction of anxiety has occurred—otherwise the disorder may be exacerbated rather than ameliorated.

For most forms of psychotherapy, there is little evidence to justify the belief that specific treatment components produce effects that are independent of expectancy. This is especially true of treatments for disorders involving maladaptive nonvolitional responses; for example, anxiety and depression. In treating phobias, for example, graduated hierarchies are not necessary, and treatment can be successful even if clients are allowed to leave the feared situation before their anxiety has diminished. Because of their effects on expectancy, these procedures are typically useful. Graduated hierarchies and the experience of diminishing anxiety promote positive expectations by providing experiential feedback indicating therapeutic change. But they are not the only way of altering expectations. Staying in a feared situation until anxiety has lessened may be too difficult for some clients to tolerate. Rather than attempting to "overcome their resistance," by persuading them that it is necessary, they can be praised for their attempt and assured that they will be able to tolerate more on future trials. Instructing these clients to retreat as soon as anxiety reaches a particular level may work better than asking them to stay in the situation.

Many therapeutic procedures, including those shown to be particularly effective, appear to function like hypnotic inductions in that the effectiveness of their specific components depends on how those components are perceived by clients. For this reason, successful therapists adapt their procedures to the attitudes and beliefs of their clients, rather than adhering rigidly to specific procedures. The colloquial wisdom "different strokes for different folks" applies equally to hypnotic inductions and psychotherapy.

Finally, flexibility is needed in both planning an intervention and implementing it. No matter how clever we are or how good at assessing our clients, some of our interventions will not work. A number of therapeutic strategies, commonly used by experienced hypnotists, can be used in these situations. For example, an apparent failure can be reinterpreted as a success. One might point out how well the client coped with this "failure." Additionally, it can be noted that the client was "not quite ready for" this particular step, carrying the implication that he or she will succeed at that task in the future. "Less than perfect" performance can also be interpreted as an indication that easier subgoals should be carried out first. If the choice of task was made by the client, the therapist can praise his or her courage in taking on such a formidable challenge so quickly. If the choice was made by the therapist, the error can quite truthfully be accepted as that of the therapist, not of the client. Finally, the therapist can point out that failure is as much a part of life as success, and learning to cope with its occurrence is an important part of treatment. A depressed client, for example, must learn to accept being depressed at times, without interpreting it as a sign of "illness."

Many of these strategies are the stock and trade of experienced hypnotists. They are also the expectancy modification strategies recommended in Chapter 7 on the basis of research on cognitive-behavior therapy. Hypnosis is psychotherapy in miniature. It begins with the establishment of rapport, proceeds to an assessment of the individual's beliefs and expectations, continues with the presentation of a rationale that corrects misconceptions, and utilizes individually tailored and flexibly administered rituals for producing changes in experience and behavior. For these reasons, regardless of whether the word "hypnosis" is used, the principles of hypnosis can be used to enhance psychotherapeutic outcome.

CAUSAL MECHANISMS

How Expectancy Produces Change

The data reviewed in this book leave little room for doubt that expectancy has wide-ranging effects on experience, behavior, and physiological function. Furthermore, many of these effects are clinically significant. Response expectancy plays an important role in the treatment of anxiety and depression. It is also an essential aspect of hypnosis, a procedure that can be a useful adjunct to various forms of psychotherapy.

This is by no means an exhaustive list of the clinically significant effects of response expectancies. For example, there is a growing body of current research on alcohol-related response expectancies as predictors of alcohol use and abuse (reviewed by Goldman et al., in press). These expectancies include the beliefs that drinking alcohol transforms subjective experiences in a positive manner; that it enhances social and physical pleasure; that it increases sexual arousal, assertiveness, power, and aggressiveness; and that it reduces tension. Individual differences in expectancies about the effects of alcohol are related to differences in drinking patterns among adolescents, adults, alcoholics, and nonalcoholics. In fact, they are as good or even better at predicting problem drinking than such demographic variables as parental attitudes toward alcohol, parental drinking patterns, or the presence of an alcoholic in the family.

One might suspect that these expectancies are nothing more than reflections of the pharmacologically-induced effects that people experience after drinking alcoholic beverages. Maybe it is these pharmacologically-induced effects, rather than the expectancy of their occurrence, that lead people to drink. However, various aspects of the data argue against this interpretation and suggest that expectancy is a cause of alcohol use. First, balanced placebo studies have shown that some of these effects—enhanced sexual arousal and aggressiveness, for example—are not produced by alcohol pharmacologically (see Chapter 2). They occur when people think they have consumed alcohol, regardless of the actual content of their beverages, but they do not occur when people have unknowingly consumed alcohol. Second, the expectations of adolescents about the effects of alcohol develop before they begin drinking and undergo relatively little change as a function of subsequent experience with alcohol (Christiansen, Goldman, &

Inn, 1982). Third, expectancies measured during adolescence predict the subsequent onset of problem drinking (Smith, Hoehling, Christiansen, & Goldman, 1986). Finally, the alcohol expectancies of alcoholics have been shown to be good predictors of treatment outcome (Brown, 1985).

Once it is accepted that response expectancies have important effects, the most frequently asked question is "How are those effects produced?" In other words, what are the mechanisms by which response expectancies affect experience, behavior, and physiology?

In answering that question, we must separate two kinds of effects associated with response expectancies. Nonvolitional responses are often consequences of voluntary behaviors, and anticipation of these responses affects behavior in the same way that other outcome expectancies do. One of the most well-established principles of social learning theory is that behavior can be predicted by the expectancy that it will lead to particular outcomes, and by the value of those outcomes (Mischel, 1973; Rotter, 1954, 1982; also see Ajzen & Fishbein, 1980). As applied to response expectancies, examples of this include phobic avoidance of public places because of the expectancy of a panic attack, and the consumption of an alcoholic beverage because of the expectancy that it will make one feel good.

This effect of expectancy on behavior seems intuitively obvious, perhaps explaining why the question of how it is produced is so seldom asked. However, response expectancies have other effects that are not shared with other kinds of outcome expectancies. These are related to the tendency for response expectancies to be self-confirming. It is the self-confirming nature of response expectancies that raises questions about intervening mechanisms. The question is, "Why are response expectancies self-confirming?" A number of mediating mechanisms have been proposed to account for various self-confirming expectancy effects. In the following sections, we will look at the most common of these hypotheses.

Classical Conditioning

Classical conditioning has been proposed as an alternative to expectancy theory in accounting for placebo effects (Gliedman, Gantt, & Teitelbaum, 1957; Herrnstein, 1962; Wickramasekera, 1980). According to these theorists, expectancy is, at best, an epiphenomenon or by-product of Pavlovian conditioning, without any genuine causal impact on behavior. From this point of view, the many active medical treatments experienced by people during the course of their lives constitute conditioning trials. Active treatments are unconditioned stimuli (USs), and the vehicles in which they are delivered (pills, capsules, and syringes) are conditioned stimuli (CSs). Through repeated pairings of the CSs and USs, the vehicles acquire the capacity to evoke therapeutic effects as conditioned responses (CRs).

Conditioning theorists have proposed a number of procedures that can be used as "litmus tests" for determining whether a phenomenon can be attributed to classical conditioning (Turkkan, 1989; Wickramasekera, 1980). As applied to placebo effects, these include the following tests:

1. The strength of the placebo effect should increase as a function of the amount of experience the person has had with the active medication.

2. The magnitude of the placebo effect should be proportional to the intensity of the active medication.

3. The placebo should affect the same responses that are affected by the active medication.

4. Repeated application of placebos should result in extinction of the placebo effect.

5. The placebo effect ought to be weaker than the pharmacological effect of the active medication.

All of these tests have been failed in various studies of placebo effects. According to test number 1, for example, prior experience with an active drug (conditioning trials) should enhance the placebo effect. Studies of placebo tranquilizers demonstrate the opposite: Instead of strengthening the placebo effect, conditioning trials weaken it (Meath, Feldberg, Rosenthal, & Frank, 1956; Pihl & Altman, 1971; Rickels, Lipman, & Raab, 1966; Segal & Shapiro, 1959; Zukin, Arnold, & Kessler, 1959).

According to the second litmus test, the magnitude of the placebo response should be proportional to the strength of the active medication. Although this relationship has been reported for placebo analgesia (Evans, 1974), the opposite has been found for placebo tranquilizers, in which case there is an inverse relation between the strength of the US and the magnitude of the CR (Rickels et al., 1966).

The third litmus test is that the placebo effect should be specific to the pharmacological properties of the active drug. This does not seem to be the case with respect to placebo alcohol. Placebo alcohol produces a wide variety of effects, but they are not the same effects that are produced by alcohol pharmacologically (Hull & Bond, 1986; also see the data reviewed in Chapter 2). Instead of being specific to the pharmacological properties of alcohol, these effects are specific to beliefs that vary from one culture to another (MacAndrew & Edgerton, 1969). Similarly, some of the effects of placebo caffeine (decaffeinated coffee) vary as a function of the person's beliefs about the effects of caffeine (Kirsch & Weixel, 1988).

Placebos also fail the extinction test, in that continued administration of a placebo does not seem to reduce its effectiveness. For example, eight weeks of daily placebo administration failed to reduce the effectiveness of placebo treatment for panic disorder and agoraphobia (Coryell & Noyes, 1988); placebos retained their effectiveness in the treatment of angina pectoris over a six-month period (Boissel et al., 1986); and continued placebo treatment of rheumatoid arthritis was shown to be effective for as long as 30 months (Traut & Passarelli, 1957). These are hardly typical extinction curves!

Finally, the data reviewed in Chapter 2 demonstrated that placebo effects can be as strong or stronger than the effects of active drugs (Frankenhaeuser et al., 1964; Lyerly et al., 1964; Ross et al., 1962). Taken together, these failures of the "litmus test" for classical conditioning indicate that placebo effects cannot be explained as conditioned responses.

187

This does not mean that associative learning processes are unrelated to response expectancies. Conditioning models of the placebo effect are based on a view of classical conditioning widely regarded as outmoded (Bolles, 1972; Brewer, 1974; Rescorla, 1988). It is now known that the pairing of conditioned and unconditioned stimuli is not sufficient for learning to occur. Conditioned responses occur only when the CS provides the organism with information about the occurrence of the US. Instead of being a means by which one stimulus acquires the capacity to evoke the response of another, Pavlovian conditioning is now regarded as one of several means by which people and other organisms learn about the relationship between events. When two stimuli are repeatedly paired, one (the CS) can come to function as a cue for the occurrence of the other (the US). In other words, whenever the conditioned stimulus occurs, the organism expects the unconditioned stimulus to follow. The conditioned response is due to the organism's anticipation of the unconditioned stimulus.

Classical conditioning is one (but not the only) means by which stimulus expectancies are acquired. Response expectancies can be acquired via a similar mechanism. Direct experience with active drugs is one way in which people learn that certain medications have particular effects, but it is not the only way. People also acquire response expectancies through observational learning—that is, by observing the responses of others to various stimuli—and by the provision of verbal information. Most importantly, even if a conditioning-like process can account for the acquisition of some response expectancies, it cannot explain how those expectancies generate self-confirming effects.

Hope and Faith

Expectancy effects in psychotherapy were first linked to feelings of hope and faith by Freud (1905/1953). The most extensive and influential development of this view is that proposed by Jerome Frank (1973). Frank argued that negative emotional states increase vulnerability to physical disease, aggravate existing illness, and retard the process of healing. Conversely, the positive emotional state of hopefulness, which can be produced by placebo treatment, might not only encourage symptomatic relief, but might also promote physical healing.[1]

According to Frank, the effects of psychotherapy are due to a similar process. Most people who enter therapy are suffering from demoralization and a sense of hopelessness. The promise of improvement remoralizes patients and restores their faith in the future. Because hopelessness is a large part of what brought them into treatment, the restoration of hope constitutes a large part of the cure.

---

[1]Considerable data indicate that negative emotions affect physical health, most likely via their impact on the immune system (Irwin et al., 1987; Krantz, Grunberg, & Baum, 1985). In contrast, little attention has been paid to testing the converse hypothesis that positive emotional states can enhance physical health. This is both surprising and unfortunate, given the practical and theoretical import that positive findings would have.

A number of testable predictions can be derived from Frank's hypothesis that improvement due to positive treatment expectations is mediated by feelings of hope. One of these is the surprising hypothesis that changes in psychological well-being ought to occur before a treatment is actually administered (Goldstein, 1962; Kirsch, 1978). In fact, it is this hypothesis that has generated the strongest empirical support for the hope and faith perspective. Before reviewing these data, however, let us briefly examine the logic behind the hypothesis they support.

Consider what happens to many clients who enter therapy suffering from a sense of hopelessness about their condition. They are interviewed by a therapist and possibly given some psychological tests. The therapist then accepts them into treatment, provides some information about the nature of the treatment, and conveys the impression that it will lead to improvement. It is at this point in time, before formal treatment has begun, that clients may come to believe that they really will get better. Once these positive outcome expectations have been acquired, people should no longer feel hopeless. Instead of expecting to remain distressed, they now believe that they will improve. If their distress was caused by the belief that their situation was hopeless, then their new-found hope should be accompanied by immediate improvement.

Significant and often substantial improvement has in fact been reported to follow an initial diagnostic interview and the promise of treatment (Frank, Nash, Stone, & Imber, 1963; Kellner & Sheffield, 1971; Piper & Wogan, 1970; Shapiro, Struening, & Shapiro, 1980). The design of these studies are quite similar. At their initial visit to a clinic, clients are asked to complete measures of their symptoms and mood states. They are then given further evaluation or placed on a waiting list and given a promise of subsequent treatment. Prior to actually receiving treatment, their symptom and mood levels are once again assessed. These studies have shown clinically and statistically significant improvement merely as a function of the promise of treatment. This effect appears to be long-lasting (Frank, 1973), and the degree of pretreatment improvement reported is substantially correlated with people's expectations about the eventual effects of treatment (Friedman, 1963; Goldstein, 1960).[2]

This effect of expectancies for eventual improvement on general measures of psychological distress is consistent with the data reviewed in Chapter 9 on treatments for depression. On the other hand, many of the established effects of response expectancies cannot be explained in terms of hopefulness. These include side effects produced by placebo medication; effects that are specific to particular expectancy manipulations; and placebo effects obtained in nondistressed subjects.

If response expectancy effects were entirely due to feelings of hopefulness, then one would expect them to be invariably benign. However, the occurrence of "toxic" side effects in response to placebo administration has been well docu-

---

[2] As noted earlier, however, many studies have reported that patients receiving placebo treatments improved more than those placed on a waiting list.

mented (see Beecher, 1955; Pogge, 1963). Among the more common side effects attributed to placebos are drowsiness, headache, nervousness, nausea, constipation, vertigo, dry mouth, cramps, vomiting, fatigue, and difficulty concentrating.

These side effects are not likely to be produced by feelings of hope and faith. However, they might be produced by the opposite of these feelings. As Frank (1973) has noted:

> Some patients fear drugs and distrust doctors. In these patients a placebo may produce severe untoward physiological reactions including nausea, diarrhea, and skin eruptions [p. 140].

The most salient feature of Frank's explanation of placebo side effects is the implication that they should not occur in people who experience positive placebo effects. If we accept the idea that all beneficial effects are due to hopefulness and all negative effects are due to hopelessness, then those who improve and those who experience side effects should constitute distinct sets of people: the former trusting doctors and having faith in medication, the latter distrusting doctors and fearing drugs.

However, the data clearly reveal that negative and positive placebo effects frequently occur in the same individual (Loranger, Prout, & White, 1961; Rickels et al., 1967; Shapiro et al., 1980). In fact, some of these data suggest that the experience of side effects might enhance the therapeutic effectiveness of a placebo. This is a logically predictable relationship because side effects might help convince a person that he or she is in fact receiving an effective drug (Moscucci et al., 1987; Ney et al., 1986), but it cannot be explained by the hopefulness hypothesis. A person does not feel hopeful and hopeless at the same time. If the improvement was produced by enhanced feelings of hopefulness, the side effects could not have been produced by decreased feelings of hopefulness.

Another problem with the hopefulness hypothesis is that it cannot account for the specificity of many expectancy effects. According to the hope and faith hypothesis, it is not the specific belief that matters, but rather its emotional consequences. Thus the same effects should be produced by different specific expectancies, so long as those expectancies have comparable effects on people's sense of hopelessness. However, many of the effects of response expectancies are very specific to the content of the expectancy. Placebo-induced side effects, for example, are specific to the type of medication that subjects think they are receiving. When summarizing results from 67 studies involving 3,549 subjects and 14 different kinds of medication, Pogge (1963) discovered that drowsiness was reported by approximately 8% of patients given placebo analgesics, antihistamines, or tranquilizers, but by fewer than 3% of subjects given placebos with other labels. Similarly, constipation was relatively common following placebo antidepressants (13%), antispasmodics (18%), and "geriatric products" (24%), but uncommon following all other placebos (2%). Headaches were elicited by placebo antidepressants (19%) and antihistimines (7%), but far less frequently by other placebos (2%). Vomiting was occasionally produced by placebo estrogen (8%), but rarely by any other placebo (0.003%). If these effects were due to a sense of hopelessness, they should not be so specifically linked to the type of medication that the person thinks he or she is taking.

Finally, expectancy effects have been demonstrated in people who are suffering from psychological or physical distress. Placebos and hypnosis have been used with healthy volunteer subjects in many experimental studies. There is no reason to believe that these healthy volunteers are experiencing hopelessness when they enter the experiment or that the experimental manipulation induces feelings of hope. Further, the responses displayed by subjects in these situations are specific to the nature of the expectancy manipulation. They become more relaxed when given placebo tranquilizers, but less relaxed when given placebo stimulants (see Chapter 2). In hypnosis studies, they may display selective amnesia, automatic movements, psychogenic paralysis, perceptual distortions, or any of a number of other responses, depending on the suggestions that are given (see Chapters 4 and 5). It is difficult to fathom how these expectancy effects could be explained by general feelings of hope.

Endorphin Release

Endorphins are normal constituents of the brain that are pharmacologically identical to narcotic analgesics. Considerable excitement has been evoked by a study in which the effects of placebos on clinical pain appeared to be mediated by these endogenous opioids (Levine, Gordon, & Fields, 1978). In that study, the administration of naloxone, a substance that blocks opiate receptors, inhibited the effects of placebo medication on postoperative pain. However, the interpretation of these data are clouded by the fact that naloxone can enhance many types of pain, including postsurgical pain, independently of placebo administration. In a subsequent study, hidden infusions of naloxone were administered to patients who were unaware that it was being given (Gracely, Dubner, Wolskee, & Deeter, 1983). In this study, naloxone increased pain regardless of whether a placebo had been administered, and the placebo reduced pain regardless of whether naloxone had been administered. These data suggest that placebos and naloxone alter pain by different mechanisms and that the effects of placebos cannot be explained by endorphin release. On the other hand, naloxone has been shown to partially inhibit the effect of placebos on experimental ischemic pain. Unlike postoperative pain, ischemic pain (pain produced by obstructing blood flow) is not increased by naloxone alone (Grevert, Albert, & Goldstein, 1983).

The degree to which endorphins mediate placebo pain reduction has not yet been established. Nevertheless, it is clear that endorphin release cannot fully explain expectancy effects. First, it does not seem plausible that endorphins could account for all of the response-expectancy effects that have been demonstrated. Second, even if the endorphin release is associated with some of these effects, it does not constitute an explanation of them. Instead, it presents a new dilemma: How does placebo analgesia enhance endorphin release? Rather than being a cause of expectancy effects, endorphin release is one more effect that needs to be explained.

Expectancy As an Immediate Cause of Subjective Experience

Although some expectancy effects might be due to feelings of hopefulness, and others might be associated with the release of endorphins in the brain, no mechanism has been proposed that is capable of accounting for all of the different self-confirming expectancy effects that have been documented. It is possible that different effects are mediated by different mechanisms, but this would leave us with too much of a coincidence. How is it that so many different mechanisms produce the same kind of effect—that is, the confirmation of response expectancies? The ubiquity of the effect and the consistency of its direction—that is, the fact that the direction of change generally appears to be consistent with the direction of the expectancy—suggest the operation of a common mechanism.

Response expectancies affect three different response systems: subjective experience, overt behavior, and physiological function. In the search for a common set of mechanisms, it may be helpful to consider each of these response systems separately, beginning in this section with the self-reported subjective effects produced by expectancy manipulations.

Once something is found to produce an effect, we frequently ask how that effect is produced. Typically, this question is answered by implicating some intervening variable that mediates the effect of the independent variable on the dependent variable. But this immediately raises two new questions: How does the independent variable produce an effect on the mediating variable, and how does the mediating variable produce an effect on the dependent variable? For example, suppose it were established that placebos reduce pain by lowering anxiety. This would raise the questions: How do placebos lower anxiety, and how does lowered anxiety reduce pain? Answers to these questions would involve the discovery of additional mediating variables which would raise similar questions.

Within the confines of any one scientific discipline, this process must at some point come to an end. Further explanation requires the coordination of findings of one scientific discipline with those of another. At least in principle, there should be some point at which we would conclude that a purely psychological explanation of an event is complete. At that point, further understanding of the event requires an investigation of the relation between psychological and physiological variables.

Consider, for example, the effect of outcome expectancies and subjective values on behavior. How is that effect produced? Most expectancy theorists treat the effect as a given and do not search for additional intervening variables (see Feather, 1982). Ajzen and Fishbein (1980), however, note that the effect is limited to voluntary behaviors and suggest that it is mediated by intentions. People intend to do things that they believe will produce positively valued outcomes, and so long as it is within their ability to do so, people do what they intend to do.

This seems intuitively obvious, but one might nevertheless ask how intentions produce voluntary behaviors. The answer that Ajzen and Fishbein (1980) give is that the effect of intention on behavior is immediate; that is, it is not mediated by any other psychological variables. One might, of course, search for physiological mechanisms associated with the effect of intentions on behavior, but at the purely psychological level, the relation is hypothesized to be immediate or direct.

It has been hypothesized that the self-confirming effect of response expectancy on subjective experience might be analogous to the effect of intention on behavior; that is, it might not be mediated by any additional intervening variables (Kirsch, 1985a). In some instances, the connection between expectancies and the subjective experiences they affect is intuitively obvious. For example, we are afraid of events that are very aversive. We do not think to ask how the anticipation of an aversive event produces the feeling of fear, except perhaps to inquire about the physiology of fear. Psychologically, we accept as direct the relation between a perceived threat and fear. There is no need to hypothesize any other psychological state intervening between the anticipation of harm and the experience of fear. Similarly, the belief that an aversive state of affairs is not going to end makes us feel sad, and the relation between the belief and the feeling can be easily accepted as unmediated.

Fear and sadness are aversive emotional states. For that reason, the expectancy of intense fear is sufficient to cause its occurrence, and the belief that feelings of sadness cannot be alleviated is sufficient to maintain depression. Other self-confirmatory effects are less intuitively obvious. Nevertheless, it is possible that they too are immediate consequences of expectancies. In fact, it was this immediate consequence of response expectancies that led to the downfall of introspective experimental psychology and its replacement by behaviorism. Complaining about the degree to which beliefs about consciousness were self-confirming, Raymond Dodge (1912) wrote, "If a factor is expected, it is ipso facto in consciousness. . . . New and previously unsuspected facts may be readily introspected as soon as there is theoretical ground for belief that they exist" (p. 227).

The hypothesis of a direct, unmediated link between expectancy and subjective response is, in effect, a null hypothesis. As such, it cannot be proven true, but it can be disconfirmed. All that is required is the empirical demonstration of a mechanism or mechanisms by means of which expectancy effects are obtained. What needs to be shown is that response expectancies produce self-confirmatory experiences only when they affect one or another intervening variable.

Physiological Effects of Response Expectancies: A Metatheoretical Framework

Besides affecting subjective experiences, interventions designed to manipulate response expectancies have reliable effects on physiological states. Placebo stimulants, for example, produce increases in pulse rate and blood pressure, while placebo tranquilizers have opposite effects (see Chapter 2). How are these physiological effects produced? The discovery of mediating variables as an answer to this question inevitably raises additional questions. Should we find that physical changes are mediated by some psychological state that is a consequence of expectancy (feelings of hope and optimism, for instance), we must next ask how that psychological state produced those physical consequences. Conversely, if we find a physiological mediator between an expectancy and a physical change (endorphin release, for instance), we must inquire as to how the expectancy affected the physiological mediating variable. Thus we are always left with an unanswered question of how some mental state has caused a change in some physiological state.

Michael Hyland (1985) has argued that questions about psychological states as causes or consequences of physiological states are unanswerable because they are improperly formulated. According to Hyland, psychological constructs and physiological constructs may refer to the same underlying event, just as Muhammed Ali and Cassius Clay are different names for the same person, and water and H_2O are different descriptions of the same substance. Because they refer to the same thing, it is improper to speak of one causing the other. Water does not cause, nor is it caused by, H_2O. Similarly, because they are one and the same person, Muhammed Ali cannot cause Cassius Clay. When a mentalistic variable and a physiological variable are assumed to refer to the same underlying event, the two variables are said to be *identified* with each other, and the implication of a direct causal connection is precluded.

Hyland (1985) has proposed that we think of psychological variables and physiological variables as different types of descriptions. Neither type is capable of fully representing the described event, but each description complements the other, so that a more complete representation can be obtained by using both language systems. As a heuristic for theory construction, Hyland proposed that we avoid hypothesizing direct causal connections between variables that belong to different language systems. According to his principle of *complementarity,* psychological variables can be causally related to other psychological variables, and physiological variables can be causally related to other physiological variables, but the only direct relation that is possible between a physiological variable and a psychological variable is one of identity.

There are compelling data indicating that psychological states can have physical consequences and that changes in physical states can produce psychological effects. How are these psychophysiological phenomena to be explained? According to Hyland, this question can best be answered by recognizing two types of relations between events: causal relations and identity relations. It is reasonable to assume that there is a physiological substrate to any mental event.[3] Because the relation between a psychological event and its physiological substrate is one identity, causal sequences involving mentalistic variables and causal sequences involving physiological variables can be linked together.

Figure 11–1 (page 196) illustrates how two kinds of causal sequences, one involving mentalistic variables and the other involving physiological variables, can be linked through identity relations. In this example, feelings of depression are hypothesized to be due to negative expectations. Because feelings and

---

[3]The converse assumption is not made. It seems certain that some physiological states do not have mental counterparts.

194

immune function are different types of events, the former being a psychological variable and the latter a physiological variable, one cannot directly affect the other. However, as with all psychological states, we assume that these feelings have a physiological substrate. After all, one cannot think or feel without a brain. Properly speaking, changes in immune function are not caused by depression; they are caused by the physiological state with which those feelings are identified. When we hypothesize that feelings might affect the immune system, our statement should be understood as a convenient shorthand for a model involving a combination of causal and identity relations (Kirsch & Hyland, 1987).

Hyland's (1985) concept of mind-brain complementarity was not intended as a metaphysical statement (see Hyland & Kirsch, 1988). It is not an assertion about the real nature of the relation of mind to brain. Instead of being about minds and brains, complementarity was proposed as heuristic convention for using mentalistic constructs and physiological constructs in theory construction. Complementarity is not linked to any particular mind-brain philosophy. In fact, Kirsch and Hyland (1987) have shown that it is a necessary consequence of virtually all monist mind-body theories.[4] More importantly, with respect to the present discussion, complementarity avoids the infinite regress to which interactionist[5] assumptions lead and thereby allows the possibility of complete causal models of psychophysiological events.

Figure 11–2 (page 196) illustrates a logical consequence of the principle of mind-brain complementarity. One of the assumptions that we have made is that there is a physiological state that corresponds to every psychological state—that whenever a person is thinking, something must be happening in his or her brain.[6] If this is true, then for every instance in which one mental state causes another mental state, there is a corresponding causal sequence in which one physiological state has caused another physiological state. For example, if a person expects to be depressed forever, that expectation must somehow be represented in the person's nervous system. If a person is feeling sad, that too has a physiological substrate. Therefore, if it is true that negative expectancies cause depression, then it must also be true that the physiological substrates of these expectancies cause the physiological substrates of depression.

[4]There are two types of mind-body philosophies. *Dualist* philosophies (for example, interactionism, parallelism, and occasionalism) assume that the univers contains two different types of substances—mental and physical. *Monist* theories (for example, materialism, idealism, and double-aspect monism) assert that the world is composed of only one type of substance.

[5]Interactionism is a dualist mind-body philosophy. From an interactionist perspective, mind and body are two fundamentally different substances that are nevertheless capable of affecting each other directly. The most common objection to interactionism is that the question of how these substances can affect each other is unanswerable.

[6]This assumption is made for particular instances of mental events; for example, the depressed feeling that John Smith had at 3:45 p.m., on November 24, 1989. The assumption that there is some specific physiological state that can be identified with any instance of a mental event—that is, a thought or feeling—is called "token physicalism" by philosophers. It may also be true that one *type* of physiological event corresponds to each type of mental event; for example, that all instances of depression are identified with one particular type of physiological state. This latter claim, which is called "type identity," cannot be assumed. Instead, it should be treated as an empirically testable hypothesis.

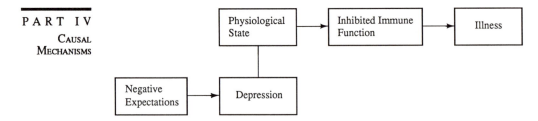

FIGURE 11–1 A model of how causal sequences involving mentalistic variables can be linked through identity relations.

This principle of "causal isomorphism" (Kirsch, 1985a; Kirsch & Hyland, 1987; Hyland & Kirsch, 1988) provides a framework for answering questions about the physiological effects of response expectancies, as well as the physical effects of other psychological variables. As an example, let us consider the well-established finding that besides altering subjectively experienced mood states, placebo stimulants lead to an increase in pulse rates (see Chapter 2). For the sake of simplicity, let us assume that there are no psychological states intervening between the feelings of increased tension that are produced by placebo stimulants and the person's expectation that the "drug" will produce increased tension. In other words, we are assuming that on the purely psychological level, the causal relation between expectancy and experience is direct and immediate.

The appropriate question to ask in regard to how expectancies cause changes in pulse rate is illustrated in Figure 11–3. As shown in the figure, the increase in pulse rate is not caused by the expectancy of its occurrence. Rather, it is caused by the brain state with which the expectancy is identified. At the purely psychological level, the explanation is complete. However, a complete psychophysiological explanation would require discovering the specific brain states that correspond to response expectancies.

Most of the physiological effects that are associated with expectancy fit the model illustrated in Figure 11–3. They are the physiological concomitants of the subjective states that are elicited by expectancy. These include increases in penile tumescence that accompany expectancy-induced increases in sexual arousal; changes in gastric function that accompany changes in the experience of nausea;

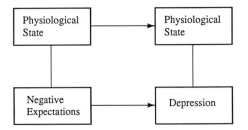

FIGURE 11–2 An illustration of causal isomorphism.

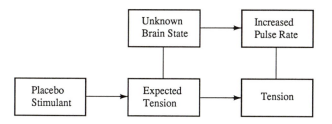

FIGURE 11-3 A heuristic model of how expectancies cause changes in pulse rate.

and alterations in physiological indices of arousal that accompany changes in anxiety, alertness, relaxation, and tension. However, other types of physiological changes may also be linked to changes in expectancy. This is true because many aspects of brain physiology are not represented in consciousness. Changes in endorphin release, for example, may be instances of a nonconscious physiological process.

Let us assume for the moment that endorphin release is reliably associated with expectancy-induced pain reduction. (As we have seen, the data are not conclusive.) As illustrated in Figure 11-4, endorphins might be related to placebo pain reduction in four possible ways: (1) endorphin release may be part of the brain state with which expected pain reduction is identified; (2) it may be a nonconscious consequence of that brain state; (3) it could be an aspect of the brain state with which a change in experienced pain is identified; or (4) it could be a consequence of that latter physiological state. The establishment of a physiological marker of a change in experience is an important discovery, but it raises more questions than it answers. The point was made before (see Chapter 2). Changes in endorphin release are not explanations; they are phenomena that need to be explained.

Response Expectancy and Overt Behavior

Finally, we come to the question of how response expectancies influence overt behavior. One way in which response expectancies affect behavior is due to the

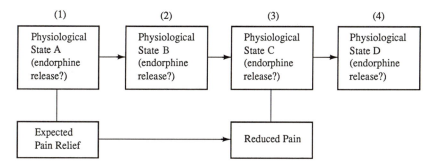

FIGURE 11-4 Four possible ways in which endorphins might be related to placebo pain reduction.

197

fact that they are a subcategory of outcome expectancies; that is, they are desired or undesired consequences of behavior. The decision to engage or persist in a voluntary behavior is a function of expectancies that the behavior will produce various outcomes, and of the value of those outcomes to the individual. Emotional reactions and other nonvolitional responses are among the outcomes that people consider in deciding whether to engage in a behavior. It is this mechanism that accounts for much of phobic avoidance, for example.

Some behaviors are public expressions of subjective states. For example, we grimace when we are in pain, and we tolerate a painful stimulus longer when we experience less pain. This is a second way in which response expectancies influence behavior. Many of the overt responses by which hypnotizability is measured are responses of this sort. For example, people may be asked to respond to a hallucinated voice, to report a hypnotically suggested dream, to brush away a hallucinated fly or mosquito, or to tell an experimenter whether they can taste the sourness of an imagined lemon. Because most people do not normally fake hypnotic responses unless asked to do so (see Chapter 8), most of these can be interpreted as voluntary responses that reflect expectancy-induced changes in experience. Others may occur unintentionally, as when a person unthinkingly grimaces at the taste of a vividly imagined lemon. But in either case, they can be regarded as overt expressions of subjective experience. In principle, they are not different from the verbal self-reports by means of which subjective states are most frequently assessed.

These two mechanisms explain most of the effects of response expectancy on overt behavior. There remains, however, one type of hypnotic response that raises some questions. These are called *ideomotor* responses. Hypnotized subjects are asked to imagine that their arms are becoming lighter or heavier, or that their hands are being drawn together or pushed apart. It is possible that these responses can also be interpreted as expressions of subjective experience. Perhaps people intentionally engage in movements that are consistent with their nonvolitional internal experiences. However, most hypnotic subjects report that the movements themselves are involuntary. How are these reports to be explained?

Spanos (1986) has argued that people intentionally make these movements, but then convince themselves that they have occurred nonvolitionaly. According to Spanos, subjects' response expectancies may enable them to experience their behavioral responses as nonvolitional, even though the responses are in fact completely voluntary. These subjects may not be lying about their experience of involuntariness, but Spanos believes that they are mistaken. In other words, their responses are intentional, despite their experience of them as nonvolitional.

For the most part, this account of ideomotor responses is consistent with response expectancy theory. However, it is not clear how Spanos (1986) is using the term *involuntary*. I have defined *nonvolitional responses* as "responses that are *experienced* as occurring automatically; that is, without volitional effort" (Kirsch, 1985a, p. 1189, emphasis added). The reason for defining *volition* in terms of subjective experience is that it may be the only way of circumventing the unsolvable issue of free will versus determinism. As scientists, we assume that all events are determined, until and unless data lead us to a contrary conclusion for some precisely specified domain of events (as has occurred in 20th century theoretical physics). The reason for this assumption is that one of the central tasks of psychology is to discover the determinants of behavior, including those behaviors that are experienced as voluntary. But to say that a behavior is voluntary in some more fundamental sense is to say that it is indeterminate—hence the definition of *volition* in terms of experience. Given this definition, a response is necessarily nonvolitional if it is experienced as such. Clearly, Spanos is using a different definition of *volition*, but what that definition is remains unclear.[7]

The experienced nonvolitional character of ideomotor responses seems exceptional because we generally regard such gross motor responses as voluntary. However, many of the movements with which we carry out our daily activities occur without an awareness of volition, and this may provide a clue to how ideomotor hypnotic responses can be experienced as nonvolitional. A frequently cited example of this is the phenomenon of driving to a familiar location while absorbed in thought or conversation and realizing, upon arrival, that one does not remember driving there. This phenomenon, which has been referred to as "highway hypnosis," is even more dramatic when a person has intended to go somewhere other than a usual destination, but finds that he or she has unthinkingly and unintentionally gone to the wrong place.

The execution of motor movements without conscious volitional effort is far more common than such exceptional examples as highway hypnosis might suggest. Even when driving with full attention to where we are going, we typically do not think about all the minor adjustments we make to steering and speed. Similarly, when reading a book, we may turn the pages automatically, without having to think about each page that we turn; we write without thinking of each letter; we eat without being aware of voluntarily lifting the fork each time we do so; when we experience an itch, we may become aware of scratching it only afterwards, and so on.

There is an important difference between these common automatic movements and hypnotic ideomotor responses. During hypnosis, the person's attention is directed toward the movement, whereas nonhypnotic automatic responses most commonly occur when the person's attention is directed elsewhere. However, Lynn, Rhue, and Weekes (1989) have provided an excellent example of a nonhypnotic situation in which behavioral responses that are normally under voluntary control are frequently emitted involuntarily. In the children's game "Simon Says," one person recites a list of simple instructions (for example, "Raise your hand"), prefacing each with the phrase "Simon says." Then, without warning, an instruction is given without the prefatory phrase. As Lynn et al. note,

[7]The term *involuntary* is often used to mean "against one's will." However, hypnotic responses are not usually claimed to occur against one's will. Hypnotic responses are nonvolitional only in the sense that they are experienced as occurring as an outcome rather than as an action. They may, however, be experienced as a consequence of a volitional act. For example, actors sometimes imagine distressing events in order to produce tears, but the tears themselves may be experienced as automatic consequences of their involved imaginings. Similarly, people can be quite ingenious in devising strategies to facilitate hypnotic responding (see Chapter 4). It is precisely to avoid the stronger meaning of the term *involuntary* that I use the less common term *nonvolitional*.

"Anyone who has played this game knows how difficult it is to inhibit the response when it is not preceded by 'Simon says'" (p. 17).

The degree to which hypnotic responses and automatic movements in non-hypnotic contexts are brought about by a common mechanism remains to be established. But at the very least, nonhypnotic automatic movements may provide people with a sense of what it is like to experience a nonvolitional movement, and this knowledge may make it easier to experience hypnotically suggested movements as nonvolitional.

Cautions and Prospects

The strategy of this text has been to stay rather close to research data and to build cautiously on existing theory. Although an attempt has been made to pull together findings from diverse areas of investigation (for example, placebo effects, hypnosis, and cognitive-behavior therapy), I have not proposed an all-encompassing theory of any of these phenomena, let alone of psychotherapy or behavior in general. Response expectancy is not the only important variable in hypnosis, anxiety disorders, or depression. It is certainly not the central mechanism by which all therapies work.

On the other hand, it is clear that response expectancies play an important role in hypnosis, in the maintenance of many emotional disorders, and in all forms of psychotherapy. The evidence that response expectancy is an important aspect of these phenomena is strong enough to warrant careful attention to optimizing them in therapy. Treatment procedures and rationales should be adapted to clients' existing beliefs, and efforts should be taken to provide experiential confirmation of therapeutic change.

Much remains to be learned about the causes and effects of response expectancies. Among the topics worthy of further research are the following: How can response expectancies be altered more effectively? What are the mechanisms by which response expectancies produce self-confirming experiences? How do response expectancies interact with other factors in affecting experience and behavior? Do some response expectancies (or more precisely, their physiological substrates) affect the immune system, and can they be utilized in the treatment of physical disorders? What role does response expectancy play in the etiology, maintenance, and treatment of insomnia, erectile disorder (impotence), inhibited female orgasm, and other conditions involving nonvolitional responses? It is my hope that this book will stimulate research to answer these questions.

References

ABBOT, F. K., MACK, M., & WOLF, S. (1952). The action of banthine on the stomach and duodenum of man with observations of the effects of placebos. *Gastroenterology, 20,* 249–269.

ABRAMS, D. B., & WILSON, G. T. (1979). Effects of alcohol on social anxiety in women: Cognitive versus physiological processes. *Journal of Abnormal Psychology, 88,* 161–173.

ABRAMSON, L. Y., SELIGMAN, M. E. P., & TEASDALE, J. (1978). Learned helplessness in humans: Critique and reformulation. *Journal of Abnormal Psychology, 87,* 49–74.

AJZEN, I., & FISHBEIN, M. (1980). *Understanding attitudes and predicting social behavior.* Englewood Cliffs, NJ: Prentice-Hall.

ALLEN, G. J. (1971). Effectiveness of study counseling and desensitization in alleviating test anxiety in college students. *Journal of Abnormal Psychology, 77,* 282–289.

ALLINGTON, H. V. (1952). Review of the psychotherapy of warts. *A. M. A. Archives of Dermatology and Syphilology, 66,* 316–326.

ALLISON, R. B. (1974). A new treatment approach for multiple personalities. *American Journal of Clinical Hypnosis, 17,* 15–32.

ALLOY, L. B., & ABRAMSON, L. Y. (1979). Judgment of contingency in depressed students: Sadder but wiser? *Journal of Experimental Psychology: General, 108,* 441–485.

AMERICAN PSYCHIATRIC ASSOCIATION (1987). *Diagnostic and statistical manual of mental disorders* (3rd ed., rev.). Washington, DC: Author.

ANDREWS, G., & HARVEY, R. (1981). Does psychotherapy benefit neurotic patients? A reanalysis of the Smith, Glass, and Miller data. *Archives of General Psychiatry, 36,* 1203–1208.

BÄCKMAN, H., KALLIOLA, H., & ÖSTLING, G. (1960). Placebo effect in peptic ulcer and other gastroduodenal disorders. *Gastroenterologia, 94,* 11–20.

BAKER, S., & KIRSCH, I. (1987, August). Hypnotic and placebo analgesia in subjects not selected for hypnotizability. In J. Chaves (Chair), *Hypnotic analgesia, placebo effects, and expectancy.* Symposium conducted at the meeting of the American Psychological Association, New York.

BANDURA, A. (1977). Self-efficacy: Toward a unifying theory of behavioral change. *Psychological Review, 84,* 191–215.

BANYAI, E. & HILGARD, E. R. (1976). A comparison of active-alert hypnotic induction with traditional relaxation induction. *Journal of Abnormal Psychology, 85,* 218–224.

BARBER, T. X. (1959). Toward a theory of pain: Relief of chronic pain by prefrontal leucotomy, opiates, placebos, and hypnosis. *Psychological Bulletin, 56,* 430–460.

BARBER, T. X. (1964). Hypnotizability, suggestibility, and personality: V. A critical review of research findings. *Psychological Reports, 14,* 299–320.

BARBER, T. X. (1969). *Hypnosis: A scientific approach.* New York: Van Nostrand Reinhold.

BARBER, T. X. (1978). Hypnosis, suggestions, and psychosomatic phenomena: A new look from the standpoint of recent experimental studies. *The American Journal of Clinical Hypnosis, 21,* 13–27.

BARBER, T. X., SPANOS, N. P., & CHAVES, J. F. (1974). *Hypnosis, imagination, and human potentialities.* New York: Pergamon.

BARKER, S. L, FUNK, S. C., & HOUSTON, B. K. (1988). Psychological treatment versus nonspecific factors: A meta-analysis of conditions that engender comparable expectations for improvement. *Clinical Psychology Review, 8,* 579–594.

BARLOW, D. H. (Ed.). (1985). *Clinical handbook of psychological disorders.* New York: Guilford.

BARLOW, D. H., LEITENBERG, H., AGRAS, W. S., & WINCZE, J. P. (1969). The transfer gap in systematic desensitization: An analogue study. *Behaviour Research and Therapy, 7,* 191–196.

BARLOW, D. H., & WADDELL, M. T. (1985). Agoraphobia. In D. H. Barlow (Ed.), *Clinical handbook of psychological disorders* (pp. 1–68). New York: Guilford.

BECK, A. T. (1976). *Cognitive therapy and the emotional disorders.* New York: International Universities Press.

BECK, A. T., & EMERY, G. (1985). *Anxiety disorders and phobias.* New York: Basic Books.

BECK, A. T., RUSH, A. J., SHAW, B. F., & EMERY, G. (1979). *Cognitive therapy of depression.* New York: Guilford.

BEECHER, H. K. (1955). The powerful placebo. *Journal of the American Medical Association, 159,* 1602–1606.

BEECHER, H. K. (1956). The subjective response and reaction to sensation: The reaction phase as the effective site for drug action. *American Journal of Medicine, 20,* 107–113.

BEECHER, H. K. (1957). The measurement of pain: Prototype for the quantitative study of subjective responses. *Pharmacological Review, 9,* 59–209.

BEECHER, H. K. (1961). Surgery as placebo: A quantitative study of bias. *Journal of the American Medical Association, 176,* 1102–1107.

BELLIVEAU, R. (1988). The therapist role-playing the client [Summary]. *Proceedings of the Eleventh National Conference on Student Development* (p. 46). Storrs, CT: University of Connecticut.

BENNETT, H. L., BENSON, D. R., & SAIGO, S. H. (1985, August). Preoperative suggestions for decreased bleeding during spine surgery. In C. Margolis (Chair), *Clinical applications of hypnosis: Case presentations and consultation.* Symposium conducted at the meeting of the American Psychological Association, Los Angeles.

BILLINGS, A. G., & MOOS, R. H. (1984). Coping, stress, and social resources among adults with unipolar depression. *Journal of Personality and Social Psychology, 46,* 877–891.

BLACKWELL, B., BLOOMFIELD, S. S., & BUNCHER, C. R. (1972). Demonstration to medical students of placebo responses and non-drug factors. *The Lancet, 19,* 1279–1282.

BLANEY, P. H. (1986). Affect and memory: A review. *Psychological Bulletin, 99,* 246–299.

BLISS, E. L. (1980). Multiple personalities: A report of 14 cases with implications for schizophrenia and hysteria. *Archives of General Psychiatry, 37,* 1388–1397.

BLISS, E. L. (1986). *Multiple personality, allied disorders, and hypnosis.* New York: Oxford University Press.

202

BLUMENTHAL, D. S., BURKE, R., & SHAPIRO, K. (1974). The validity of "identical matching placebos." *Archives of General Psychiatry, 31,* 214–215.

BOISSEL, J. P., PHILIPPON, A. M., GAUTHIER, E., SCHBATH, J., DESTORS, J. M., & the B. I. S. RESEARCH GROUP. (1986). Time course of long-term placebo therapy effects in angina pectoris. *European Heart Journal, 7,* 1030–1036.

BOLLES, R. C. (1972). Reinforcement, expectancy, and learning. *Psychological Review, 79,* 394–409.

BOOTZIN, R. R., & LICK, J. R. (1979). Expectancies in therapy research: Interpretive artifact or mediating mechanism? *Journal of Consulting and Clinical Psychology, 47,* 852–855.

BORKOVEC, T. D., & NAU, S. D. (1972). Credibility of analogue therapy rationales. *Journal of Behavior Therapy and Experimental Psychiatry, 3,* 257–260.

BORKOVEC, T. D., & SIDES, J. (1979). The contribution of relaxation and expectancy to fear reduction via graded imaginal exposure to feared stimuli. *Behaviour Research and Therapy, 7,* 191–196.

BOWER, G. (1981). Mood and memory. *American Psychologist, 36,* 129–148.

BOWERS, K. S. (1966). Hypnotic behavior: The differentiation of trance and demand characteristic variables. *Journal of Abnormal Psychology, 1966, 71,* 42–51.

BREIER, A., CHARNEY, D. S., & HENINGER, G. R. (1986). Agoraphobia with panic attacks. *Archives of General Psychiatry, 43,* 1029–1036.

BREUER, J., & FREUD, S. (1955). *Studies on Hysteria* (J. Strachey & A. Freud, Trans. & Eds.). New York: Basic Books. (Original work published 1895)

BREWER, W. F. (1974). There is no convincing evidence for operant or classical conditioning in adult humans. In W. B. Weimer & D. S. Palermo (Eds.), *Cognition and the symbolic processes* (pp. 1–42). Hillsdale, NJ: Lawrence Erlbaum.

BREWIN, C. R. (1985). Depression and causal attribution: What is their relation? *Psychological Bulletin, 98,* 297–309.

BRIDDELL, D. W., RIMM, D. C., CADDY, G. K., KRAWITZ, G., SHOLIS, D., & WUNDERLIN, J. (1978). Effects of alcohol and cognitive set on sexual arousal to deviant stimuli. *Journal of Abnormal Psychology, 87,* 418–430.

BRODEUR, D. W. (1965). The effects of stimulant and tranquilizer placebos on healthy subjects in a real-life situation. *Psychopharmacologia, 7,* 444–452.

BROWN, S. A. (1985). Reinforcement expectancies and alcoholism treatment outcome after a one-year follow-up. *Journal of Studies on Alcohol, 46,* 304–308.

BROWN, S. A., GOLDMAN, M. S., INN, A., & ANDERSON, L. R. (1980). Expectations of reinforcement from alcohol: Their domain and relation to drinking patterns. *Journal of Consulting and Clinical Psychology, 48,* 419–426.

BUCKALEW, L. W. (1972). An analysis of experimental components in a placebo effect. *The Psychological Record, 22,* 113–119.

CAMATTE, R., GEROLAMI, A., & SARLES, H. (1969). Comparative study of the action of different treatments and placebos on pain crises of gastro-duodenal ulcers. *Clinica Terapeutica, 49,* 411–419.

CATANESE, R. A., ROSENTHAL, T. L., & KELLEY, J. E. (1979). Strange bedfellows: Reward, punishment, and impersonal distraction strategies in treating dysphoria. *Cognitive Therapy and Research, 3,* 299–305.

CATANZARO, S. J., & MEARNS, J. (1987, August). *A scale measuring generalized expectancies for coping with negative moods.* Paper presented at the meeting of the American Psychological Association, New York.

CAUTELA, J. R. (1967). Covert sensitization. *Psychological Reports, 20,* 459–468.

REFERENCES

CHAMBLESS, D. L., CAPUTO, G. C., BRIGHT, P., & GALLAGHER, R. (1984). Assessment of fear of fear in agoraphobics: The body sensation questionnaire and the agoraphobic cognitions questionnaire. *Journal of Consulting and Clinical Psychology, 52,* 1090–1097.

CHARCOT, J. M. (1893). The faith-cure. *New Review, 8,* 18–31.

CHRISTIANSEN, B. A., GOLDMAN, M. S., & INN, A. (1982). Development of alcohol-related expectancies in adolescents: Separating pharmacological from social-learning influences. *Journal of Consulting and Clinical Psychology, 50,* 336–344.

COE, W. C. (1983, August). *Trance: A problematic metaphor for hypnosis.* Paper presented at the meeting of the American Psychological Association, Anaheim, CA.

COLLINS, R. L., & SEARLES, J. S. (1988). Alcohol and the balanced-placebo design: Were experimenter demands in expectancy really tested? Comment on Knight, Barbaree, and Boland (1986). *Journal of Abnormal Psychology, 97,* 503–507.

COMINS, J., FULLAM, F., & BARBER, T. X. (1975). Effects of experimenter modeling, demands for honesty, and initial level of suggestibility on response to hypnotic suggestions. *Journal of Consulting and Clinical Psychology, 43,* 668–675.

CONFER, W. N., & ABLES, B. S. (1983). *Multiple personality: Etiology, diagnosis, and treatment.* New York: Human Sciences.

COPPOLA, R., & GRACELY, R. H. (1983). Where is the noise in SDT pain assessment? *Pain, 17,* 257–266.

CORYELL, W., & NOYES, R. (1988). Placebo response in panic disorder. *American Journal of Psychiatry, 145,* 1138–1140.

COUNCIL, J. R., KIRSCH, I., & HAFNER, L. P. (1986). Expectancy versus absorption in the prediction of hypnotic responding. *Journal of Personality and Social Psychology, 50* 182–189.

COUNCIL, J. R., KIRSCH, I., VICKERY, A. R., and CARLSON, D. (1983). "Trance" vs. "skill" hypnotic inductions: The effects of credibility, expectancy, and experimenter modeling. *Journal of Consulting and Clinical Psychology, 51,* 432–440.

CRAIK, K. J. W. (1943). *The nature of explanation.* Cambridge, England: Cambridge University Press.

CRITELLI, J. W., & NEUMANN, F. K. (1984). The placebo: Conceptual analysis of a construct in transition. *American Psychologist, 39,* 32–39.

DANIELS, A. M., & SALLIE, R. (1981). Headache, lumbar puncture, and expectation. *The Lancet,* 1003.

DAVISON, G. C. (1968). Systematic desensitization as a counterconditioning process. *Journal of Abnormal Psychology, 73,* 91–99.

DE GROOT, H. P., GWYNN, M. I., & SPANOS, N. P. (1988). The effects of contextual information and gender on the prediction of hypnotic susceptibility. *Journal of Personality and Social Psychology, 54,* 1049–1053.

DEVINE, D. A., & FERNALD, P. S. (1973). Outcome effects of receiving a preferred, randomly assigned or nonpreferred therapy. *Journal of Consulting and Clinical Psychology, 41,* 104–107.

DIAMOND, M. J. (1972). The use of observationally presented information to modify hypnotic susceptibility. *Journal of Abnormal Psychology, 79,* 174–180.

DODGE, R. (1912). The theory and limitations of introspection. *American Journal of Psychology, 23,* 214–229.

DRAKE, S. D., NASH, M. R., SPINLER, D. G., & WEISBERG, J. N. (1986, August). *Imaginative involvement and hypnotic susceptibility: A relationship mediated by context?* Paper presented at the meeting of the American Psychological Association, Washington, DC.

204

DUBREUIL, D. L., SPANOS, N. P., & BERTRAND, L. D. (1983). Does hypnotic amnesia dissipate with time? *Imagination Cognition and Personality, 2,* 103–113.

DWORKIN, S. F., CHEN, A. C. N., LERESCHE, L., & CLARK, D. W. (1983). Cognitive reversal of expected nitrous oxide analgesia for acute pain. *Anesthesia and Analgesia, 62,* 1073–1077.

DWORKIN, S. F., CHEN, A. C. N., SCHUBERT, M. M., & CLARK, D. W. (1984). Cognitive modification of pain: Information in combination with N_2O. *Pain, 19,* 339–351.

EDMONSTON, W. E. (1981). *Hypnosis and relaxation: Modern verification of an old equation.* New York: Wiley.

ELKIN, I., PARLOFF, M. B., HADLEY, S. W., & AUTRY, J. H. NIMH treatment of depression collaborative research program: Background and research plan. *Archives of General Psychiatry, 42,* 305–316.

ELKIN, I., SHEA, T., IMBER, S., PILKONIS, P., SOTSKY, S., GLASS, D., WATKINS, J., LEBER, W., & COLLINS, J. (1986, May). *NIMH treatment of depression collaborative research program: Initial outcome findings.* Unpublished abstract, American Association for the Advancement of Science.

ELLENBERGER, H. F. (1970). *The discovery of the unconscious: The history and evolution of dynamic psychiatry.* New York: Basic Books.

EMMELKAMP, P. M. G. (1982). *Phobic and obsessive-compulsive disorders: Theory, research, and practice.* New York: Plenum.

EMMELKAMP, P. M. G., & Ultee, K. A. (1974). A comparison of successive approximation and self-observation in the treatment of agoraphobia. *Behavior Therapy, 5,* 605–613.

ENGLE, K. B., & WILLIAMS, T. K. (1972). Effect of an ounce of vodka on alcoholic's desire for alcohol. *Quarterly Journal of Studies on Alcohol, 33,* 1099–1105.

ERICKSON, M. H. (1980). *The nature of hypnosis and suggestion.* New York: Irvington.

EVANS, F. J. (1974). The placebo response in pain reduction. *Advances in Neurology, 4,* 289–296.

FARAVELLI, C., Webb, T., AMBONETTI, A., FONNESU, F., & SESSAREGO, A. (1985). Prevalence of traumatic early life events in 31 agoraphobic patients with panic attacks. *American Journal of Psychiatry, 142,* 1493–1494.

FARKAS, G. M., & ROSEN, R. C. (1976). Effect of alcohol on elicited male sexual response. *Journal of Studies on Alcohol, 37,* 265–272.

FAZIO, R. H., & ZANNA, M. P. (1981). Direct experience and attitude-behavior consistency. *Advances in Experimental Social Psychology, 14,* 161–202.

FEATHER, N. T. (Ed.). (1982). *Expectations and actions: Expectancy-value models in psychology.* Hillsdale, NJ: Lawrence Erlbaum.

FENNELL, M. J. V., & TEASDALE, J. D. (1987). Cognitive therapy for depression: Individual differences and the process of change. *Cognitive Therapy and Research, 11,* 253–271.

FERSTER, C. B. (1973). A functional analysis of depression. *American Psychologist, 28,* 857–870.

FIELD, P. B. (1965). An inventory scale of hypnotic depth. *International Journal of Clinical and Experimental Hypnosis, 26,* 238–249.

FISH, J. M. (1973). *Placebo therapy.* San Francisco: Jossey-Bass.

FISHBEIN, M., & AJZEN, I. (1975). *Belief, attitude, intention, and behavior: An introduction to theory and research.* Reading, MA: Addison-Wesley.

FOA, E. B., GRAYSON, J. B., STEKETEE, G. S., DOPPELT, H. G., TURNER, R. M., & LATIMER, P. R. (1983). Success and failure in the behavioral treatment of obsessive-compulsives. *Journal of Consulting and Clinical Psychology, 51,* 287–297.

FOA, E. B., & KOZAK, M. J. (1986). Emotional processing of fear: Exposure to corrective information. *Psychological Bulletin, 99,* 20–35.

REFERENCES

FRANK, J. D. (1973). *Persuasion and healing* (rev. ed.). Baltimore, MD: Johns Hopkins University Press.

FRANK, J. D., NASH, E. H., STONE, A. R., & IMBER, S. D. (1963). Immediate and long-term symptomatic course of psychiatric outpatients. *American Journal of Psychiatry, 120,* 429–439.

FRANKENHAEUSER, M., JARPE, G., SVAN, H., & WRANGSJÖ, B. (1963). Physiological reactions to two different placebo treatments. *Scandinavian Journal of Psychology, 4,* 245–250.

FRANKENHAEUSER, M., POST, B., HAGDAHL, R., & WRANGSJÖ, B. (1964). Effects of a depressant drug as modified experimentally-induced expectation. *Perceptual and Motor Skills, 18,* 513–522.

FRANKLIN, B., MAJAULT, LEROY, SALLIN, BAILLY, D'ARCET, DE BORIE, GUILLOTIN, & LAVOISIER. (1970). Report on animal magnetism. In M. M. Tinterow, *Foundations of hypnosis: From Mesmer to Freud* (pp. 82–128). Springfield, IL: Charles C. Thomas. (Original work published 1785)

FREMONT, J., & CRAIGHEAD, L. W. (1987). Aerobic exercise and cognitive therapy in the treatment of dysphoric moods. *Cognitive Therapy and Research, 11,* 241–251.

FREUD, S. (1953). Psychical (or mental) treatment. In J. Strachey (Ed. and Trans.), *The standard edition of the complete psychological works of Sigmund Freud* (Vol. 7). London: Hogarth Press. (Original work published 1905)

FREUD, S. (1959a). Obsessions and phobias; their psychical mechanisms and their aetiology. In E. Jones (Ed.), *Sigmund Freud: Collected papers* (Vol. 1, pp. 128–137). New York: Basic Books. (Original work published 1895)

FREUD, S. (1959b). Turnings in the ways of psycho-analytic therapy. In E. Jones (Ed.), *Sigmund Freud: Collected papers* (Vol. 2, pp. 392–402). New York: Basic Books. (Original work published 1919)

FRIEDMAN, H. J. (1963). Patient-expectancy and symptom reduction. *Archives of General Psychiatry, 8,* 61–67.

GATCHEL, R. J., HATCH, J. P., MAYNARD, A., TURNS, R., & TAUNTON-BLACKWOOD, A. (1979). Comparison of heart rate biofeedback and systematic desensitization in reducing speech anxiety: Short- and long-term effectiveness. *Journal of Consulting and Clinical Psychology, 47,* 620–622.

GATCHEL, R. J., HATCH, J. P., WATSON, P. J., SMITH, D., & GAAS, E. (1977). Comparative effectiveness of voluntary heart rate control and muscular relaxation as active coping skills for reducing speech anxiety. *Journal of Consulting and Clinical Psychology, 45,* 1093–1100.

GAUTHIER, J. G., LABERGE, B., DUFOUR, L., & FEVRE, A. (1987, August). Therapeutic expectancies and exposure in the treatment of phobic anxiety. In S. L. Williams (Chair), *Psychological mechanisms in performance based treatment of severe phobias.* Symposium conducted at the meeting of the American Psychological Association, New York.

GAUTHIER, J. G., & MARSHALL, W. L. (1977). The determination of optimal exposure to phobic stimuli in flooding therapy. *Behaviour Research and Therapy, 15,* 403–410.

GELDER, M. G., BANCROFT, J. H., GATH, D. H., JOHNSTON, D. W., MATHEWS, A. M., & SHAW, P. M. (1973). Specific and non-specific factors in behaviour therapy. *British Journal of Psychiatry, 123,* 445–462.

GELFAND, S., ULLMANN, L. P., & KRASNER, L. (1963). The placebo response: An experimental approach. *Journal of Nervous and Mental Disease, 136,* 379–387.

GFELLER, J. D., LYNN, S. J., & PRIBBLE, W. E. (1987). Enhancing hypnotic susceptibility: Interpersonal and rapport factors. *Journal of Personality and Social Psychology, 52,* 586–595.

GIBBONS, D. E. (1976). Hypnotic vs. hyperempiric induction procedures: An experimental comparison. *Perceptual and Motor Skills, 42,* 834.

GLASS, L. B., & BARBER, T. X. (1961). A note on hypnotic behavior, the definition of the situation, and the placebo effect. *Journal of Nervous and Mental Diseases, 132,* 539–541.

GLIEDMAN, L. H., GANTT, W. H., & TEITELBAUM, H. A. (1957). Some implications of conditional reflex studies for placebo research. *American Journal of Psychiatry, 113,* 1103–1107.

GOLDFRIED, M. R., & GOLDFRIED, A. P. (1977). Importance of hierarchy content in the self-control of anxiety. *Journal of Consulting and Clinical Psychology, 45,* 124–134.

GOLDFRIED, M. R., & TRIER, C. S. (1974). Effectiveness of relaxation as an active coping skill. *Journal of Abnormal Psychology, 83,* 348–355.

GOLDMAN, M. S., BROWN, S. A., & CHRISTIANSEN, B. A. (in press). Expectancy theory: Thinking about drinking. In H. T. Blane & K. E. Leonard (Eds.), *Psychological theories of drinking and alcoholism.* New York: Guilford.

GOLDSTEIN, A. J., & CHAMBLESS, D.L. (1978). A reanalysis of agoraphobia. *Behavior Therapy, 9,* 47–59.

GOLDSTEIN, A. P. (1960). Patient's expectancies and non-specific therapy as a basis for (un)spontaneous remission. *Journal of Clinical Psychology, 16,* 399–403.

GOLDSTEIN, A. P. (1962). *Therapist-patient expectancies in psychotherapy.* New York: Pergamon.

GORASSINI, D. P., & SPANOS, N. P. (1986). A social-cognitive skills approach to the successful modification of hypnotic susceptibility. *Journal of Personality and Social Psychology, 50,* 1004–1012.

GRACELY, R. H., DUBNER, R., WOLSKEE, P. J., & DEETER, W. R. (1983). Placebo and naloxone can alter post-surgical pain by separate mechanisms. *Nature, 306,* 264–265.

GREVERT, P., ALBERT, L. H., & GOLDSTEIN, A. (1983). Partial antagonism of placebo analgesia by naloxone. *Pain, 16,* 129–143.

GRIMM, L. G. (1980). The evidence for cue-controlled relaxation. *Behavior Therapy, 11,* 283–293.

GRUENEWALD, D. (1971). Hypnotic techniques without hypnosis in the treatment of dual personality: A case report. *Journal of Mental and Nervous Disease, 153,* 41–66.

GRUENEWALD, D. (1984). On the nature of multiple personality: Comparisons with hypnosis. *International Journal of Clinical and Experimental Hypnosis, 32,* 170–190.

GRÜNBAUM, A. (1985). Explication and implications of the placebo concept. In L. White, B. Tursky, & G. E. Schwartz (Eds.), *Placebo: Theory, research, and mechanisms* (pp. 9–36). New York: Guilford.

HALL, H. (1984). Imagery and cancer. In A.A. Sheikh (Ed.), *Imagination and Healing* (pp. 159–170). Farmingdale, NY: Baywood.

HAM, M. L., RADTKE, H. L., & SPANOS, N. P. (1981). *The effects of suggestion type and the experience of involuntariness on the breaching of hypnotic amnesia.* Unpublished manuscript, Carleton University.

HAMMER, A. G. & ARKINS, W. J. (1964). The role of photic stimulation in the induction of hypnotic trance. *International Journal of Clinical and Experimental Hypnosis, 12,* 81–87.

HEATON, R. K. (1975). Subject expectancy and environmental factors as determinants of psychedelic flashback experiences. *Journal of Nervous and Mental Disease, 161,* 157–165.

HEIBY, E. L. (1986). Social versus self-control skills deficits in four cases of depression. *Behavior Therapy, 17,* 158–169.

HEIDE, F. J., & BORKOVEC, T. D. (1984). Relaxation-induced anxiety: Mechanisms and theoretical implications. *Behaviour, Research, and Therapy, 22*, 1–12.

HENDLER, C. S., & REDD, W. H. (1986). Fear of hypnosis: The role of labeling in patients' acceptance of behavioral interventions. *Behavior Therapy, 17*, 2–13.

HENRY, D. (1985). *Subjects' expectancies and subjective experience of hypnosis.* Unpublished doctoral dissertation, University of Connecticut, Storrs, CT.

HERRNSTEIN, R. (1962). Placebo effect in the rat. *Science, 138*, 677–678.

HEWETT, F. M. (1965). Teaching speech to an autistic child through operant conditioning. *American Journal of Orthopsychiatry, 35*, 927–936.

HILGARD, E. R. (1979a). Divided consciousness in hypnosis: The implications of the hidden observer. In E. Fromm & R. E. Shor (Eds.), *Hypnosis: Developments in research and new perspectives* (rev. ed., pp. 45–79). New York: Aldine Publishing Co.

HILGARD, E. R. (1979b). The Stanford Hypnotic Susceptibility Scales as related to other measures of hypnotic responsiveness. *American Journal of Clinical Hypnosis, 21*, 68–83.

HILGARD, E. R. (1984). The hidden observer and multiple personality. *International Journal of Clinical and Experimental Hypnosis, 32*, 248–253.

HILGARD, J. R. (1979). *Personality and hypnosis: A study of imaginative involvement* (2nd ed.). Chicago: University of Chicago Press.

HILLIS, B. R. (1952). The assessment of cough suppressing drugs. *Lancet*, 1230–1235.

HODGSON, J. W. (1981). Cognitive versus behavioral-interpersonal approaches to the group treatment of depressed college students. *Journal of Counseling Psychology, 28*, 243–249.

HOGAN, R. A., & KIRCHNER, J. H. (1968). Implosive, eclectic verbal and bibliotherapy in the treatment of fears of snakes. *Behaviour Research and Therapy, 6*, 106–111.

HOLLON, S. D., DeRUBEIS, R. J., & EVANS, M. D. (1987). Causal mediation of change in treatment for depression: Discriminating between nonspecificity and noncausality. *Psychological Bulletin, 102*, 139–149.

HOLLOWAY, W., & McNALLY, R. J. (1987). Effects of anxiety sensitivity on the response to hyperventilation. *Journal of Abnormal Psychology, 96*, 330–334.

HOLROYD, K. A. (1976). Cognition and desensitization in the group treatment of test anxiety. *Journal of Consulting and Clinical Psychology, 44*, 991–1001.

HONIGFELD, G. (1964). Non-specific factors in treatment: I. Review of placebo reactions and placebo reactors. *Diseases of the Nervous System, 25*, 145–156.

HORVATH, P. (1987). Demonstrating therapeutic validity versus the false placebo-therapy distinction. *Psychotherapy, 24*, 47–51.

HORVATH, P. (1988). Placebos and common factors in two decades of psychotherapy research. *Psychological Bulletin, 104*, 214–225.

HOWARD, M. L., & COE, W. C. (1980). The effects of context and subjects' perceived control in breaching posthypnotic amnesia. *Journal of Personality, 48*, 342–359.

HULL, C. L. (1933). *Hypnosis and suggestibility: An experimental approach.* New York: Appleton-Century Crofts.

HULL, J. G., & BOND, C. F. (1986). Social and behavioral consequences of alcohol consumption and expectancy: A meta-analysis. *Psychological Bulletin, 99*, 347–360.

HYLAND, M. E. (1985). Do person variables exist in different ways? *American Psychologist, 40*, 1003–1010.

HYLAND, M. E., & KIRSCH, I. (1988). Methodological complementarity: With and without reductionism. *Journal of Mind and Behavior, 9*, 5–12.

IKEMI, Y., & NAKAGAWA, S. (1962). A psychosomatic study of contagious dermatitis. *Kyoshu Journal of Medical Science, 13*, 335–350.

208

Irwin, M., Daniels, M., Bloom, E. T., Smith, T. L., & Weiner, H. (1987). Life events, depressive symptoms, and immune function. *American Journal of Psychiatry, 144,* 437–441.

Jacobson, E. (1929). *Progressive relaxation.* Chicago: University of Chicago Press.

Johnson, J., & Strenstrum, R. (1986, August). *Hypnotic suggestion and placebo in the treatment of warts.* Paper presented at the meeting of the American Psychological Association, Washington, DC.

Johnston, J. D. (1987). *The effects of aerobic and sedentary self-improvement activities on psychological well-being: Aerobic training, psychological expectancy, and measurement issues.* Unpublished doctoral dissertation, University of Connecticut, Storrs, CT.

Jones, M. C. (1924). The elimination of children's fears. *Journal of Experimental Psychology, 7,* 383–390.

Kanfer, F. H., & Grimm, L. G. (1978). Freedom of choice and behavioral change. *Journal of Consulting and Clinical Psychology, 46,* 873–878.

Kantor, T. G., Sunshine, A., Laska, E., Meisner, M., & Hopper, M. (1966). Oral analgesic studies: Pentazocien, hydrochloride, codeine, aspirin, and placebo and their influence on response to placebo. *Clinical Pharmacology and Therapeutics, 7,* 447–454.

Kaplan, H. S. (1974). *The new sex therapy.* New York: Brunner/Mazel.

Katz, N. (1978). Hypnotic inductions as training in self-control. *Cognitive Therapy and Research, 2,* 365–369.

Katz, N. (1979). Comparative efficacy of behavioral training, training plus relaxation, and a sleep/trance induction in increasing hypnotic susceptibility. *Journal of Consulting and Clinical Psychology, 47,* 119–127.

Kazdin, A. E., & Wilcoxon, L. A. (1976). Systematic desensitization and non-specific treatment effects: A methodological evaluation. *Psychological Bulletin, 83,* 729–758.

Kellner, R., & Sheffield, B. F. (1971). The relief of distress following attendance at a clinic. *British Journal of Psychiatry, 118,* 195–198.

Kenny, D. A. (1979). *Correlation and causality.* New York: Wiley.

Kessler, R. C., Price, R. H., & Wortman, C. B. (1985). Social factors in psychopathology: Stress, social support, and coping processes. *Annual Review of Psychology, 36,* 531–572.

Kiesler, D. J. (1966). Some myths of psychotherapy research and the search for a paradigm. *Psychological Bulletin, 65,* 110–136.

Kihlstrom, J. F. (1985). Hypnosis. *Annual Review of Psychology, 36,* 385–418.

Kihlstrom, J. F., Evans, F. J., Orne, M. T., & Orne, E. C. (1980). Attempting to breach posthypnotic amnesia. *Journal of Abnormal Psychology, 89,* 603–616.

Kirsch, I. (1978a). The placebo effect and the cognitive-behavioral revolution. *Cognitive Therapy and Research, 2,* 255–264.

Kirsch, I. (1978b). Teaching clients to be their own therapists. *Psychotherapy: Theory, Research and Practice, 15,* 302–305.

Kirsch, I. (1982). Efficacy expectations or response predictions: The meaning of efficacy ratings as a function of task characteristics. *Journal of Personality and Social Psychology, 42,* 132–136.

Kirsch, I. (1985a). Response expectancy as a determinant of experience and behavior. *American Psychologist, 40,* 1189–1202.

Kirsch, I. (1985b). Self-efficacy and expectancy: Old wine with new labels. *Journal of Personality and Social Psychology, 49,* 824–830.

Kirsch, I. (1985c). The logical consequences of the common-factor definition of the term placebo. *American Psychologist, 40,* 237–238.

REFERENCES

KIRSCH, I. (1986a). Early research on self-efficacy: What we already know without knowing we knew. *Journal of Social and Clinical Psychology, 4,* 339–358.

KIRSCH, I. (1986b). Unsuccessful redefinitions of the term *placebo. American Psychologist, 41,* 844–845.

KIRSCH, I. (1986c). Response expectancy and phobic anxiety: A reply to Wilkins and Bandura. *American Psychologist, 41,* 1391–1393.

KIRSCH, I., & BARTON, R. D. (1988). Hypnosis in the treatment of multiple personality: A cognitive-behavioural approach. *British Journal of Experimental and Clinical Hypnosis, 5,* 131–137.

KIRSCH, I., COUNCIL, J. R., & MOBAYED, C. (1987). Imagery and response expectancy as determinants of hypnotic behavior. *British Journal of Experimental and Clinical Hypnosis, 4,* 25–31.

KIRSCH, I., COUNCIL, J. R., & VICKERY, A. R. (1984). The role of expectancy in eliciting hypnotic responses as a function of type of induction. *Journal of Consulting and Clinical Psychology, 52,* 708–709.

KIRSCH, I., & HENRY, D. (1977). Extinction vs. credibility in the desensitization of speech anxiety. *Journal of Consulting and Clinical Psychology, 45,* 1052–1059.

KIRSCH, I., & HENRY, D. (1979). Self-desensitization and meditation in the treatment of public speaking anxiety. *Journal of Consulting and Clinical Psychology, 47,* 536–541.

KIRSCH, I., & HYLAND, M. E. (1987). How thoughts affect the body: A metatheoretical framework. *Journal of Mind and Behavior, 8,* 417–434.

KIRSCH, I., MEARNS, J., & CATANZARO, S. J. (1988). *Coping expectancies, coping responses, depression, and health problems.* Manuscript submitted for publication.

KIRSCH, I., SILVA, C. E., CARONE, J. E., JOHNSTON, J. D., & SIMON, B. (1989). The surreptitious observation design: An experimental paradigm for distinguishing artifact from essence in hypnosis. *Journal of Abnormal Psychology, 98,* 132–136.

KIRSCH, I., TENNEN, H., WICKLESS, C., SACCONE, A. J., & CODY, S. (1983). The role of expectancy in fear reduction. *Behavior Therapy, 14,* 520–533.

KIRSCH, I., & WEIXEL, L. (1988). Double-blind versus deceptive administration of a placebo. *Behavioral Neuroscience, 102,* 319–323.

KLEIN, M. H., GREIST, J. H., GURMAN, A. S., NEIMEYER, R. A., LESSER, D. P., BUSHNELL, N. J., & SMITH, R. E. (1985). A comparative outcome study of group psychotherapy vs. exercise treatments for depression. *International Journal of Mental Health, 13,* 148–177.

KLERMAN, G. L., & WEISSMAN, M. M. (1982). Interpersonal psychotherapy: Theory and research. In A. J. Rush (Ed.), *Short-term psychotherapies for depression: Behavioral, interpersonal, cognitive, and psychodynamic approaches* (pp. 88–106). New York: Guilford.

KLOPFER, B. (1957). Psychological variables in human cancer. *Journal of Projective Techniques, 21,* 331–340.

KNIGHT, L. J., BARBAREE, H. E., & BOLAND, F. J. (1986). Alcohol and the balanced-placebo design: The role of experimenter demands in expectancy. *Journal of Abnormal Psychology, 95,* 335–340.

KORNBLITH, S. J., REHM, L. P., O'HARA, M. W., & LAMPARSKI, D. M. (1983). The contribution of self-reinforcement training and behavioral assignments to the efficacy of self-control therapy for depression. *Cognitive Therapy and Research, 7,* 499–528.

KRANTZ, D. S., GRUNBERG, N. E., & BAUM, A. (1985). Health psychology. *Annual Review of Psychology, 36,* 349–383.

210

KROGER, W. S. & SCHNEIDER, S. A. (1959). An electronic aid for hypnotic induction: A preliminary report. *International Journal of Clinical and Experimental Hypnosis, 7*, 93–98.

LADER, M. H. (1967). Palmer skin conductance measures in anxiety and phobic states. *Journal of Psychosomatic Research, 11*, 271–281.

LADER, M. H., & WING, L. (1969). Physiological measures in agitated and retarded depressed patients. *Journal of Psychiatric Research, 7*, 89–100.

LANDMAN, J. T., & DAWES, R. M. (1982). Psychotherapy outcome: Smith and Glass' conclusions stand up under scrutiny. *American Psychologist, 37*, 504–516.

LANG, A. R., GOECKNER, D. J., ADESSO, V. J., and MARLATT, G. A. (1975). Effects of alcohol on aggression in male social drinkers. *Journal of Abnormal Psychology, 84*, 508–518.

LANG, A. R., SEARLES, J., LAUERMAN, R., & ADESSO, V. (1980). Expectancy, alcohol, and sex guilt as determinants of interest in and reaction to sexual stimuli. *Journal of Abnormal Psychology, 89*, 644–653.

LANG, P. J., MELAMED, B. G., & HART, J. (1970). A psychophysiological analysis of fear modification using an automated desensitization procedure. *Journal of Abnormal Psychology, 76*, 220–234.

LANSKY, D., & WILSON, G. T. (1981). Alcohol, expectations, and sexual arousal in males: An information processing analysis. *Journal of Abnormal Psychology, 90*, 35–45.

LAZARUS, A. A. (1971). *Behavior therapy and beyond.* New York: McGraw-Hill.

LEIBLUM, S. R., & PERVIN, L. A. (Eds.). (1980). *Principles and practice of sex therapy.* New York: Guilford.

LENT, R. W. (1983). Perceptions of credibility of treatment and placebo by treated and quasi-control subjects. *Psychological Reports, 52*, 383–386.

LENT, R. W., RUSSELL, R. K., & ZAMOSTNY, K. P. (1981). Comparison of cue-controlled desensitization, rational restructuring, and a credible placebo in the treatment of speech anxiety. *Journal of Consulting and Clinical Psychology, 49*, 608–610.

LEVINE, J. D., GORDON, N. C., & FIELDS, H. L. (1978). The mechanism of placebo analgesia. *Lancet, 2*, 654–657.

LEWINSOHN, P. M., & HOBERMAN, H. M. (1982). Depression. In A. S. Bellack, M. Hersen, & A. E. Kazdin (Eds.), *International handbook of behavior modification and therapy* (pp. 397–431). New York: Plenum.

LEWINSOHN, P. M., MISCHEL, W., CHAPLIN, W., & BARTON, R. (1980). Social competence and depression: The role of illusory self-perception? *Journal of Abnormal Psychology, 80*, 203–212.

LEWINSOHN, P. M., SULLIVAN, J. M., & GROSSCUP, S. J. (1982). Behavior therapy: Clinical applications. In A. J. Rush (Ed.), *Short-term psychotherapies for depression: Behavioral, interpersonal, cognitive, and psychodynamic approaches* (pp. 50–87). New York: Guilford.

LEY, R. (1985). Blood, breath, and fears: A hyperventilation theory of panic attacks and agoraphobia. *Clinical Psychology Review, 5*, 271–285.

LIBERMAN, R. (1964). An experimental study of the placebo response under three different situations of pain. *Journal of Psychiatric Research, 2*, 233–246.

LICK, J. (1975). Expectancy, false galvanic skin response feedback, and systematic desensitization in the modification of phobic anxiety. *Journal of Consulting and Clinical Psychology, 43*, 557–567.

LICK, J., & BOOTZIN, R. (1975). Expectancy factors in the treatment of fear: Methodological and theoretical issues. *Psychological Bulletin, 82*, 917–931.

LORANGER, A. W., PROUT, C. T., & WHITE, M. A. (1961). The placebo effect in psychiatric drug research. *Journal of the American Medical Association, 176*, 920–925.

LUBORSKY, L., SINGER, B., & LUBORSKY, L. (1975). Comparative studies in psychotherapy. *Archives of General Psychiatry, 32*, 995–1008.

LYERLY, S. B., ROSS, S., KRUGMAN, A. D., & CLYDE, D. J. (1964). Drugs and placebos: The effects of instructions upon performance and mood under amphetamine sulphate and chloral hydrate. *Journal of Abnormal and Social Psychology, 68*, 321–327.

LYNN, S. J., NASH, M. R., RHUE, J. W., FRAUMAN, D. C., & SWEENEY, C. A. (1984). Nonvolition, Expectancies, and Hypnotic Rapport. *Journal of Abnormal Psychology, 93*, 295–303.

LYNN, S. J., RHUE, J. W., & WEEKES, J. R. (1989). *Hypnotic involuntariness: A social-cognitive analysis.* Manuscript submitted for publication.

LYNN, S. J., SEEVARATNAM, J., RHUE, J., NEUFIELD, V., & DUDLEY, K. (1985, August). *A cross-cultural investigation of hypnosis and imagination.* Paper presented at the meeting of the American Psychological Association, Los Angeles.

LYNN, S. J., SNODGRASS, M., RHUE, J. W., & HARDAWAY, R. (1987). Goal-directed fantasy, hypnotic susceptibility, and expectancies. *Journal of Personality and Social Psychology, 53*, 933–938.

MACANDREW, C., & EDGERTON, R. B. (1969). *Drunken comportment: A social explanation.* Chicago: Aldine-Atherton.

MALESKI, E. F. (1971). Effects of contingency awareness and suggestion on systematic desensitization: Unplanned therapist differences. *Journal of Consulting and Clinical Psychology, 37*, 446.

MARCIA, J. E., RUBIN, B. M., & EFRAN, J. S. (1969). Systematic desensitization: Expectancy change or counter-conditioning? *Journal of Abnormal Psychology, 74*, 382–387.

MARKS, I. M., GELDER, M. G., & EDWARDS, A. (1968). Hypnosis and desensitization for phobias: A controlled prospective trial. *British Journal of Psychiatry, 114*, 1263–1274.

MARLATT, G. A., DEMMING, B., & REID, J. B. (1973). Loss of control drinking in alcoholics: An experimental analogue. *Journal of Abnormal Psychology, 81*, 233–241.

MARLATT, G. A., & ROHSENOW, D. J. (1980). Cognitive processes in alcohol use: Expectancy and the balanced placebo design. In N. K. Mello (Ed.), *Advances in substance abuse: Behavioral and Biological Research*, (pp. 159–199). Greenwich, CT: JAI Press.

MATHEWS, W. J., KIRSCH, I., & MOSHER, D. (1985). The "double" hypnotic induction: An initial empirical test. *Journal of Abnormal Psychology, 94*, 92–95.

MAVISSAKALIAN, M. (1987). The placebo effect in agoraphobia. *Journal of Nervous and Mental Disease, 175*, 95–99.

MAVISSAKALIAN, M. (1988). The placebo effect in agoraphobia: II. *Journal of Nervous and Mental Disease, 176*, 446–448.

MCCONKEY, K. M. (1986). Opinions about hypnosis and self-hypnosis before and after hypnotic testing. *International Journal of Clinical and Experimental Hypnosis, 34*, 311–319.

MCCONKEY, K. M., and SHEEHAN, P. W. (1981). The impact of videotape playback of hypnotic events on posthypnotic amnesia. *Journal of Abnormal Psychology, 90*, 46–54.

MCGLASHAN, T. H., EVANS, F. J., & ORNE, M. T. (1969). The nature of hypnotic analgesia and placebo response to experimental pain. *Psychosomatic Medicine, 31*, 227–246.

MCGLYNN, F. D., GAYNOR, R., & PUHR, J. (1972). Experimental desensitization of snake-avoidance after an instructional manipulation. *Journal of Clinical Psychology, 28*, 224–227.

McGlynn, F. D., Reynolds, E. J., & Linder, L. H. (1971). Experimental desensitization following therapeutically oriented and physiologically oriented instructions. *Journal of Behavior Therapy and Experimental Psychiatry, 2*, 13–18.

McGuire, W. J. (1969). Suspiciousness of experimenter's intent. In R. Rosenthal & R. L. Rosnow (Eds.), *Artifact in behavioral research* (pp. 13–57). New York: Academic Press.

McKnight, D. L., Nelson, R. O., Hayes, S. C., & Jarrett, R. B. (1984). Importance of treating individually assessed response classes in the amelioration of depression. *Behavior Therapy, 15*, 315–335.

McLean, P. D., & Hakstian, A. R. (1979). Clinical depression: Comparative efficacy of outpatient treatments. *Journal of Consulting and Clinical Psychology, 47*, 818–836.

McNally, R. J., & Steketee, G. S. (1985). The etiology and maintenance of severe animal phobias. *Behaviour, Research, and Therapy, 23*, 431–435.

McNamara, K., & Horan, J. J. (1986). Experimental construct validity in the evaluation of cognitive and behavioral treatments for depression. *Journal of Counseling Psychology, 33*, 23–30.

McReynolds, W. T., Barnes, A. R., Brooks, S., & Rehagen, N. J. (1973). The role of attention-placebo influences in the efficacy of systematic desensitization. *Journal of Consulting and Clinical Psychology, 41*, 86–92.

McReynolds, W. T., & Grizzard, R. H. (1971). A comparison of three fear reduction procedures. *Psychotherapy: Theory, Research and Practice, 8*, 264–268.

Meath, J. A., Feldberg, T. M., Rosenthal, D., & Frank, J. D. (1956). Comparison of resperine and placebo in treatment of psychiatric outpatients. *A. M. A. Archives of Neurology and Psychiatry, 76*, 207–214.

Merry, J. (1966). The "loss of control" myth. *Lancet, 1*, 1257–1258.

Merton, R. K. (1948). The self-fulfilling prophecy. *Antioch Review, 8*, 193–210.

Mesmer, F. A. (1980). Dissertation on the discovery of animal magnetism. In G. J. Bloch (Ed. and Trans.), *Mesmerism: A translation of the original medical and scientific writings of F. A. Mesmer, M.D.* (pp. 43–76). Los Altos, CA: William Kaufmann. (Original work published in 1779)

Miller, S. B. (1972). The contribution of therapeutic instructions to systematic desensitization. *Behaviour Research and Therapy, 10*, 159–170.

Mischel, W. (1973). Toward a cognitive social reconceptualization of personality. *Psychological Review, 80*, 252–283.

Morgan, A. H., Johnson, D. L., & Hilgard, E. R. (1974). The stability of hypnotic susceptibility: A longitudinal study. *International Journal of Clinical and Experimental Hypnosis, 22*, 249–257.

Morganstern, K. P. (1973). Implosive therapy and flooding procedures: A critical review. *Psychological Bulletin, 79*, 313–334.

Morris, L. A., & O'Neal, E. (1974). Drug-name familiarity and the placebo effect. *Journal of Clinical Psychology, 30*, 280–282.

Moscucci, M., Byrne, L., Weintraub, M., & Cox, C. (1987). Blinding, unblinding, and the placebo effect: An analysis of patients' guesses of treatment assignment in a double-blind clinical trial. *Clinical Pharmacology & Therapeutics, 41*, 259–265.

Mosher, D. L. (1966). The development and multitrait-multimethod matrix analysis of three measures of three aspects of guilt. *Journal of Consulting Psychology, 30*, 23–29.

Ney, P. G., Collins, C., & Spensor, C. (1986). Double blind: Double talk or are there ways to do better research. *Medical Hypotheses, 21*, 119–126.

213

NIETZEL, M. T., RUSSELL, R. L., KELLY, A. H., & GRETTER, M. L. (1987). Clinical significance of psychotherapy for unipolar depression: A meta-analytic approach to social comparison. *Journal of Consulting and Clinical Psychology, 55*, 156–161.

O'LEARY, K. D., & WILSON, G. T. (1975). *Behavior therapy: Application and outcome.* Englewood Cliffs, NJ: Prentice-Hall.

ORNE, M. T. (1959). The nature of hypnosis: Artifact and Essence. *Journal of Abnormal Psychology, 58*, 277–299.

ORNE, M. T. (1979). On the simulating subject as a quasi-control group in hypnosis research: What, why, and how. In E. Fromm & R. E. Shor (Eds.), *Hypnosis: Developments in research and new perspectives* (2nd ed., pp. 519–601). New York: Aldine.

PARK, L. C., & COVI, L. (1965). The non-blind placebo trial. *Archives of General Psychiatry, 12*, 335–345.

PAUL, G. L. (1966). *Insight vs. desensitization in psychotherapy.* Stanford, CA: Stanford University Press.

PAUL, G. L. (1967a). Strategy of outcome research in psychotherapy. *Journal of Consulting Psychology, 31*, 109–118.

PAUL, G. L. (1967b). Insight versus desensitization in psychotherapy two years after termination. *Journal of Consulting Psychology, 31*, 333–348.

PAYKEL, E. S., & HOLLYMAN, J. A. (1984). Life events and depression: A psychiatric view. *Trends in Neuroscience, 7*, 478–481.

PHELPS, J. L. (1986). *Effects of expectancy enhancement, client expectancy and therapist expectancy on therapy outcome.* Unpublished doctoral dissertation, University of Connecticut, Storrs, CT.

PIHL, R. O., & ALTMAN, J. (1971). An experimental analysis of the placebo effect. *Journal of Clinical Pharmacology, 11*, 91–95.

PIHL, R. O., ZEICHNER, A., NIAURA, R. NAGY, K., & ZACCHIA, C. (1981). Attribution and alcohol-mediated aggression. *Journal of Abnormal Psychology, 90*, 468–475.

PIPER, W. E., & WOGAN, M. (1970). Placebo effect in psychotherapy: An extension of earlier findings. *Journal of Consulting and Clinical Psychology, 34*, 447.

PLOTKIN, W. B. (1979). The alpha experience revisited: Biofeedback in the transformation of psychological state. *Psychological Bulletin, 86*, 1132–1148.

POGGE, R. (1963). The toxic placebo. *Medical Times, 91*, 773–778.

POSNER, J., & BURKE, C. A. (1985). The effects of naloxone on opiate and placebo analgesia in healthy volunteers. *Psychopharmacology, 87*, 468–472.

PRIOLEAU, L., MURDOCK, M., & BRODY, N. (1983). An analysis of psychotherapy versus placebo studies. *Behavioral and Brain Sciences, 6*, 275–310.

RACHMAN, S., CRASKE, M., TALLMAN, K., & SOLYOM, C. (1986). Does escape behavior strengthen agoraphobic avoidance? *Behavior Therapy, 17*, 366–384.

REHM, L. P. (1977). A self-control model of depression. *Behavior Therapy, 8*, 787–804.

REHM, L. P., KASLOW, N. J., & RABIN, A. S. (1987). Cognitive and behavioral targets in a self-control therapy program for depression. *Journal of Consulting and Clinical Psychology, 55*, 60–67.

REISS, S. (1987). Theoretical perspectives on the fear of anxiety. *Clinical Psychology Review, 7*, 585–596.

REISS, S., & McNALLY, R. J. (1985). The expectancy model of fear. In S. Reiss & R. R. Bootzin (Eds.), *Theoretical issues in behavior therapy* (pp. 107–121). New York: Academic Press.

REISS, S., PETERSON, R. A., GURSKY, D. M., & McNALLY, R. J. (1986). Anxiety sensitivity, anxiety frequency and the prediction of fearfulness. *Behaviour, Research, and Therapy, 24*, 1–8.

RESCORLA, R. A. (1988). Pavlovian conditioning: It's not what you think it is. *American Psychologist, 43*, 151–160.

REYNOLDS, W. M., & COATS, K. I. (1986). A comparison of cognitive-behavioral therapy and relaxation training for the treatment of depression in adolescents. *Journal of Consulting and Clinical Psychology, 54*, 653–660.

RHUE, J., LYNN, S. J., VINOCOUR, S., CLARK, K., & WEISS, F. (1986, October). *The effects of contextual factors on the relationship between absorption and hypnotizability.* Paper presented at the Ninth American Imagery Conference, Los Angeles.

RICKELS, K., LIPMAN, R., & RAAB, E. (1966). Previous medication, duration of illness, and placebo response. *The Journal of Nervous and Mental Disease, 142*, 548–554.

RICKELS, K., SNOW, L., UHLENHUTH, H., LIPMAN, R. S., PARK, L. C., & FISHER, S. (1967). Side reactions on meprobromate and placebo. *Diseases of the Nervous System, 28*, 39–45.

ROHSENOW, D. J., & BACHOROWSKI, J. A. (1984). Effects of alcohol and expectancies on verbal aggression in men and women. *Journal of Abnormal Psychology, 93*, 418–432.

ROSEN, G. M. (1976). The development and use of nonprescription behavior therapies. *American Psychologist, 31*, 139–141.

ROSENTHAL, D., & FRANK, J. D. (1956). Psychotherapy and the placebo effect. *Psychological Bulletin, 53*, 294–302.

ROSENTHAL, R. (1969). Interpersonal expectations: Effects of the experimenter's hypothesis. In R. Rosenthal & R. L. Rosnow (Eds.), *Artifact in behavioral research* (pp. 181–277). New York: Academic Press.

ROSENTHAL, R., & RUBIN, D. B. (1978). Interpersonal expectancy effects: The first 345 studies. *Behavioral and Brain Sciences, 3*, 377–415.

ROSS, M., & OLSON, J. M. (1982). Placebo effects in medical research and practice. In J. R. Eiser (Ed.), *Social Psychology and Behavioral Medicine,* (pp. 441–458). New York: Wiley.

ROSS, S., KRUGMAN, A. D., LYERLY, S. B., & CLYDE, D. J. (1962). Drugs and placebos: A model design. *Psychological Reports, 10*, 383–392.

ROTTER, J. B. (1954). *Social learning and clinical psychology.* Englewood Cliffs, NJ: Prentice-Hall.

ROTTER, J. B. (1966). Generalized expectancies for internal versus external control of reinforcement. *Psychological Monographs, 80* (1, Whole No. 609).

ROTTER, J. B. (1982). *The development and application of social learning theory: Selected Papers.* New York: Praeger.

ROTTER, J. B., CHANCE, J. E., & PHARES, E. J. (1972). *Applications of a social learning theory of personality.* New York: Holt, Rinehart & Winston.

ROUNSAVILLE, B. J., & CHEVRON, E. (1982). Interpersonal psychotherapy: Clinical Applications. In A. J. Rush (Ed.), *Short-term psychotherapies for depression: Behavioral, interpersonal, cognitive, and psychodynamic approaches* (pp. 107–142). New York: Guilford.

ROY-BYRNE, P. P., GERACI, M., & UHDE, T. W. (1986). Life events and the onset of panic disorder. *American Journal of Psychiatry, 143*, 1424–1427.

RUBIN, H. B., & HENSON, D. E. (1976). Effects of alcohol on male sexual responding. *Psychopharmacology, 47*, 123–134.

RUSH, A. J., BECK, A. T., KOVACS, M., & HOLLON, S. (1977). Comparative efficacy of cognitive therapy and pharmacotherapy in the treatment of depressed outpatients. *Cognitive Therapy and Research, 1*, 17–38.

SACKEIM, H. A., NORDLIE, J. W., & GUR, R. C. (1979). A model of hysterical and hypnotic blindness: Cognition, motivation, and awareness. *Journal of Abnormal Behavior, 88,* 474–489.

ST. JEAN, R. (1986). Hypnosis: Artichoke or onion? *Behavioral and brain sciences, 9,* 482.

SALKOVSKIS, P. M., WARWICK, H. M. C., CLARK, D. M., & WESSELS, D. J. (1986). A demonstration of acute hyperventilation during naturally occurring panic attacks. *Behaviour, Research, and Therapy, 24,* 91–94.

SARBIN, T. R. (1950). Contributions to role-taking theory: I. Hypnotic behavior. *Psychological Review, 57,* 225–270.

SARBIN, T. R., & COE, W. C. (1972). *Hypnosis: A social psychological analysis of influence communication.* New York: Holt, Rinehart & Winston.

SARBIN, T. R., & COE, W. C. (1979). Hypnosis and psychopathology: Replacing old myths with fresh metaphors. *Journal of Abnormal Psychology, 88,* 506–526.

SCHREIBER, Y. L. (1961). The method of indirect suggestion as used in hysteria. In R. B. Winn (Trans. & Ed.), *Psychotherapy in the Soviet Union.* New York: Philosophical Library.

SCHUYLER, B. A., & COE, W. C. (1981). A physiological investigation of volitional and nonvolitional experience during posthypnotic amnesia. *Journal of Personality and Social Psychology, 40,* 1160–1169.

SEGAL, M., & SHAPIRO, K. L. (1959). A clinical comparison study of the effects of resperine and placebo on anxiety. *Archives of Neurology and Psychiatry, 81,* 392–398.

SELIGMAN, M. E. P. (1975). *Helplessness.* San Francisco: W. H. Freeman.

SEWITCH, S., & KIRSCH, I. (1984). The cognitive content of anxiety: Naturalistic evidence for the predominance of threat-related thoughts. *Cognitive Therapy and Research, 8,* 49–58.

SHAPIRO, A. K. (1960). A contribution to a history of the placebo effect. *Behavioral Science, 5,* 109–135.

SHAPIRO, A. K., & MORRIS, L. A. (1978). The placebo effect in medical and psychological therapies. In S. L. Garfield & A. E. Bergin (Eds.), *Handbook of psychotherapy and behavior change* (2nd ed.). New York: Wiley.

SHAPIRO, A. K., STRUENING, E., & SHAPIRO, E. (1980). The reliability and validity of a placebo test. *Journal of Psychiatric Research, 15,* 253–290.

SHAPIRO, D. A. (1981). Comparative credibility of treatment rationales: Three tests of expectancy theory. *British Journal of Clinical Psychology, 20,* 111–122.

SHAPIRO, D. A., & SHAPIRO, D. (1982). Meta-analysis of comparative therapy outcome studies: A replication and refinement. *Psychological Bulletin, 92,* 581–604.

SHAW, B. F. (1977). Comparison of cognitive therapy and behavior therapy in the treatment of depression. *Journal of Consulting and Clinical Psychology, 45,* 543–551.

SHEEHAN, P. W., & PERRY, C. W. (1976). *Methodologies of hypnosis.* Hillsdale, NJ: Lawrence Erlbaum.

SHOR, R. E. (1971). Expectations of being influenced and hypnotic performance. *International Journal of Clinical and Experimental Hypnosis, 19,* 154–166.

SHOR, R. E., & ORNE, E. C. (1962). *Harvard Group Scale of Hypnotic Susceptibility, Form A.* Palo Alto, CA: Consulting Psychologists Press.

SILVA, C. E., & KIRSCH, I. (1987). Breaching amnesia by manipulating expectancy. *Journal of Abnormal Psychology, 96,* 325–329.

SIMONS, A. D., GARFIELD, S. L., & MURPHY, G. E. (1984). The process of change in cognitive therapy and pharmacotherapy for depression. *Archives of General Psychiatry, 41,* 45–51.

SIMONS, A. D., MURPHY, G. E., LEVINE, J. L., & WETZEL, R. D. (1986). Cognitive therapy and pharmacotherapy for depression. *Archives of General Psychiatry, 43*, 43–48.

SLOANE, R. B., STAPLES, F. R., CRISTOL, A. H., YORKSTON, N. J., & WHIPPLE, K. (1975). *Psychotherapy versus behavior therapy.* Cambridge, MA: Harvard University Press.

SMITH, G. T., ROEHLING, P. V., CHRISTIANSEN, B. A., & GOLDMAN, M. S. (1986, August). *Alcohol expectancies predict early adolescent drinking: A longitudinal study.* Paper presented at the meeting of the American Psychological Association, Washington, DC.

SMITH, M. L., GLASS, G. V., & MILLER, T. I. (1980). *The benefits of psychotherapy.* Baltimore, MD: Johns Hopkins University Press.

SMITH, S. A. (1985). *Utilization and standardized hypnotic inductions: Response expectancy manipulations.* Unpublished doctoral dissertation, University of Connecticut, Storrs, CT.

SOUTHWORTH, S. (1986). *The role of expectancy in the treatment of agoraphobia by in vivo exposure.* Doctoral dissertation, University of Connecticut, Storrs, CT.

SOUTHWORTH, S., & KIRSCH, I. (1988). The role of expectancy in exposure-generated fear reduction in agoraphobia. *Behaviour Research and Therapy, 26*, 113–120.

SPANOS, N. P. (1982). A social psychological approach to hypnotic behavior. In G. Weary & H. L. Mirels (Eds.), *Integrations of clinical and social psychology* (pp. 231–271). New York: Oxford University Press.

SPANOS, N. P. (1986). Hypnotic behavior: A social-psychological interpretation of amnesia, nalgesia, and "trance logic." *The Behavioral and Brain Sciences, 9*, 499–502.

SPANOS, N.P., COBB, P.C., & GORASSINI, D. (1985). Failing to resist hypnotic test suggestions: A strategy for self-presenting as deeply hypnotized. *Psychiatry, 48*, 282–292.

SPANOS, N.P., DE GROH, M., & DE GROOT, H. (1987). Skill training for enhancing hypnotic susceptibility and word list amnesia. *British Journal of Experimental and Clinical Hypnosis, 4*, 15–23.

SPANOS, N. P., & GOTTLIEB, J. (1979). Demonic possession, mesmerism, and hysteria: A social psychological perspective on their historical interrelations. *Journal of Abnormal Psychology, 88*, 527–546.

SPANOS, N. P., & HEWITT, E. C. (1980). The hidden observer in hypnotic analgesia: Discovery or experimental creation? *Journal of Personality and Social Psychology, 39*, 1201–1214.

SPANOS, N. P., KENNEDY, S. K., & GWYNN, M. I. (1984). Moderating effects of contextual variables on the relationship between hypnotic susceptibility and suggested analgesia. *Journal of Abnormal Psychology, 93*, 285–294.

SPANOS, N. P., RADTKE, H. L., & BERTRAND, L. D. (1984). Hypnotic amnesia as a strategic enactment: Breaching amnesia in highly susceptible subjects. *Journal of Personality and Social Psychology, 46*, 1155–1169.

SPANOS, N. P., WEEKES, J. R., & DE GROH, M. (1984). The "involuntarily" countering of suggested requests: A test of the ideomotor hypothesis of hypnotic responsiveness. *British Journal of Experimental and Clinical Hypnosis, 1*, 3–11.

SPINHOVEN, P. (1987). Hypnosis and behavior therapy: A review. *International Journal of Clinical and Experimental Hypnosis, 35*, 8–31.

STAM, H. J. (1987, August). Hypnotic analgesia and placebo analgesia: The effects of context on pain. In *Hypnotic analgesia, placebo effects, and expectancy.* Symposium conducted at the meeting of the American Psychological Association, New York.

STAVA, L. J., & JAFFA, M. (1988). Some operationalizations of the neodissociation and their relationship to hypnotic susceptibility. *Journal of Personality and Social Psychology, 54*, 989–996.

REFERENCES

STONE, L. (1972). *The causes of the English revolution 1529–1642.* New York: Harper & Row.

SUE, D. (1972). The role of relaxation in systematic desensitization. *Behaviour Research and Therapy, 10,* 153–158.

TAYLOR, F. G., & MARSHALL, W. L. (1977). Experimental analysis of a cognitive-behavioral therapy for depression. *Cognitive Therapy and Research, 1,* 59–72.

TEASDALE, J. D. (1983). Negative thinking in depression: Cause, effect, or reciprocal relationship? *Advances in Behaviour Research and Therapy, 5,* 3–25.

TEASDALE, J. D. (1985). Psychological treatments for depression: How do they work? *Behaviour Research and Therapy, 23,* 157–165.

THIGPEN, C. H., & CLECKLEY, H. A. (1957). *The three faces of Eve.* New York: McGraw-Hill.

THOMSEN, J., BRETLAU, P., TOS, M., & JOHNSEN, N. J. (1983). Placebo effect in surgery for Meniere's disease: Three-year follow-up. *Otolaryngology—Head and Neck Surgery, 91,* 183–186.

THYER, B. A., & HIMLE, J. (1985). Temporal relationship between panic attack onset and phobic avoidance in agoraphobia. *Behaviour Research and Therapy, 23,* 607–608.

TOLMAN, E. C. (1932). *Purposive behavior in animals and men.* New York: Appleton-Century Crofts.

TORI, C., & WORELL, L. (1973). Reduction of human avoidant behavior: A comparison of counterconditioning, expectancy and cognitive information approaches. *Journal of Consulting and Clinical Psychology, 41,* 269–278.

TRAUT, E. F., & PASSARELLI, E. W. (1957). Placebos in the treatment of rheumatoid arthritis and other rheumatic conditions. *Annals of the Rheumatic Diseases, 16,* 18–22.

TRUAX, C. B. (1966). Reinforcement and nonreinforcement in Rogerian psychotherapy. *Journal of Abnormal Psychology, 71,* 1–9.

TURKKAN, J. S. (1989). Classical conditioning: The new hegemony. *Behavioral and Brain Sciences, 12,* 121–179.

TYLER, D. B. (1946). The influence of a placebo, body position and medication on motion sickness. *American Journal of Physiology, 146,* 458–466.

UDOLF, R. (1987). *Handbook of hypnosis for professionals* (2nd ed). New York: Van Nostrand Reinhold.

VALINS, S., & RAY, A. A. (1967). Effects of cognitive desensitization on avoidance behavior. *Journal of Personality and Social Psychology, 7,* 345–350.

VICKERY, A. R., & KIRSCH, I. (1985, August). Expectancy and skill-training in the modification of hypnotizability. In S. J. Lynn (Chair), *Modifying hypnotizability.* Symposium conducted at the meeting of the American Psychological Association, Los Angeles.

VICKERY, A. R., KIRSCH, I., SIRKIN, M. I., & COUNCIL, J. R. (1985). Cognitive skill and traditional trance hypnotic inductions: A within-subject comparison. *Journal of Consulting and Clinical Psychology, 53,* 131–133.

VINAR, O. (1978). Addiction to placebo. *American Journal of Psychiatry, 135,* 1000.

VOLGYESI, F. A. (1954). "School for patients", hypnosis-therapy and psycho-prophylaxis. *British Journal of Medical Hypnotism, 5,* 8–17.

WADDEN, T. A., & ANDERTON, C. H. (1982). The clinical use of hypnosis. *Psychological Bulletin, 91,* 215–243.

WAGSTAFF, G. F. (1981). *Hypnosis, compliance and belief.* New York: St. Martin's Press.

WATSON, J. B., & RAYNER, R. (1920). Conditioned emotional reactions. *Journal of Experimental Psychology, 3,* 1–14.

WATSON, J. P., GAIND, R., & MARKS, I. M. (1972). Physiological habituation to continuous phobic stimulation. *Behaviour Research and Therapy, 10,* 269–293.

WEITZENHOFFER, A. M., & HILGARD, E. (1959). *Stanford Hypnotic Susceptibility Scale: Forms A and B.* Palo Alto, CA: Consulting Psychologists Press.

WEITZENHOFFER, A. M., & HILGARD, E. (1962). *Stanford Hypnotic Susceptibility Scale: Form C.* Palo Alto, CA: Consulting Psychologists Press.

WICKER, A. W. (1969). Attitudes vs. actions: The relationship of verbal and overt behavioral responses to attitude objects. *Journal of Social Issues, 25,* 41–78.

WICKLESS, C., & KIRSCH, I. (1988). Cognitive correlates of anger, anxiety, and sadness. *Cognitive Therapy and Research, 12,* 367–377.

WICKLESS, C., & KIRSCH, I. (in press). The effects of verbal and experiential expectancy manipulations on hypnotic susceptibility. *Journal of Personality and Social Psychology.*

WICKRAMASEKERA, I. (1980). A conditioned response model of the placebo effect: Predictions from the model. *Biofeedback and Self-Regulation, 5,* 5–18.

WILBER, C. B. (1984). Multiple personality and child abuse: An overview. *Psychiatric Clinics of North America, 7,* 3–7.

WILKINS, W. (1971). Desensitization: Social and cognitive factors underlying the effectiveness of Wolpe's procedure. *Psychological Bulletin, 76,* 311–317.

WILKINS, W. (1979a). Getting specific about nonspecifics. *Cognitive Therapy and Research, 3,* 319–329.

WILKINS, W. (1979b). Expectancies in therapy research: Discriminating among heterogeneous nonspecifics. *Journal of Consulting and Clinical Psychology, 47,* 837–845.

WILKINS, W. (1986a). Placebo problems in psychotherapy research: Social-psychological alternatives to chemotherapy concepts. *American Psychologist, 41,* 551–556.

WILKINS, W. (1986b). Invalid evidence for expectancies as causes: Comment on Kirsch. *American Psychologist, 41,* 1387–1389.

WILLIAMS, S. L. (1985). On the nature and measurement of agoraphobia. *Progress in Behavior Modification, 19,* 109–144.

WILLIAMS, S. L., DOOSEMAN, G., & KLEIFIELD, E. (1984). Comparative effectiveness of guided mastery and exposure treatments for intractable phobias. *Journal of Consulting and Clinical Psychology, 52,* 505–518.

WILLIAMS, S. L., TURNER, S., & PEER, D. (1985). Guided mastery and performance desensitization treatments for severe acrophobia. *Journal of Consulting and Clinical Psychology, 53,* 237–247.

WILLIAMS, S. L., & WATSON, N. (1985). Perceived danger and perceived self-efficacy as cognitive determinants of acrophobic behavior. *Behavior Therapy, 16,* 136–146.

WILSON, D. L. (1967). The role of confirmation of expectancies in hypnotic induction. *Dissertation Abstracts International, 28,* 4787-B. (University Microfilms No. 66-6781)

WILSON, G. T., & ABRAMS, D. (1977). Effects of alcohol on social anxiety and physiological arousal: Cognitive versus pharmacological processes. *Cognitive Therapy and Research, 1,* 195–210.

WILSON, G. T., & LAWSON, D. M. (1976). Expectancies, alcohol, and sexual arousal in male social drinkers. *Journal of Abnormal Psychology, 85,* 587–594.

WILSON, G. T., & LAWSON, D. M. (1978). Expectancies, alcohol, and sexual arousal in women. *Journal of Abnormal Psychology, 87,* 358–367.

WILSON, P. H., GOLDIN, J. C., & CHARBONNEAU-POWIS, M. (1983). Comparative efficacy of behavioral and cognitive treatments of depression. *Cognitive Therapy and Research, 7,* 111–124.

REFERENCES

WILSON, S. C., & BARBER, T. X. (1978). The Creative Imagination Scale as a measure of hypnotic responsiveness: Applications to experimental and clinical hypnosis. *American Journal of Clinical Hypnosis, 20,* 235–249.

WILSON, S. C., & BARBER, T. X. (1983). The fantasy-prone personality: Implications for understanding imagery, hypnosis, and parapsychological phenomena. In A. A. Sheikh (Ed.), *Imagery: Current theory, research, and application* (pp. 340–387). New York: Wiley.

WINTER, C. A. (1980). *Credibility of therapy style as a function of pre-existing subject beliefs.* Unpublished doctoral dissertation, University of Connecticut, Storrs, CT.

WOLF, S. (1950). Effects of suggestion and conditioning on the action of chemical agents in human subjects—the pharmacology of placebos. *Journal of Clinical Investigation, 29,* 100–109.

WOLF, S. (1959). The pharmacology of placebos. *Pharmacological Review, 11,* 689–705.

WOLF, S. (1962). Placebos: Problems and pitfalls. *Clinical Pharmacology and Therapeutics, 3,* 254–257.

WOLPE, J. (1958). *Psychotherapy by reciprocal inhibition.* Stanford, CA: Stanford University Press.

YOUNG, J., & COOPER, L. M. (1972). Hypnotic recall amnesia as a function of manipulated expectancy. *Proceedings of the 80th Annual Convention of the American Psychological Association, 7,* 857–858.

ZAJONC, R. (1980). Feeling and thinking: Preferences need no inferences. *American Psychologist, 35,* 151–175.

ZAMANSKY, H. S. (1977). Suggestion and countersuggestion in hypnotic behavior. *Journal of Abnormal Psychology, 86,* 346–351.

ZEISS, A. M., LEWINSOHN, P. M., & MUÑOZ, R. F. (1979). Nonspecific improvement effects in depression using interpersonal skills training, pleasant activity schedules, or cognitive training. *Journal of Consulting and Clinical Psychology, 47,* 427–439.

ZUKIN, P., ARNOLD, D. G., & KESSLER, C. (1959). Comparative effects of phenaglycodol and meprobromate on anxiety reactions. *Journal of Nervous and Mental Disease, 129,* 193–195.

Author Index

SUBJECT INDEX